THE AUTHOR: Shūichi Katō is Professor of Japanese Intellectual History at the International Division, Sophia University, Tokyo. He was born in Tokyo in 1919 and graduated in medicine from Tokyo University in 1943, taking his doctorate in medicine in 1950 and, during the 1950s, pursuing medical research there.

Since 1960 he has held chairs in Asian Studies at the University of British Columbia and the Free University of Berlin. He has also been a Visiting Professor at the University of Munich, the University of Oxford and Sophia University, Tokyo, and a Visiting Lecturer in Far Eastern Studies at Yale University.

Among his books in English are *Form, Style, Tradition: Reflections on Japanese Art and Society* and *The Japan-China Phenomenon*.

THE TRANSLATOR: Don Sanderson graduated in English from the University of Reading in 1968. He spent several years working and studying in Japan and was a research student at the University of Hokkaido and a research fellow at the University of Kyoto. He returned to England in 1981 and is presently completing a doctoral thesis at the School of Oriental and African Studies, University of London.

Also by Shuichi Kato (in English)
FORM, STYLE, TRADITION
THE JAPAN–CHINA PHENOMENON

Other volumes in this work

A HISTORY OF JAPANESE LITERATURE

Volume 2
The Years of Isolation

SHUICHI KATO

TRANSLATED by DON SANDERSON

FOREWORD by RENÉ E. ETIEMBLE

KODANSHA INTERNATIONAL
Tokyo • New York • London

First published in English in 1979 by Macmillan Press Ltd., London and Basingstoke.

Published by Kodansha International Ltd., 17-14, Otowa 1-chome, Bunkyo-ku, Tokyo 112 and Kodansha America, Inc., 114 Fifth Avenue, New York, New York 10011. Copyright © 1979 by Shuichi Kato. Translation © 1979 by Paul Norbury Publications Limited. All rights reserved. Printed in Japan.

LCC 77-75967
ISBN 4-7700-1546-1

First paperback edition, 1990

To Midori and Paul
and
in memory of David

Contents

Foreword

My meetings with the author would alone have amply sufficed to make me aware of the close affinity which exists between us in so many respects. When the first volume of this *History* appeared it only confirmed my affectionate admiration for its author. Then came *Six Lives, Six Deaths* (New Haven & London: Yale University Press, 1979), published under the joint names of Robert Jay Lifton, Shuichi Kato and Michael R. Reich. The last portrait, that of Mishima Yukio, 'The Man who Loved Death', is analysed by Shuichi in terms so close to my own diagnosis that our explanations can be superimposed on one another like two equal isosceles triangles.

I find, therefore, that despite my lack of detailed knowledge, the value-judgements which I have formed in half a century of reading Japanese literature, from the *Kojiki* to the novels of Kawabata, have been both reinforced and greatly enhanced through reading Shuichi Kato. For example, I can now better understand why, of all the writers of *haiku* that I first got to know, it was Kikaku who was the most accessible and the most familiar to me. It is because he talks about down to earth subjects like courtesans, *sake* and brothels; in short about the real life which Rimbaud pretended not to exist, and about its oppressive features, which, aided by Hitler and Stalin, affects all of us, indeed sometimes overwhelms us from all sides.

Again, and this confirms a long discussion we had one night in Hiroshima on whether or not alliteration has a role to play in *haiku* – the author shows, on pages 100–1, when dealing with Bashō, that those who maintain that alliteration is of negligible importance as an element in the prosody of this particular verse form are probably wrong. But if Shuichi Kato is not one of these narrow-minded historians of literature who turn their backs on formal analyses, one should not think of him, for that reason, as lacking in flesh and blood or as uninterested in social questions, or ideologies, dominant or otherwise. If he finds in Bashō an exponent of what French critics have called 'art for art's sake' it is because he does not hesitate to put him into his proper context in relation to the social and religious environment of his time: 'For this poet, uncommitted to the values of the *samurai* or the *chōnin*, and unconcerned with the other-worldly doctrines of Buddhism, the "Way of Elegance" came inevitably to be the only value in which he believed and by which he lived. There were few if any examples of such a thorough commitment in the secularized culture of the seventeenth century.'

Here, then, is something to compensate us for all the non-sense which we accumulate in this Europe of ours, in its frantic search for *yin* and *yang*, for *zen* on the cheap, as though it were so much hashish or heroin; here we can find solace in the *haiku* of Bashō, and I for one, can better understand why this poet has become such a favourite of mine. Here, there will be surprise and disappointment for some when they learn that the victory of Nobunaga was the result of the equal contempt felt on the one hand for Shinto, the religion of the Yamato, and on the other hand, for the intruding creed which had come from India, through its Chinese version of *tch'an* (the future Zen). It was with merciless logic that Japanese pragmatism examined all things temporal or spiritual.

Indeed, how can anyone reading this second volume fail to agree with the author's conclusions on page 112: 'Hakuseki and Saikaku, although one used the vocabulary of Sung Confucianism and the other that of *chōnin* and *haikai*, were alike in trying to grasp the reality of their respective worlds and were thus both excellent observers. Both stood out from their contemporaries. Sorai and Chikamatsu, being poets, were masters of language. Hakuseki and Saikaku produced their incomparable prose not primarily from a concern with language but from a concern with reality.'

We who fall indiscriminately for everything which comes from Japan – cars, motorcycles, cameras – could say, like my wife, Jeannine Kohn-Etiemble, who includes in her general literature course quite a few Japanese works, 'Honda for every-one, but Bashō for no one'. She means that those of us who approach Bashō, approach him head down and eyes tight shut, understanding nothing, just as, for example, the Japanese reacted to Neo-Confucianism, and to the contributions of the Dutch. As for the Dutch, it was simple; one learnt their language to be able to borrow their knowledge of anatomy, their dissection technique and their fire-arms technology.

Yes, now at last I begin to understand why I am writing an Introduction for my dear friend Shuichi Kato: it is because he deals with his Japanese literature in the way in which, in my view, all literature should be handled: without isolating it from the economic and sociological conditions in which it arose, but at the same time not treating it simply as a mirror reflecting these conditions.

Every great work of literature has its birth pangs in that crucial moment of exquisite pain in which the social environment becomes refracted – rather than reflected – in a lucid and sorrowful conscience under which an *id* is aspiring to become an *ego*: *wo es war, soll ich werden*. Should I say that this is a secular view of literature? Why not?

René E. Etiemble

Glossary of Terms

See also the glossaries in Volumes 1 and 3.

Ainu   Previously known as Ezo. The indigenous people of Japan. In Tokugawa times they were confined to the north of Honshū and Hokkaidō.

Amaterasu (ōmikami)   The Sun Goddess of Japanese mythology. Associated with the Imperial family and Ise Shrine.

Analects of Confucius   A record of the sayings of the Chinese philosopher Kong Qiu (known as Master Kong or Kong-zi, 551–479 B.C.) prepared by his disciples. The primary text of the Confucian school which came to dominate Chinese philosophy.

Ashigaru   Originally common infantry. In the Tokugawa period the lowest rank of *samurai*.

Benkei   See *Yoshitsune*.

Bugei   The martial arts.

Bunjin   The literati, a style consciously adopted by a type of Japanese artist who sought inspiration from the Chinese literati school. Where the Chinese had been for the most part retired or disgraced officials living a life of cultured leisure, the Japanese literati had to adapt this style to the economic realities of their less-exalted station.

Bunraku   A later term for *ningyō jōruri*; taken from the Bunra-kuza theatre in Ōsaka (now the Asahi-za).

Bushidō   'The Way of the Warrior'. The code of behaviour for members of the warrior caste. Necessary virtues include fidelity, self-sacrifice, loyalty, modesty, propriety, fastidiousness, frugality, economy, martial spirit, honour and love.

Chajin   A 'tea-person', someone devoted to the cult and ceremony of tea.

Cheng brothers   Cheng I (1033–1108) and Cheng Hao (1032–85), Neo-Confucianist philosophers and initiators of, respectively, the school which was completed by Zhu Xi and the school which was completed by Wang Yangming. The former, roughly speaking, held that the universe was not legislated by the mind, the latter that it was.

Chōnin 'Burghers'. The mercantile, urban classes, lowest in the official Tokugawa hierarchy.

Dutch studies and Dutch scholars During the Tokugawa period the only foreigners with whom the Japanese came into contact were the Dutch traders at Nagasaki. This meant that the language used as a medium for anyone interested in studying European culture was Dutch, and the study itself became known as 'Dutch studies'.

Giri 'Duty'; what is owing to society as a whole.

Haikai Short poem in the syllable pattern 5–7–5. Later known as *haiku*.

Handayū bushi A style of *jōruri*, originating with the performer Handayū in Edo. Popular from the 1680s to the 1770s.

Jōruri Dramatic chanted ballad, the substance of which is often simultaneously acted out by puppets (*ningyō jōruri*).

Junshi The act of committing suicide on the death of one's lord as an act of loyalty.

Kakekotoba A play on the different meanings of a word used to link two successive phrases so that the meaning of the word in the second phrase is different from its meaning in the first. It is possible to demonstrate in English – 'I sit beneath the pine for my love'– but seldom possible to translate.

Kami A 'god'; any thing, animal or person of transcendent quality.

Kanazōshi Short stories written in simple, classically influenced Japanese, popular in the late seventeenth century.

Kirishitan 'Christian' (from the Portuguese *Cristāo*), a general term for the converts of the missionaries who came with and after Francisco Xavier in the middle to late sixteenth century.

Kōdō 'The Way of Incense'. An elegant avocation in which the adept tries to appreciate and identify various kinds of incense. There are games which can be played combining one's skill at *kōdō* with knowledge of other arts.

Kojiki Japan's oldest extant history. Completed early in the eighth century. Centred on the mythological and legendary history of the Imperial house.

Kokoro   The essence or core of any phenomenon. In people the mind/heart/spirit.

Koku   A unit used to measure rice, approximately 180 litres. *Samurai* were paid in rice measured in *koku*; the wealth and power of *daimyō* were in turn signified by the amount of rice the central government decided it was possible to grow on their land.

Koto   A stringed instrument, played by plucking. A 'Japanese zither'.

Kouta   Popular songs adopted and sophisticated by the more cultured classes.

Kuruwa   The licensed quarters. The authorities sought to regularize prostitution by confining it to distinct areas, surrounded by a wall. These areas came to be a kind of separate world within which the restraints of the ordered existence were relaxed, although in practice prostitution often flourished outside them as well.

Kyōka   A comic *tanka*.

Machi-shū   The term used for *chōnin* in the Kyōto-Ōsaka area in the early part of the Tokugawa period and before.

Manyōshū   Japan's first poetry collection. Completed in the mid-eighth century.

Mencius   Meng-zi (371?–289? B.C.), whose teaching systematized and developed the work of Confucius.

Michiyuki   Literally, 'a journey'. A scene of travel in either *Nō* or *jōruri*. In *jōruri* the journey is typically the flight of lovers to their glorious death, and the textual and theatrical style at this point is suitably poetical and charged with emotion.

Nanga   'Southern paintings', a style of monochrome ink painting originating with the 'southern' Chan (Zen) Sect in China. Subtle, evocative and fluid in line, this was the style favoured by the *bunjin* (literati) painters of Japan.

Nihonshoki   A Japanese history produced in the early eighth century.

Ningyō jōruri   Puppet play accompanied by the chanting of *jōruri* (q.v.).

Ninjō   'Human feelings', especially those of a personal and private nature.

Ninjōbon   'Books of human feelings'. Sentimental romantic novels popular in the first half of the nineteenth century.

Ōbaku-shū A sect of Zen which entered Japan during the isolationist policies of the *Bakufu* and was consciously Chinese in style.

Okagemairi Sudden enthusiastic mass pilgrimages to the Grand Shrine of Ise (in present-day Mie Prefecture). When the urge to join in hit them, no obligations, whether to other family members or to social superiors, kept the pilgrims at home, and often they took up and left without making any preparations for their journey.

Pure Land Sect (Jōdo-shū) A sect of Buddhism founded in the late twelfth century by Hōnen. The central tenet is the need for complete faith in Amida Buddha and future salvation in the Pure Land. Thus self-improvement is unnecessary, a feature which contributed to the sect's wide popularity.

Renga Linked verse. Several poets would attempt to 'cap' each other's verses. The thematic links between successive verses were extremely subtle.

Rōnin A masterless *samurai*. As the *samurai* was devoted to service, to be masterless was a contradiction.

Sabi A mood or quality of elegant simplicity, especially associated with the poetry of Matsuo Bashō and his school.

Sakoku 'Closed country'. The isolationist policy adopted by the Tokugawa regime.

Sarugaku A comic entertainment, featuring mimicry and vocal comedy, popular in the Heian period.

Satori 'Realization, awakening'. One aim of Buddhism, especially associated with Zen: to perceive things as they really are.

Senryū A short comic verse.

Seppuku Suicide by disembowelment, considered an honourable end for a warrior.

Sewamono A domestic piece, that is, a kind of puppet play or *Kabuki* which deals with the life of 'ordinary people' as opposed to the fantastic figures and actions of the historical plays.

Shinjū Love suicide, the suicide of a pair of lovers whose love is impossible in their society and who choose death as an apotheosis of passion. Most sublimely represented in the work of Chikamatsu Monzaemon (1653–1724).

Shuinsen 'Red-seal ships'. Vessels granted a license to trade with foreign countries during the period when Japan was being unified and before the exclusionist policies of the Tokugawa government.

Six Classics The *Book of Changes* (I Jing), the *Book of Odes* (Shi Jing), the *Book of History* (Shu Jing), the *Book of Rites* (Li Jing), the *Book of Music* (Yue Jing) and the *Spring and Autumn Annals* (Chun Qiu). The earliest works of Chinese philosophy and the foundation of the Confucianist school and other of the literati schools of philosophy.

Soga brothers Historically these two brothers avenged their father's death in 1193; on the stage and later in fiction they became types representing filial piety and heroism. The theme of their revenge, as well as the characters themselves, were woven into other plots, often anachronistic, usually highly implausible.

Suiboku-ga Chinese-style ink and brush paintings, especially those of the Muromachi period.

Sushi Pieces of fish, often raw, served on vinegared rice-balls.

Tanka A verse form with the syllable pattern 5–7–5–7–7.

Terakoya The temple schools which gave a basic education to the less-privileged classes who could afford it throughout the Tokugawa period.

True Pure Land Sect (Jōdo shin-shū) A sect which was developed out of the Pure Land Sect in the thirteenth century by Shinran.

Ukiyo-e 'Pictures of the floating world', woodblock prints of the eighteenth and nineteenth centuries often depicting famous courtesans, actors, landscapes or scenes from life.

Uta See *Waka*.

Wabi A mood or quality of tranquillity, especially of a rustic nature. Associated with the tea ceremony and *haikai*.

Waka A generic term for Japanese verse, later used exclusively to mean *tanka*.

Way of the Former Kings The notion, found in Confucius, that there had in the past existed perfect rulers, especially, for Confucius, the Duke of Zhou. Later the Japanese philosopher Ogyū Sorai (1666–1728) used this notion as a norm against which to judge the development of Confucianist thought.

Yamato The old name for Japan, especially before the influence of Chinese culture.

Yamato-e A specifically Japanese style of painting, largely free of Chinese influence, using purely Japanese subject matter derived from Japanese poetry and tales.

Yinyang The two cosmic principles or forces of Chinese philosophy. *Yin* represents such qualities as femininity, passivity, cold, darkness, wetness, softness. *Yang* represents masculinity, activity, heat, brightness, dryness, hardness. *Yin* and *yang* are complementary and through their interaction are produced all the phenomena of the universe.

Yomihon 'Reading books'. A genre of fiction popular in the first half of the nineteenth century, mostly consisting of historical romances influenced by Chinese colloquial fiction.

Yoshitsune Minamotono Yoshitsune, historical figure and legendary hero. Born shortly before the defeat of his clan, the Genji, Yoshitsune was (in later popular legend at least) slight of build, elegant, magically proficient in combat and doomed to eventual defeat, all factors that have contributed to his popularity. He defeated Benkei, the massive and warlike priest, in a duel on a Kyōto bridge, and thus gained a devoted lieutenant.

Yoshiwara The licensed quarters of Edo and the centre of the culture which was not officially sanctioned, this being a considerable proportion of the literature and art of the time.

Zazen 'Sitting Zen'. Zen meditation.

Translator's Note

The obvious limitations and inherent compromises that inevitably obtain when rendering in another language a large number of originals from different authors and periods is to state the obvious. Sorai's Chinese, for example, is more precise and succinct than an English translation will show; whereas Norinaga's Japanese is more rambling than English can express without being comical. In a longer translation of any one writer's work there is the opportunity for the spirit of the author to be revealed. Here, we must accept what Katō says about each writer without being able, within the pages of this volume, to experience their style. Any inadequacies of translation, therefore, will, I hope, provoke the reader to seek more complete versions of the work, or, ideally, the original itself. And then it is well worth returning to Katō's account of literature: it is more illuminating the more there is to be illuminated.

The wide range which this history covers means more than difficulties in translation. It extends far beyond what an Anglophone reader would expect from the word 'literature' (although not beyond the definition of the Japanese *bungaku*). This redefinition is stimulating. We are forced to challenge the comfortable conventions of what is and is not literature and admit that there are many ways for a person to record his or her thoughts and feelings, all of which can be interesting and tell us something of the person and the age.

If there is any justification for translation it lies here – in the unsettling of settled definitions. This ability to disturb also has something to do with Katō's style. He is known in Japan as a 'western-oriented' writer and his knowledge of western culture is indeed formidable. As one might expect, one finds in his style a relatively high proportion of 'western' terms and concepts. These are, however, never used to display irrelevant erudition or bolster up a sagging argument. He uses them with a precision and economy which is all the more remarkable when one remembers that the subject of this volume is the Japan before the incursion of the West, an area in which western approaches can only be used with the greatest tact. One is struck again and again by a use of Japanese which is not 'western' but rather the most incisive expression which he could find, whatever the source; the aim is not to impress or overawe the reader but to communicate with him or her with the greatest clarity. Again much is lost in translation; but not, I hope, all.

My profound gratitude is due to Masako Saitō who helped me with this translation with immense kindness, patience and erudition; and to Irene for her help and much else.

Don Sanderson

Note on Orthography and Titles

Developments in Asian studies since the publication of Volume 1 have led to two orthographic changes being introduced into this and the following volume of the *History* . The letter 'm' representing the *n* sound before the consonants 'b', 'm' and 'p' in romanized Japanese words has been replaced by the letter 'n'. Chinese proper names and book titles are now given in *pinyin*, the romanization system officially adopted by the Chinese government in 1979. A third major change is the use here of English titles to refer to most works in Japanese. Japanese titles are, however, given in romanized form at the first citation of each work in the text and are retained subsequently for older works discussed at length in Volume 1 and where translation is unnecessary or problematic.

Chapter 1

The Third Turning Point

CONTACT WITH THE WEST

The hundred years from the middle of the sixteenth century were a period of two kinds of change and marked the third turning point in Japan's history and thus her literature. In the wider international sphere, the influence of the West reached Japan for the first time. This phase can be said to have begun when Portuguese castaways brought the first firearms to Japan (in 1543 or possibly 1542) and the Society of Jesus began to spread Christianity (with the arrival of Francis Xavier in 1549). It ended when the Tokugawa authorities ordered a policy of exclusion (*sakoku*) in 1635, forbidding Japanese and their trading ships to sail for foreign ports.

Firearms brought great changes to the perennial struggles of the *samurai*. In 1575, just over thirty years after they were first imported, Oda Nobunaga assembled three thousand guns for the battle of Nagashino, with devastating effect, and firearms played no small part in his comprehensive victory in the civil wars.

The other new import, Christianity, was adopted with comparable enthusiasm. Not only did it gain converts among the *daimyō* (feudal lords) of Kyūshū but it also spread to the Kyōto region and gained widespread success among the peasants. In the early years of the seventeenth century the number of converts is said to have reached 700,000. At that time Kyōto, the capital, had a population of only 300,000, less than half that figure. (This can be contrasted with the situation in Japan since the Meiji Restoration, when Christian missionary work was once again permitted. At no time since 1868 has the number of Christians reached even a third of the population of the capital.) Trade also flourished. After the arrival of the first Portuguese came commerce with Spain (from 1580), the Netherlands (1609) and Britain (1613). At the beginning of the seventeenth century Japanese merchant ships regularly visited ports in Southeast Asia, Taiwan and the Philippines, and between 1604 and 1635 there were about 355 ships licensed for international trade. These were known as 'red-seal ships' or *shuinsen*.

The other sphere of change was internal. The power of the *samurai* since the thirteenth century had shown a marked tendency towards decentralization. But this tendency now began to decline. It continued doing so throughout a period which included Oda Nobunaga's military unification of the country, the dominance of Toyotomi Hideyoshi, the rule of Tokugawa Ieyasu and the early years of the Tokugawa regime – successive military dictatorships that concentrated at the centre a greater and greater degree of power. Nobunaga was assassinated before he could achieve final unification of the country and was replaced by the powerful figure of Hideyoshi, who succeeded in establishing a system of central government supported by semi-autonomous *daimyō*, divided against themselves. The government that Tokugawa Ieyasu then established in 1603 spent the next fifty or so years weakening the feudal lords and strengthening the administrative power of the central government. Thus, by the middle of the seventeenth century the government, or Bakufu, maintained agencies for national administration, managed approximately one-sixth of the country's cultivated land, controlled most of the mines, exercised direct control over the major cities, had a monopoly in the minting of coins, regulated overseas trade and maintained its own standing army of eighty thousand men (compared with Hideyoshi's army of ten thousand). The military forces of the local lords were limited under policies which permitted only one castle to each domain and only about two thousand armed men to a *daimyō* of 100,000 *koku*, with the result that the forces of the central government were overwhelmingly superior. The government also had the authority to confiscate *daimyō* lands and to transfer them to other provinces. Whether this was feudalism, strictly speaking, is a matter of definition. But what is clear is that it represented the culmination of a hundred years of centralization and differed greatly from the system that had obtained from the fourteenth century.

Not all the fundamental reforms carried out by the Tokugawa authorities were directly concerned with the centralization of power. The grades of hereditary status were defined and fixed by the Rules for Military Houses (*bukeshohatto*) and the Rules for the Palace and the Court (*kinchūkugeshohatto*) of 1615, in which the relative positions of noble, *samurai*, peasant and *chōnin* (townsman) were clearly described and a hierarchy firmly established. The culture of the age similarly followed distinct and differing paths which corresponded to these social divisions. As we shall mention later, what is known as the Genroku culture (at the end of the seventeenth century) was clearly divided into the Chinese verse and prose of the *samurai* on the one hand and the *Kabuki* and colloquial fiction of the *chōnin* on the other, the Kanō school of painting favoured by the higher-class *samurai* and the Rinpa school patronized by the merchants. Influence and contact between these two cultures was minimal. This situation is in marked contrast to that of the fifteenth century when all Kyōto, from the *Shōgun* down, watched *sarugaku* entertainments and every level of society, from provincial peasant to aristocrat, composed *renga* linked verse. Behind this splitting of the unified 'popular culture' of the Muromachi period into two parts – that of the rulers and that of the masses – stood the society of rigidly defined status created by the Tokugawa government, and at the centre of that society was the dominant power of the government itself.

To the military leaders who were intensely active in the internal struggles of the sixteenth century, contact with Europe brought new military techniques, overseas trade and the Christian teachings of the Jesuits. Thirty years after the arrival of firearms the town of Sakai near Ōsaka was manufacturing guns in large numbers and importing saltpetre to make gunpowder. Since the trade carried on by Portuguese vessels was linked with the activities of the Christian missionaries, there appeared among the *daimyō* of Kyūshū, who were well aware of the profits to be had from trade, converts to the new religion. Most of them, with the notable exception of men such as Takayama Ukon and Konishi Yukinaga, renounced their faith when Hideyoshi, having unified the country, sought to impose ideological uniformity on the *daimyō* and ordered the expulsion of the missionaries in 1587. Hideyoshi himself was interested in foreign trade rather than Christianity. That he allowed missionaries to work, and then only for a relatively short time, was for no other reason than to ensure the smooth progress of commerce. The same can be said of Ieyasu the subsequent Tokugawa *Shōgun*.

Although Hideyoshi expelled foreign missionaries he did not suppress popular belief in Christianity, and the faith, now forced out of higher *samurai* circles, found a home among the common people. The Tokugawa authorities, still able to recall the risings of the Ikkō Sect, came almost inevitably to suppress this potentially troublesome new religion, to ban the entry of Portuguese ships into Japanese ports (in 1639) and to trade instead with the Dutch, who did not mix proselytizing with business. In short, the attitude towards the West of Japanese policymakers, from the Kyūshū *daimyō* to Hideyoshi and Ieyasu, was a mixture of an interest in technology, especially military technology, a desire for the profits of trade and feelings of concern about the political role of Christianity, with its dangers of colonization and its potential for fomenting unrest amongst the people. This attitude, which was constant throughout this period, was not unlike the one adopted by the Japanese government the next time it was compelled to deal with the West, in the second half of the nineteenth century.

In the period immediately after Japan's first contacts with the West this attitude was exemplified by Oda Nobunaga who, as we have already mentioned, made extensive use of troops armed with guns in his victory in the civil wars, overwhelming his more conservative rivals and opening the way to the military unification of the country. Nobunaga made his first bases in the productive agricultural areas of Owari and Mino (in central Honshū) and later in Ōmi; he also became a patron of the commercial town of Sakai, which supplied him with firearms. He trained troops of *ashigaru* musketeers and overcame the individual valour of the professional warrior with the more pragmatic strategies concerned with the handling of troops.

Why was it Nobunaga alone who did this? Certainly courage, decisiveness and cunning were qualities in no short supply among the *daimyō* who came through the long period of civil strife. But Nobunaga, who began his all-conquering career as the lowly Deputy of Owari, had the special advantage of being free from the constrictions of established military practice, traditional systems of values and the Buddhist-Shintō world-view. He chose a simple objective and pursued it with great thoroughness, using the most effective means at his disposal and involving himself in no wider consideration. The result was a triumph of pitiless logic.

According to the account of a perceptive Jesuit, Luis Frois, Nobunaga despised Shintō and Buddhist worship as super-stition and recognized no absolute values. His philosophy of life was entirely temporal and his character practical, an expression, in his case on the battlefield, of the inclination towards pragma-tic rationalism typical of the Japanese. (Ieyasu showed the same tendency as dictator.) The religious authority of the Buddhist Tendai Sect presented no obstacle to Nobunaga when, in 1571, he burned the temple complex of Hieizan near Kyōto and with it his enemies who had fled there; the wholesale massacres which were part of his suppression of the Ikkō Sect in Echizen in 1575 caused him no qualms. He ignored contemporary military practice in his use of musketeers and of the seven ironclad warships which enforced the blockade of Ishiyama Honganji castle, the Ikkō headquarters in Ōsaka, and helped to bring about its fall in 1580. In his bitter struggle against this sect Nobunaga had no hesitation in using the Christian missionaries whose residence in Kyōto he had permitted in 1569, but the man who despised Buddhism and Shintō can scarcely be imagined as not despising Catholicism. The concern of this brutal man was for the Church as an organization, not as a faith. His motives were not to be found in any religion; rather he viewed all religions as mere tools for the accomplishment of his ends.

The activities of the Jesuits did not result in a Japanese translation of the Bible, but versions of other works were published and distributed, such as the catechism *Dochirina kirishitan* (first edition 1591), Thomas à Kempis' *De Imitatio Christi* (*Kontentsusu munji*), published in roman script in Amaku-sa in 1596 and in a mixture of Chinese characters and *kana* (phonetic symbols) in Kyōto in 1610, and an adaptation of Ignatius Loyola's *Exercitia Spiritualia* (*Supiritsuaru shugyō*, 1607). The translations were written either in roman script or a mixture of characters and *kana* with special terms transliterated or neologisms coined. Religious terms, transliterated using *kana* or characters, remained unexplained (*Deus*, for example, became *deusu*, *fides* became *hiidesu*) or were translated into Japanese ('Devil' as *tengu*, 'God's love' as *gotaisetsu*). In their earlier work the Jesuits followed a policy of translating the more important concepts – 'God', for example, could become *dainichi* or 'great sun', a term also used to denote the Buddhist Mahavairocana; or *tentei*, 'the lord of heaven', associated with the Buddhist Sakra devanam Indra; or *tendō*, 'the Way of Heaven', another phrase loaded with Buddhist associations. Later, however, they often used the Portuguese or Latin term transliterated into Japanese without any effort to render it into a local idiom. This change in policy was possibly prompted by the thought that to render these concepts in the Japanese idiom would be likely to cause misunderstanding. The Japanese of the Meiji period took a completely different line in their relatively voluminous translation, putting all western terminology, including that of religion and philosophy, into Japanese. The effects of the methods are opposite: to avoid translation helps to preserve the pristine clarity but is likely to impede the easy spread of ideas; to translate helps the spread of ideas – and obviously speeded the diffusion of western knowledge in the Meiji period – but the resulting translation may well not be faithful to the original idea, as the many and various Meiji translations show.

How the Japanese intellectuals of the late sixteenth and early seventeenth century viewed Christianity can be surmised from the evidence of two kinds of work, apologetics written by Japanese and anti-Christian polemics, especially those written from a Buddhist or Confucian standpoint. Fukan Fabian (1565–1621?) was a Japanese who became a Jesuit in 1586, studied at Catholic schools in Ōsaka and Nagasaki and worked as a language instructor at Amakusa. Returning to Kyōto he wrote an apology for Christianity in dialogue form (*Myōtei mondō*, 1605), engaged in a written dispute with the brothers of Hayashi Razan in 1606 and then left the faith and wrote an attack on it (*Ha-daiusu*, *Anti-Christ*, 1620). He died, probably only a year later, in Nagasaki.

There are three volumes in *Myōtei mondō*. The first, which is now known as the independent work *Buppo no shidai ryakubassho*, is a critique of Buddhism; the second is an attack on Confucianism and Shintō; and the third is an exposition of Christian doctrine. The main points of Fabian's criticism of

Buddhism are firstly that Sakyamuni and Amitabha were human and as such could not bring salvation to mankind ('If they were human then they would be unable to save [other] humans in the afterlife') and secondly that the doctrine of the indivisibility of good and evil (*zen'akufuji*) lacks a Lord who would punish evil and thus preserve morality ('In this world's laws too, if [people] do not know that there is a fearful Lord above them, then the Way is not such as the Way should be' [i.e. people break the law].).

Part of Fabian's attack on Confucianism is concerned with the origins of the universe. Everything has a beginning and it is improbable, despite Confucianist claims, that the beginning is spontaneous ('Had there not been some other force which caused it, it would no have come about'). The Confucian theory that everything springs from *yinyang* (the two cosmic principles or forces, complementary and inseparable) he attacks with the comment that it does not explain the origin of *yinyang* ('Where do you think that the universal *yinyang* sprang from?'). Shintō myths are dismissed as sexual fables ('Shintō secrets are in the end only the way of *yinyang* in the sexual relationship of man and woman'), and Shintō mysteries are shallow and insignificant ('All these "mysteries" that must be hidden are not at all profound'). He disputes the belief that men came to inhabit the Japanese islands on the command of the Shintō Sun Goddess, Amaterasu, saying that in fact they arrived from neighbouring countries.

Fabian contrasts the inadequacies of Buddhism with the Christian doctrine that God became man in Christ and so brought 'salvation in the afterlife' to mankind. On the problem of good and evil he denies that the two are indivisible and asserts that man possesses an *anima rashonaru* (*anima rationalis*) and that if he keeps the Ten Commandments he will find peace in this and the next life. To correct the weaknesses he finds in Confucian metaphysics, he replaces the universal *yinyang* with the Christian God (*Deusu*) and continues: 'How then did *Deusu* begin? ... For *Deusu* there was no such thing as a beginning. Everything reaches a point beyond which it cannot rise and beyond that there is an extreme which it is impossible to question.' This theory is not consistent with his criticism of Neo-Confucianist theories of universal *yinyang*. The criticism of the Confucian theory can as fairly be applied to the Christian doctrine and the notion of the 'extreme which it is impossible to question' can just as well be used to defend the *yinyang* theory. Fabian himself must have been aware of this contradiction. That he persisted in this approach gives some indication of the stress that the Jesuit missionaries put on the doctrine of the Creation; that he fell into self-contradiction shows the difficulties he faced in accepting it.

The arguments of *Anti-Christ* are the mirror-image of those of *Myōtei mondō*. The points Fabian made against Shintō and Buddhism are now directed against Christianity, and the arguments previously used to support Christian doctrine are used to advance the cause of the other religions. Thus in *Ha-daiusu* he says that 'to regard Buddha and the gods as merely human is the mistaken view of the ignorant'. Also: 'With Joseph as his father and Mary as his mother he was not the true image of *Daiusu*. When Christ was born it was as a man.' And men, as he said in *Myōtei mondō*, cannot bring salvation to their fellows, for man, as he reasserts in *Anti-Christ*, 'is not the Lord of the universe'. Similarly the premise of his argument on creation, in *Myōtei mondō*, that everything has a beginning and needs some outside force to come into being, is denied in *Ha-daiusu*: 'Willows are green, flowers are crimson ... this is the original form of all nature.' And: 'It is always the way that branches have things which are not of the root.' Fabian seems to have regarded the problem of the spontaneity of creation as a matter neither of faith nor of ascertainable fact; he disposed of this fundamental problem arbitrarily whenever it arose.

Fabian probably knew something of Scholasticism and includes some theological disputation in *Anti-Christ*, mainly concerning the Devil and the origins of human sin. The Fall, which he had already touched upon in the earlier work, he now takes to be contradictory to the notion of an omnipotent and merciful God. 'After all, did God not know that Adam would break the vow? If He did not know, then he does not know all of the past and future. If He did know, it would have been merciful and just for Him to have prevented Adam and Eve from falling into sin.'

Fabian's religious critiques indicate the shallowness of his understanding of Buddhism and his knowledge of Christianity seems far from profound. Also it is difficult to know from his writings what he regarded as a question of faith and what a matter of reason. In the third part of *Myōtei mondō* he states that Christianity teaches people to worship God and next to Him 'to revere from the depths of their hearts their [temporal] lords' starting with the Emperor and the *Shōgun*. In a Christian country there is no rebellion or treason and 'though there is no law of the Buddha, the law of the monarch flourishes'. From this he comes to the conclusion that 'unless all Japanese become Christian ultimately they will not be governable'. In *Anti-Christ* his conclusion is that 'when the law of Buddhism and Shintō prevail the law of the monarch flourishes. And it is when the law of the monarch is present that the authority of Buddhism and Shintō increases.' It is wrong 'to break the law of the monarch, to extinguish Buddhism and Shintō and to put aside the customs of Japan' and 'to consider how to seize the country for oneself'. 'The law of the monarch' here means the established authority of the state, specifically that of Ieyasu. The defeats suffered by the Christian *daimyō* Ōtomo Sōrin and Konishi Yukinaga and the burning of other Christians are instanced as being the fault not of the oppressors but of the oppressed: 'When the Portuguese priests listened indulgently [presumably in confession] to a great treason that would overthrow the state, and said that the crime would be forgiven they were in effect saying that it would be permissible for them to commit the crime.' Therefore, 'the Portuguese priests are leaders of bandits, teachers and guides to assassins.'

Clearly Fabian's apostasy was not simply a matter of conversion from Christianity to Buddhism, from one international religion to another. Rather he changed from a system of universal principles and values to an attitude that placed the specific interests of Japan above all else, moving from a set of transcendent values to the denial of all values which transcended the confines of one specific group, the state of which he was a citizen. Naturally the value judgements used to support a religion can be inverted to attack it and arguments used in apology can be used with great accuracy in condemnation. The value system established by the founder of any religion (be it God, Buddha or *yinyang*) can conveniently be turned inside-out, and it is the apostate who does this with the greatest skill. In

Fabian's case the particular phenomenon (the Japanese state) which outweighed any argument and the abstract reasoning which he used to justify his change of faith form two parallel but separate, and intellectually unconnected strands of thought. Their connection was non-intellectual; reasoning followed where the demands of state led.

The events that were the immediate cause of Fabian's apostasy are not known. From *Ha-daiusu* we gather that it may well have been a consequence of Ieyasu's ruthless suppression of Christianity. Also his experience with foreign missionaries had sometimes been trying. 'They are arrogant people and do not think of the Japanese as human,' he says. These two factors – official oppression and mutual dislike and betrayal – must have been behind many of the apostasies of the seventeenth century.

There are also some anti-Christian works by Buddhist priests which are worthy of note. *Ha-kirishitan* (A Refutation of Christianity) by Suzuki Shōsan (1579–1655) was possibly published in 1642, six years before the *Taiji jashū-ron* (Treatise on How to Deal with the Pernicious Belief Christianity) of Sessō Sōsai (dates of birth and death unknown). The first is in Japanese, the second in Chinese; both authors were Zen priests. The argument of *A Refutation* is that the Christian outlook was in reality an extension of individual thoughts and delusions and that the theory that the body is mortal but the soul immortal had been refuted by Buddha as heresy. Sessō's *Treatise* argues that Jesus had been a follower of Buddha but had produced a heresy: 'Jesus followed Lord Buddha but [only] learned the world through the senses and taking his own mistaken view created a heresy.'

Both works comment on the geographical particularity of Christianity. *A Refutation* says: '*Deusu* did not appear in any other land, only in places near these southern barbarians.' This improbable state of affairs is also noted in *Treatise*: 'In the wide world there are many lands but among these the followers of *Deusu* are only the people of the western lands.' These two works also use an argument which occurs in almost all the anti-Christian works – there is a danger that missionaries are the forerunners of a military invasion. *A Refutation* refers to 'the plan to seize this country for the southern barbarians' and *Treatise* to 'a religion which desires to seize the state'. This argument was of course entirely in tune with the opinions of the Tokugawa authorities, and the view that Christian missionary work threatened the state was widespread among the educated ruling classes.

This threat must have seemed at its most intense in 1637 when the peasants of Amakusa, Kyūshū, bolstered by their Christian faith revolted against the imposition of heavy taxes. Nobunaga had gained power employing a policy of free trade. Now his successors of the Tokugawa regime defended their power through a policy of exclusion. In 1635 the Tokugawa authorities closed the country in an effort to stabilize its social and intellectual structure and purge it of an ideology that brought with it peasant insurrection and dangerous aliens. In this they had the overwhelming support of the educated classes.

THE INTELLECTUALS

From the fourteenth to the late sixteenth century Buddhism underwent a process of secularization which in the seventeenth century was combined with systematic institutionalization of the Buddhist church by the Tokugawa authorities. In the early part of the seventeenth century the government broke the connection between the Buddhist church and the Imperial court (the *shie hatto* or Ordinance for the Buddhist Church) and attempted to use Buddhism in the suppression of Christianity (with the structural reform known as *shūmon aratame*). Furthermore all temples were put under the direct control of their parent temples and everyone was forced to register with the local temple, thus making the Buddhist church one of the administrative organs designed to centralize power.

The most substantial intellectual legacy inherited by the Tokugawa period was probably to be found in the five great Zen temples. These temples, which had had considerable contact with China and a taste for scholarship, had a strong tradition of Sinology, which meant to a considerable extent the study of Confucianism, the philosophy that informed all the public accomplishments of the Chinese 'gentleman'. Since the Song dynasty, Chinese Confucianism had been dominated by the school of Zhu Xi and, to a lesser extent, Wang Yangming. It was these schools which were most influential on the studies made by the temple scholars. The *samurai* rulers found in this body of thought an effective ideology with which to underpin the new social system and their running of it. During this period there emerged in the Zen temples and in the court (which had a tradition of Confucian studies dating back to Heian times) a number of independent Confucianists who became active as scholars, teachers, doctors and poets and sometimes as policy-makers or at least as critics of policy. From the second part of the seventeenth century to the end of the Tokugawa period the majority of intellectuals were Confucianists. This was in marked contrast with the Muromachi period when the intellectuals were almost all Zen priests.

A system which involved the use of the Buddhist church as an administrative organ and favoured Confucianist teachings on politics and ethics was taking shape by the time of Ieyasu. (To be precise the institutionalization of the Buddhist church preceded the adoption of Confucianism; the creation of administrative machinery came before the formulation of an official ideology.) The intellectuals of the time, particularly the Zen priests and the Confucianists, adapted to the new order by taking on one of four different roles. First, there were the official scholars (goyō gakusha) who were in the service of the Tokugawa authorities; second, there were those who worked for and defended the interests of samurai houses which had played some part in the civil wars; third, there were those who addressed themselves to the ordinary, that is, non-samurai, man; and fourth, there were a small number of poets who withdrew from the world and devoted themselves to writing. That four such discrete groups can be identified is an indication of the way in which the new social system was beginning to stratify society. There were separate intellectual schools for the powerful higher-class samurai, for the middle and lower-class samurai, for the masses and for the intellectuals themselves. The state of the arts at the time was of course analogous. Whereas in the fifteenth century everyone from Shōgun to ordinary citizen watched the same sarugaku performances, in the seventeenth century the samurai watched Nō and the chōnin watched Kabuki, an unusually clear and striking example of social division.

Two figures stand out among the official scholars, the Zen priest Sūden (1569–1633) and the Tendai priest Tenkai (1536?–1643). Both of them served the first three Tokugawa Shōgun,

Ieyasu, Hidetada and Iemitsu. Sūden prepared papers on foreign policy and seems to have advised on a variety of governmental problems including trade with China, the suppression of Christianity and the reorganization of the Buddhist church. Tenkai was mainly concerned with questions of religion, especially where they impinged upon government. Thus he was in charge of religious ceremonies, the adherence of the ruling *samurai* to the Tendai Sect, incantations and prayers and the administration of temples. He also expounded a variety of Shintō belief called *Sannō ichijitsu Shintō* which was said to be based on a mystic doctrine written personally by Emperor Go-Mizunoo and given to Tenkai. This stated that 'Sakyamuni is a lesser manifestation [of the godhead]; the true image is Sannō [the guardian spirit of Mt Hiei],' reversing the usual formulation in which the Shintō deity Sannō was taken as an avatar or incarnation of the Buddhist Sakyamuni. Tenkai combined this unusual doctrine with the mystical practices of esoteric Buddhism. Quite how he did this remains obscure as none of his theoretical works survive, but, as he says in a letter: 'Speaking of *Sannō Shintō*, such a wonderful thing has never been heard of in Japan or anywhere else.'

After Ieyasu's death the discussions within the Bakufu as to what posthumous name to accord him were said to have been much influenced by Tenkai. The choice lay between the Shintō *Myōjin* ('Gracious deity') and the Buddhist *Gongen* ('Enlightened One') and it was Tenkai's view that as Toyotomi Hideyoshi had already become *Myōjin*, Ieyasu should become *Gongen*. If true this story illustrates Tenkai's, and the authorities', pragmatic approach to problems. Religious niceties, whether Shintō, Buddhist or Confucianist, were not allowed to interfere.

Another intellectual who served Ieyasu and received a stipend from him was Fujiwara Seika (1561–1619). After first entering as a monk one of the five great Zen temples, Shōkokuji of the Rinzai Sect, he renounced Buddhism and took up Confucianism, a system which was in many ways different from the philosophy of Confucius. Confucianism was originally, in the *Analects* attributed to Confucius, directed towards rulers, and explained the art of government. The Confucian concept of the good ruler was inseparable from the good man and this meant that the art of government involved both political and ethical aspects. The fundamental ethical value was filial piety with its related rituals.

About a century later in the *Mencius* there appeared a systematization of the original, relatively fragmentary Confucian teachings into a rational, politico-ethical doctrine which extended and codified the moral values expounded by Confucius, notably the five moral principles which govern the relationships between ruler and subject, father and son, elder and younger brother, man and wife, and older and younger friend. The *Mencius* also established a hierarchy of five moral values: benevolence was supreme and above propriety (the rites), followed by justice, wisdom and faith. From the Han dynasty the Confucian school of thought became the dominant perspective in Chinese education. From the time of the Five Dynasties however it was increasingly challenged by Buddhism, which had a more sophisticated cosmology and metaphysics. Buddhism itself became influenced by the other major strand of Chinese philosophy, Taoism, in, for example, the doctrines of Chan (Zen). This was followed in the Song dynasty (in the twelfth century) by the response of the Confucianist thinkers to the Buddhist challenge, a response that culminated in the thought of Zhu Xi, who provided Confucianism with a new metaphysics produced partly by assimilating Buddhist notions such as the ultimate unity of interior and exterior worlds and partly by using the concepts expounded by the *Book of Changes* and subsequent Taoist tradition such as *yinyang*. Zhu Xi reinterpreted and commented on the Confucian classics in terms of his metaphysical system so that the original political and ethical Confucian teachings could be fully incorporated into his rational, comprehensive philosophical cosmology. Zhu Xi's system, which by and large is what came to be meant by Song or Neo-Confucianism, became the authority for the interpretation of texts and the framework of Chinese higher education. All subsequent educated Chinese – and these were all at some time public officials – were Confucianists of this type.

In Japan after the collapse of the aristocratic Heian regime economic and cultural contacts with China were encouraged by the *samurai* government. In the fourteenth and fifteenth centuries temples which were subsidized by the government were visited by Chinese monks whose interests went beyond Buddhist sutras and commentaries and included the Chinese classics in general. This led to the introduction into Japan of orthodox Chinese Confucianism and the commentaries and interpretations of the classics of the Zhu Xi school. The Tokugawa regime closed the country to Christian missionaries and imposed a new social order through administrative structures and education. The organization of the Buddhist church was used as a means of regulating the populace, and Confucian moral codes were taught as the basis of the moral code of the *samurai* elite. Thus the teachers of the Bakufu and at the schools in the domains were followers of the Zhu Xi approach to the classics, and education almost automatically implied Neo-Confucianism.

Neo-Confucianist cosmology is based on two concepts, Principle (*li*) and Ether (*chi*), a homogeneous basic substance which can be either *yin* or *yang*. Ether, when in a coherent form (as a being or thing) accords to the Principle proper to that object. Continuous with the Principle of each category of thing is a universal Principle, the Supreme Ultimate, which governs the universe. Thus man has Principle inherent in him and this is in turn continuous with the universal Principle which should through Ether and *yinyang* ensure the harmony of all phenomena and forms. In fact, however, man's life is not always harmonious and the reason for this is the imperfection (or 'turbidity') of his own specific Ether. His duty therefore is to 'clear' his Ether through the pursuit of virtue, although as can be seen from the rarity of truly virtuous and wise men most people will never achieve perfection in this regard. The virtues which men are to pursue are those defined by Confucius and Mencius, and Neo-Confucianism can be described as an intellectual attempt to supply the metaphysical foundation to affirm the political and ethical ideals of classical Confucianism.

The teachers and scholars of Tokugawa Japan who studied Zhu Xi's commentaries were less interested in his metaphysics than in the ethics, which were of course essentially the same as those of early Confucianism. Their position was quite unlike that of the Song philosophers; Buddhism in Japan was secularized to a large extent and what remained of its metaphysics presented no challenge. The strongest set of beliefs were those loosely grouped under the banner of Shintō, and these were animistic, practical and this-worldly. The task then was not to respond to an alien ideology but to incorporate native popular beliefs into an intellectual system, and for this was needed not Neo-Confucian cosmology but Confucian morality. At first this need was not accompanied by any clear statement that Song metaphysics were unnecessary, but eventually there emerged a thinker who had the courage and the ability to take Confucian morality and reject Neo-Confucianist 'scholasticism'. This man was Ogyū Sorai (1666–1728) and he was able, by appealing to the authority of the original Confucian texts in which there is no mention of the metaphysical notions of Song philosophy, to declare the later cosmology in error and to assert the primacy of morality and the irrelevance of metaphysics. It was perhaps no accident that this revolt against the Neo-Confucian orthodoxy happened in Japan before anything of a similar nature occurred in China, for the Chinese civil government was always highly ideological whereas the military rulers of Japan were fundamentally unconcerned with ideological and theoretical authority.

In the case of Fujiwara Seika, however, no such challenge was made and the continuous nature of the universe was of primary importance. 'If a man's thoughts and prayers are charitable, heaven will recognize them; if they are not charitable, heaven will recognize this also,' he wrote in *Kana seiri* (Plainly Written Truths and Principles, tentatively attributed to Seika). In *Seika mondō* (Seika's Dialogues), he says that the Principle 'applies to Japan, Korea, Annam and China'. Elsewhere, in *Chiyomoto-kusa*, he asserts that: 'What is known in China as Confucianism and in Japan as Shintō, is essentially the same thing, even though under different names.' The appeal of Neo-Confucianism for Seika lay in the essence (*kokoro*) it had in common with Shintō. Seika seems to have taken literally the doctrine of benevolent government and to have thought that if the actions of a statesman were ethically correct they would be politically successful. As an adviser on the actual problems of government his usefulness must have been limited.

The man who most deeply influenced succeeding generations was not Seika but his pupil Hayashi Razan (1583–1657). Razan entered service in the *Shōgun*'s court at an early age (in 1607) and served Ieyasu and his two successors. His function within the Bakufu was that of a kind of scholarly conversation partner for the *Shōgun* rather than an adviser on the problems of govern-ment. The work *Honchō kōsō-den*, which gives biographies of eminent Japanese priests, is at pains to point out the difference between his role and that of Tenkai and Sūden. In one anecdote Tenkai abruptly asks Razan to give reasons why Confucianism should dominate Buddhism, a challenge to which Razan does not rise. The anecdote, coming as it does in a book published in the early eighteenth century, may be apocryphal but it does give what seems to be an accurate picture of the relative status of the two men. In Razan's time Neo-Confucianism was not yet the officially endorsed discipline it was to become. In fact it was not until the late eighteenth century that the minister Matsudaira Sadanobu proclaimed formally that studies other than Neo-Confucianism would not be permitted (in the edict *Kansei igaku no kin* of 1790). The *Shōgun* himself however, did, employ members of the Hayashi school and patronized their private college. Successive generations of the Hayashi school followed and elaborated upon the teachings of the Chinese Neo-Confucianist Zhu Xi, and it was this branch of Song philoso-phy which was dominant throughout the seventeenth and eigthteenth centuries when Neo-Confucianism conditioned the thought of all intellectuals.

Razan, as shown by *Santokushō*, his interpretation of the Confucianist classics *The Great Learning* and *The Doctrine of the Mean*, adopted Neo-Confucian ideas *in toto*. His most detailed and interesting work, however, is *Jumon shimonroku* (A Record of Confucian Ethical Problems), in which he deals with specific ethical problems. He recounts forty-two exemplary anecdotes from ancient Chinese history and two from Japanese history and comments on the apparent conflicts between ethical values that they illustrate. For instance, if the great Emperor Shun's father committed murder, what should the man responsible for sen-tencing him do, given that he was bound by duty to Shun and Shun bound by affection to his father? The answer is that he should carry out the law. Shun, for his part, should renounce the throne and flee with his father to the seashore, abandoning all thought of government. In this Razan follows the view of Mencius and he goes on to explain further, in the Neo-Confucian manner, that the fidelity of the judge to the law is part of 'the heavenly Principle between master and servant' and

Shun's filial devotion is 'the heavenly Principle between father and son'. In his view, 'the heavenly Principle between master and servant' allows the possibility of legally punishing the master's father; this interpretation is faithful to the mainstream of Chinese Confucianism, with its stress on the reverence for law as being above fidelity. Another anecdote tells how Emperor Wu killed his lord Emperor Zhou. Razan, following Zhu Xi, argues that this apparently criminal and insurrectionary act was justified because 'he killed Zhou in order to help the people'. This view, that an evil emperor can be removed, is potentially revolutionary and is much at odds with the views of later Japanese Confucianists who made fidelity to the lord an absolute value. Razan's arguments were close to those of his Chinese models, especially Zhu Xi. Whether these arguments were an expression of his inmost beliefs, however, is another matter.

Three indications that Razan was not altogether a devoted and conventional follower of Zhu Xi can be mentioned. Firstly, in his work *Shintō denju* he equated the Neo-Confucian Supreme Ultimate and Principle with the Shintō deity Ame-no-minaka-nushi-no-mikoto, despite the fact that the Shintō deity is personified while the Confucian concepts lack any element of personification. Perhaps Razan's perception of the Confucian ideas was simply that they were convenient intellectual tools to be used where appropriate. Secondly, the apparent shallowness of his commitment to Neo-Confucianism is also indicated in the account of his meeting with the Jesuit Fukan Fabian at Nanbanji temple, Kyōto, given in his anti-Christian work *Hai-yaso* (Anti-Christ). The subjects of the debate between the two seem, as far as we can judge, to have been three in number: Is the earth round? Who or what created the universe? And which comes first, the Principle or the Lord of Heaven? The shallowness of these topics says much about Razan's lack of profound knowledge of, or commitment to, Neo-Confucianism. In comparison the previously mentioned *A Refutation of Christianity* of the Zen priest Suzuki Shōsan is penetrating indeed. Thirdly, Razan's justification of Ieyasu's attack on the remnants of the Toyotomi faction in Ōsaka castle was scarcely the work of a rigorous intellectual. The scholars who were given the task of producing an excuse for Ieyasu's apparently treacherous attack chose to concentrate on an inscription on a bell in Hōkōji temple dedicated to the memory of Toyotomi Hideyoshi. One phrase of this Chinese inscription had the characters of Ieyasu's name separated by another character. This (obviously fortuitous) disfiguring of the name was taken as inauspicious and insulting. Razan's particular contribution was to force a reading onto another part of the inscription so that it appeared to say (or was tortured into saying) that the country would flourish only if the Toyotomi family held sway, evidence of their overweening ambition.

Not all official scholars were opportunists but in Razan's case it is difficult to deny the charge. The popularity of Confucianism came not from a belief in its essential merit but from the success of the clever and opportunistic founder of the Hayashi school in running the college and in influencing figures within the inner circles of power.

At a lower level within the *samurai* class was found the second group of intellectuals, those who spoke for the individual warrior. This was, one should remember, at a time when many warriors had actual experience of war, during the period of civil strife which had ended only a few years previously. It was this experience that informed the works on swordsmanship written during the early seventeenth century, and among these there were two outstanding models of succinct and precise writing, *Fudōchi shinmyō-roku* (The Unshifting Wisdom) by the Zen priest Takuan (1573–1645) and *Gorin no sho* (The Five Circles) attributed to the founder of the 'two sword' school of fencing, Miyamoto Musashi (1584?–1645).

Takuan, a priest of the Rinzai Sect, joined two other priests in writing a letter of protest to the governor of Kyōto, Itakura Shigemune, when in 1627 he ordered the Buddhist church to re-examine all those who had entered the priesthood without Bakufu permission after 1615. Two years later, after Tōdō Takatora, Sūden and Tenkai had conferred, the Bakufu moderated the terms of the order but banished Takuan and his fellow-priests from Kyōto. Takuan spent the next ten years in exile. Then, on the invitation of the third Tokugawa *Shōgun*, Iemitsu, he founded the temple of Tōkaiji, with an endowment of land which would yield 500 *koku* of rice annually.

Takuan's *Unshifting Wisdom* is a very clear and explicit work which deals with the techniques of swordplay used in actual combat and compares them with the practice of Zen. In both Zen and in combat the supreme state is held to be a 'disengaged spirit'. A beginner in swordsmanship knows nothing of technique and so his spirit is not engaged. Practice brings technical knowledge and a concern for it, 'an engaged spirit'. True mastery means that 'one loses any consciousness of how one is holding one's body or handling the sword'. In Zen enlightenment 'the most knowledgeable man is as one who knows nothing'. This enlightenment is 'that part of a man's heart that does not shift . . . the unshifting wisdom [fudōchi]'. A man who can complement this with a comprehensive technical repertoire will be victorious – for 'even knowing the principle is useless if you cannot handle things the way you want'. It is not clear what practical experience Takuan had of swordfighting but his writing on the subject is by no means speculative. Its specific and practical tone differs greatly from the works on Bushidō written in the latter part of the seventeenth century. Takuan's readers would have had experience in combat and would perhaps still engage in it on occasion. For the later devotees of the 'Way of the Warrior', with their stipends and administrative duties, the prospects of fighting in earnest were remote.

Another writer on swordfighting, Miyamoto Musashi, dealt with the subject practically and pragmatically. Before retiring from the world he had wandered throughout Japan matching himself successfully against swordsmen of other schools. His Five Circles represents a summation of a lifetime's experience. It consists of five books, entitled 'Earth', 'Water', 'Fire', 'Wind' and 'Void' (the gorin or 'five circles' of the elements in Buddhist terminology). The volumes are arranged systematically. The 'Earth' book gives the general argument, 'Water' explains the school's techniques, 'Fire' is on tactics, 'Wind' deals with other schools and 'Void' is the conclusion. In the conclusion Musashi says: 'Having found the correct way, leave the correct way behind; the way of tactics is spontaneity and freedom.' This 'Way of the Void' is the highest state, as it is in Takuan's Unshifting Wisdom.

In The Five Circles Musashi contends that the art of tactics can be applied to all situations in human life in order to 'triumph physically over people [and] triumph mentally over people'. 'The way of tactics ... will not be defeated by others, in whatever aspect of life.' The central concern of the work, however, is not philosophical but is the solution of a specific technical problem – how to kill the opponent. As Musashi says, 'After all, you should take up your sword with thoughts of killing'. And, 'It is all for the purpose of killing people.' On 'how to compose the feelings' he advises: 'Make no change in your usual state of mind (*kokoro*).' He distinguishes between 'seeing with the spirit' (that is, perception) and seeing with the eye, stressing the need to 'see distant things [as if] near and near things [as if] distant, [make] the sight of intuition strong and the sight of the eye weak'. This is in fact eminently practical advice; it is foolish to be so concerned with immediate matters that wider issues are ignored. Footwork should be 'as if walking normally' and the long sword 'should be wielded calmly and easily'. There is much detailed practical advice: it is better to have the sun behind you and if this is not possible keep the sun on your right side. 'Inside buildings, too, keep the light behind you or from the right.' 'Know when the opponent is becoming stronger and when becoming weaker.' 'Notice people's strong and weak points.' 'When you cannot make out what is in your opponent's mind ... make a show of attacking strongly and observe how he handles it.' Once these precepts have been absorbed and rigorously practised the swordsman may reach a state where 'having learned the principles he leaves principles behind' and 'strikes spontaneously, lands the blow involuntarily'. This is the ideal.

The Five Circles encapsulates the experience of combat gained 'in more than sixty fights, when I met with warriors of different schools, as I went here and there in various provinces'. Accordingly, its argument is free from decorative quotations from Chinese classics – 'I take no ancient words from Buddhism or Confucianism; I use nothing ancient from military tales or lore' – and has no time for the abstract or speculative. 'In tactics you cannot have a part that is outer [i.e., obvious] and another part that is inner [arcane]. The artistic [schools] invariably claim to have access to inner mysteries which they call secret traditions; but when it comes to the principles of fighting with an opponent it is not a matter of fighting using the "outer" techniques or killing through the use of some "inner mystery".'

Musashi clearly is concerned with the principles (or Principle) of combat and he considers this to be essentially the same as the Principle of Heaven. 'You do not win by supreme military skill. Skill in the Way is a thing in itself; perhaps it cannot be separated from the Principle of Heaven.' This view is, however, by no means speculative; it is as directed to the purpose, the attainment of victory, as the more practical advice. In this respect *The Five Circles* is closer to Zeami's writings on *Nō* in the fifteenth century than to other Tokugawa writing on the arts. Zeami's concern, too, was to win, in his case *Nō* competitions, and his writing contains few classical quotations and much practical and specific advice, with little speculation. The highest point of Zeami's art, like Musashi's, was to know the form with absolute thoroughness and then to break it.

The third group of intellectuals, those who addressed the masses, were for the most part Zen priests. In the early years of the Tokugawa period change in the Buddhist church was not only a matter of administrative reorganization; there was also an effort on the part of some priests to educate the common people. In the first part of the seventeenth century Suzuki Shōsan was the outstanding figure in this movement and in the latter half his place was taken by Bankei Yōtaku (1622–93). Shōsan was a *samurai* of the Mikawa domain (under the lay name of Masami-tsu) and fought with Ieyasu at Sekigahara and the siege of Ōsaka castle. Bankei, whose father was a *rōnin* (masterless *samurai*) and possibly a Confucian scholar, from Shikoku, was also of *samurai* stock. Under the Tokugawa regime there appeared not only figures like Miyamoto Musashi who made arms their profession, but also those who like Shōsan turned from the sword to Zen, and others, such as Ishikawa Jōzan, whom we shall mention later, who retreated into seclusion and literary composition. What made Shōsan and, to an even greater degree, Bankei unusual was their determination to take their knowledge and faith outside the confines of *samurai* society to the majority of the people, rather than devoting themselves to arms or literature.

We have already mentioned one of Shōsan's works, the anti-Christian polemic *A Refutation of Christianity*. His most comprehensive work, however, is the collection *Banmin tokuyō* in which he expounds the knowledge necessary for the daily life of the four classes: warrior, peasant, artisan and merchant. The part for the warriors was completed in 1631 and the work first printed in 1661. He describes virtue as being of two kinds, worldly and Buddhistic. The former consists in being unselfish and following the five cardinal moral principles (that is, the five relationships of Confucianism) while the latter lies in the realization that all is illusion and in living in 'a state of natural spontaneity' (a version of Zen teachings). In addition he enjoins the reader to chant the name of Amida and in this and other ways his teachings resemble those of the Pure Land (Jōdo) Sect. Zen asceticism would of course have had less attraction for the common man than the less arduous practices of Jōdo and perhaps this accounts for their inclusion. In *Banmin tokuyō* there are also to be found the assertion that each of the four classes – warrior, peasant, artisan and merchant – is of use to society and a belief in the virtue of hard labour. Shōsan's advice to the peasant includes this: 'Entrust yourself completely to the Way of Heaven ... do work that is hard and bitter and when selfish thoughts come to you they will not trouble you.' The harsh toil of the peasants is justified secularly and in terms of religion (as preventing selfishness).

Shōsan wrote in a succinct classical Japanese with considerable use of Chinese vocabulary. Accounts of his life indicate that his personality was more vivid than his prose style. In *Hogoshū*, a collection of fragments of his writings, letters and a memoir written by a disciple, published in 1671, there is recounted an incident when a priest told Shōsan that he had achieved enlightenment 'with a cry'. When asked whether it was while he was practising *Zazen* meditation he explained that it was in fact while he was in battle and yelling as he attacked. Shōsan's response to this was to mutter, 'An empty thing!' On another occasion a *samurai* told him that he had achieved 'an inkling of the impermanence of things', that he was able to feel *mono no aware* (an intense empathy with the exterior universe). Shōsan's brisk reply was, 'What use is it to sit there and luxuriate in feelings like that? Just you brace your feelings up!' In his version of Zen, unlike others, no importance was given to the excitements of the battlefield or acute perception of the transitoriness of the world. What mattered was composure in thought and deed.

Composure was not easy to attain in an apparently futile world as two other anecdotes in *Hogoshū* illustrate. Looking at a young girl Shōsan is said to have murmured, 'What a great, great pity ... nothing is so foolish as human life.' And to a man who after four or five years of Buddhist discipline said that it did not suit him, he said, 'I have trained for seventy years and it has never suited me. I've simply become so that I can force myself to do it gritting my teeth.' This view, that the self-discipline of Zen strengthens the character, is anthropocentric in tone.

The sayings of Bankei Yōtaku are collected in *Bankei buttchi kōsai zenji oshimeshi kikigaki* (Records of the Sayings of Bankei on the Wisdom and Compassion of Buddha, published 1757), which seems to be a fairly direct record of what he said, written in a colloquial style, mostly in *kana*. When young he was ignored as a heretic or a 'Christian' but in his later years he complained, 'Too many people come to see me. ... I never have a quiet day to myself.' And in a biographical piece written fifty years after his death it is claimed that: 'His disciples now number more than fifty thousand from the elevated, marquises, earls, ministers and officials, to the lowly, the ordinary peasant men and women.' This estimate is probably an exaggeration but it is certain that his following was large.

Bankei's central doctrine was of 'the immutable Zen'. Everybody possesses a 'Buddha-heart' which is imperishable: 'The Buddha-heart is immortal and immutable and everything is in harmony.' It is only the body which is born and dies: 'The body is made for a certain time and so is born and dies; the heart is the original heart and so is not born and does not die.' Evil stems from selfish desire (*gayoku*), twisted inclinations (*kiguse*) and partiality (*mi no hiiki*), when the Buddha-heart is rejected. Selfish desire is not predetermined but is a matter of personal free will: 'Whether you steal or do not steal depends on the will and not on *karma*.' To reject selfish desires and return to the Buddha-heart is to become a Buddha, and this is the purpose of an individual's life. Bankei says: 'If you cannot become a Buddha now you will not do so in a myriad ages. You are born human in order to become a Buddha.'

Bankei's religious thought marked no new departure in the history of ideas but his popularization of Zen produced, if no new general principles, at least some original particular conclu-

sions and a thoroughgoing application of ideas whose usefulness had previously been limited to the few who understood
them. Firstly, he extended the idea that the Buddha-heart is
common to all into a kind of sexual egalitarianism: 'What
difference is there between men and women? Man is the form of
Buddha and woman too is the form of Buddha.' However, the
view that men and women are equal in having an identical
Buddha-heart made no claim for the equality of all against the
social system of hereditarily fixed hierarchy. Secondly, his use
of the colloquial meant that he was a more effective popularizer
than Shōsan, and this was quite deliberate: 'I peacefully ask and
answer questions about the Way in a manner which suits the
Japanese. The Japanese are poor at the Chinese language and
we cannot explain the Way as completely as we would like in
Chinese.'

Use of the colloquial, as well as being necessary in a popular
movement, perhaps had a further meaning for Bankei. To teach
Buddhism as a part of everyday life would have meant that the
teachings became involved with every part of his life and
formed the fibre of his existence. But the fundamental truth of
Buddhism – the universal and immutable 'Buddha-heart' –
transcended everyday life and political and cultural boundaries.
For him to interpret it in 'a manner that suits the Japanese' did
not imply that the Japanese were of a different order of existence
from other peoples, especially, for Bankei, the Chinese. Rather,
his belief in a transcendent value meant that he could judge the
Chinese on the same basis as the Japanese, as in this comment:
'Judging by recent Chinese books, I can find no "immutable"
man in China today. There too the tradition seems to have been
lost long ago.' His attitude is reminiscent of that of the thirteenth-century priest Dōgen who in his major works, written in
Japanese, criticized the Zen establishment in terms of a transcendent value, 'True Law' (shōbō), and was not overawed by the
authority of Chinese Buddhism. The commonality of the
Buddha-heart and the vernacular language are two features that
make Bankei's teachings exceptional in the history of Japanese
Buddhism.

The characteristics which Shōsan and Bankei shared were
close contact with the masses and a conservative attitude to the
society in which they found themselves. This is reminiscent on

the one hand of the popularism of the priest and woodcarver
Enkū (1632?–95), a contemporary of Bankei who travelled
throughout the country leaving behind him a vast number of
natabori ('hatchet carvings'), and the sculptor of Buddhist images
Mokujiki Gogyō (1718–1810). On the other hand there seems to
be a connection with *Shingaku*, the sect founded by Ishida
Baigan (1685–1744), carried on by Tejima Toan (1718–86) and
popular throughout the eighteenth century. *Shingaku* was primarily a popularization of Confucianist ethics, directed mainly
at the *chōnin* and defensive of the social hierarchy. That Shōsan
(in particular) and Bankei were in some way forerunners of
Shingaku is also indicated by the fact that Toan wrote a preface to
the 1778 edition of *Mōanjō*, an early work of Bankei's (completed
1619, first published 1651). The spread of ideology through the
masses, which was to characterize the Tokugawa period, had
already begun.

The final group of intellectuals which can be distinguished
was one made up of poets in retreat. Most of these had been
warriors in the civil wars. Prominent among them was Ishikawa
Jōzan (1583–1672), who was as a boy a page to Ieyasu. He
became a priest after killing an enemy soldier against orders
during the summer siege of Ōsaka castle in 1615. After some
years in Myōshinji temple in Kyōto he was introduced to
Neo-Confucianism by Seika and Razan and turned to it exclusively. In his later years, from 1640, he lived in Shisendō, the
villa on Kyōto's Mt. Higashiyama, in peaceful retirement,
gazing at 'the evening smoke of Kyōto' and was said never to
have crossed the Kamo River to the city. He was a meticulous
gardener and a skilful calligrapher in the antique *reisho* style,
and he wrote two collections of poems, *Fushōshū* and *Shinpen
fushōshū*. In these there are poems on falling leaves and dripping
eaves such as:

> Parting from the branches
> Leaves tap on door and window
> Mingling with the sound
> Of drops falling from high eaves.

And, on the joy of retreat:

> In retreat there is nothing
> To enthrall me

> Idle by nature,
> Given up to solitude.

Later writers such as Ogyū Sorai, Kan Sazan and Ōkubo Shibutsu remembered Jōzan's poetic achievement in their writing. Sazan, for instance, in the 'seven syllable' style Chinese poem *Shisendō* says:

> In his time there was only
> Ishikawa Jōzan
> A man of noble spirit,
> Who made good poetry.

The Nichiren Sect priest and poet Gensei (1623–68) began writing a little later than Jōzan. He had been a *samurai* in the service of Ii Naotaka at Edo before becoming a priest and retiring to Fukakusa in the south of Kyoto, where he led a life similar to that of Jōzan at Shisendō. He was a prolific writer, exchanging verse and prose with Kumazawa Banzan (1619–91), and was also famous for his filial piety. His Japanese short poems are collected under the title *Sōzan wakashū*, and his Chinese verse fills the thirty volumes of the collection *Sōzanshū*. Two examples, the first a *waka* on autumn:

> In the water of a pool
> Reflecting the form of a white chrysanthemum
> I see all the autumns of a thousand years.

And the last two lines of a Chinese 'five syllable' poem (also autumn):

> Boundless autumn light and unbounded thoughts,
> Blue heavens fresh and cool, white clouds floating at ease.

These reveal a poet who, like Baudelaire, loved blue sky and white clouds and delighted in the play of light. The same qualities may be seen in his Chinese 'five syllable' poem:

> A mind in the three-fold universe
> Goes and stays in freedom
> Like a cloud in the heavens
> No obstacle to its movement.

During this period a poet virtually had to go into seclusion. Not until the latter part of the century did Chinese verse become an accomplishment expected of Confucianists, and not until after the eighteenth century did it become the main concern of a significant number of them.

The above four groups account for most of the intellectuals of the time but there were of course exceptions and perhaps most exceptional of all was Nichiō (1565–1630), a Buddhist priest of the Nichiren Sect. Nichiō found himself in opposition to the military authorities and was banished by Ieyasu to Tsushima where he stayed for thirteen years before being allowed to return to Kyōto. He was scarcely less docile after his return and in 1630, the year of his death, was once more ordered into exile. His opposition to the authorities began over an issue which divided the Nichiren Sect in Kyōto. In 1595 priests of the sect were invited to take part in an interdenominational service for the souls of the dead at Hōkōji, a temple built and patronized by Toyotomi Hideyoshi. The spirit in which this 'invitation' was made was left in no doubt. Two factions formed, one maintaining that although the authorities did not look favourably on the sect, if they offered some form of patronage it would be unwise to refuse it; and the other insisting that the tradition established by Nichiren himself, that the sect should not share religious observances with non-members, had to be preserved. On one side was the authority of the state, law and order; on the other was the religious purity of the sect, 'the righteousness of the Lotus Sutra'. The two sides faced each other from fundamentally different standpoints.

Nichiō, the leader of the 'no compromise' faction, set down his views in the three volumes of Shūgi seihō-ron (1616). Written in Chinese, this consists of bitter attacks on his opponents, especially the leader of the other faction, Nikken. His main points are expressed with some clarity but the subsequent argument is often diffuse and repetitious. Nichiō's first point is that priests of the Nichiren Sect should not give support to priests of other sects (and in fact the opposing faction accepted this as a rule of the sect) and should not receive support from them (on this the opposition faction disagreed although for three hundred years, since the time of Nichiren, this rule had been observed). The fact that the Nichiren Sect had consistently refused the support of others 'even though it be by the command of the ruler of the country', leads Nichiō to his second point: When this religious law comes into conflict with the demands of the state it should not be circumvented to accommodate temporal authority; the sect should instead point out the state's error and resign itself to inevitable persecution. He supported this argument with the assertion that it was not the temporal authorities which ruled the world but Sakyamuni, and that Japan itself represented no more than a small part of Sakyamuni's domain.

This relativistic view of Japan, though distinctively Buddhistic, was analogous to the Christian viewpoint, and the Tokugawa authorities who examined the question at Ōsaka castle in 1599 and Edo castle in 1630 would certainly have seen the parallels. Both Christianity and Nichiō's faction represented theoretical challenges to the absolute authority of the state and had to be suppressed. They were declared 'forbidden religions' and Nichiō, the great exception, was effectively obliterated. With him was extinguished belief in an authority that transcended that of the state. The Tokugawa government was never again challenged in these terms. When the Bakufu fell it was replaced by another temporal authority; one worldly ideology was supplanted by another, the *Shōgun* by the Emperor.

HON'AMI KŌETSU AND HIS CIRCLE

Not all the artists of the seventeenth century were poets. Indeed from the end of the sixteenth to the middle of the seventeenth century the highest achievements of Japanese art were to be found not in literature but in the plastic arts. It was a high point in the arts with many of the truly original works of Japanese imagination completed or begun during this period. Architecture saw, on the one hand, the perfecting of the monumental style of castle with its imposing donjon and, on the other, the tea house, an extreme refinement of what at first glance might seem rustic simplicity. The gardens of Shūgakuin, the palace of the Retired Emperor Go-Mizunoo, and Katsura, the 'detached palace' of Prince Tomohito, represented a peak in the art of garden design. These gardens defined the relationship between building and garden in a distinctive way. Whereas the gardens of the Alhambra are enclosed by, and form a part of, the building and at Versailles the gardens are treated in terms of architectural space (as an extension of the building), the gardens of the two Kyōto palaces surround and absorb the buildings.

In painting, Tawaraya Sōtatsu (dates of birth and death unknown) and anonymous genre painters revived the *Yamato-e* style of painting, a tradition which stretched back to Heian times, and thus freed Japanese art from the strong mainland influence that had been felt since the Muromachi period. Sōtatsu's originality lay in his mastery of the technique of *tarashikomi* (in which paint or ink is applied to a previous coat which is not yet dry, producing a blurring or blotching effect), his bold abstraction and his distinctive spatial distribution. His style was always recognizable whether he was painting a large screen or a tiny fan – an expanse of flat colour or subtle shading in a patch of ink. He became the inspiration of Kōrin and the later Rinpa school of artists years after his death, and in his own work he drew on and distilled the tradition of an aristocratic culture which had survived the Muromachi period and dated back to Heian times. It was the literary arts of the Heian court that provided the theme for many of his paintings. Sōtatsu's genius was a summary of previous culture and at the same time a prefiguring of the art yet to come.

At the same time genre artists (almost all anonymous) were portraying a wide range of subjects – the ships of the 'southern barbarians', a flower-viewing party at Daigo, shop fronts of merchant houses, serving women, the rich and poor of Kyōto and the provinces. They combined a keen sense of observation and a fine sensibility of the beauty of colour and line. What are called 'floating world' woodblock prints (*ukiyo-e*) were not made until the second half of the seventeenth century, but the 'floating world' was already present in these paintings of the late sixteenth century.

The rough and humble taste associated with the tea ceremony, *wabi*, was further refined in the tea vessels of Oribe (Furuta Shigenari, 1544–1615), who developed the (slightly perverse) aesthetic of the distorted to a high point. Happy accidents of colour and glaze were also prized in China, but

Japan was unique in the extent to which it valued the irregular and the maculate.

At the turn of the century greater originality was to be seen in Japanese art than in any other period. Historically, however, the significance of the art of this time lay in more than its originality. From the sixth to the thirteenth century the greatest Japanese works of art (if we except certain picture scrolls) were buildings, statues and paintings connected with Buddhism. In the fourteenth century came ink painting (*suiboku-ga*), which can be regarded as an expression of the secularization of the Zen faith which nourished it, and the decorative and completely secular painting of the Kanō school, the official painters to the highest *samurai* families. The complete secularization of art did not come, however, until the period between 1550 and 1650 during which every masterpiece of architecture, garden design, painting and craftsmanship was for secular purposes and, when appropriate, of a secular subject. This division between art and religion marks clearly and definitively the end of an age; never since have the two come together again. The collapse of Buddhism as a source of artistic creation coincided, not surprisingly, with its incorporation into the machinery of government and its subsequent decline in ideological credibility. This does not imply that major artists of the time were not themselves devout Buddhists. The great calligrapher Shōkadō Shōjō (1584–1639) was a monk of the Shingon Sect and the painter Hasegawa Tōhaku (1539–1610) and the period's great 'arbiter of taste', Hon'ami Kōetsu (1558–1637), were both members of the Nichiren Sect. There is no sign, however, that Buddhism directly affected their work.

The division of literature into types to suit the strata of society had its equivalent in the fine arts where the divisions were if anything more striking. For the higher *samurai* there was, and had been since the Muromachi period, the Kanō school. The outstanding seventeenth-century painter of this school was Kanō Tan'yū (1602–74), whose career with the Bakufu started early and encompassed the sumptuous decoration of a great number of screens and sliding doors in *samurai* mansions and temples. In his larger works of twisted pines, ferocious (if not always convincing) dragons and tigers with a bold show of strength, he uses strong colours and often a ground of gold leaf.

They are typical of the Kanō style, lavish but slightly empty, trying to impress and to preserve the school's traditional authority. They also reflect the aesthetic notions of the ruling warriors, a sense of taste which found its fullest expression in this period in Ieyasu's memorial shrine, the Tōshōgū in Nikkō, north of Edo.

The arts patronized by Kyōto aristocrats, and by the *samurai* and merchants who were part of their rarefied circle, included more than palace gardens. In Sōtatsu's paintings they found not pines but grasses and flowers, not tigers but deer and, instead of dragons, waterfowl, *bugaku* court dancers and classical lovers meeting at some water's edge. Sōtatsu's line has a lyrical elegance, his colours a calm strength, and his composition is such that even the violence of subjects like the gods of wind and rain is contained in an undisturbed and harmonious tension. This aesthetic owes little to the contemporary culture of the *samurai* and the *chōnin*; it evokes and recreates the old aristocratic culture in a way only genius could achieve.

Genre paintings on the other hand depicted the ways of the *chōnin*. For whom they were painted is a matter of doubt; certainly not for the majority of the *chōnin* class, but probably for rich merchants. They were, however, the forerunners of the later and very popular *chōnin* art form, the *ukiyo-e* woodblock print.

During the age of the woodblock print, the eighteenth century, when the stratification of society had reached a condition of rigid completeness, there emerged the fourth distinctive type of graphic art, the *nanga* style of painting favoured by Confucian intellectuals. By then of course aristocratic culture had faded into insignificance and *chōnin*-supported painters such as Kōrin and his followers were prominent.

In the seventeenth century to be an artist was to be an intellectual and there were many men whose talents covered many fields. Among the aristocracy there were Karasumaru Mitsuhiro (1579–1638), who was a noted calligrapher and a fine writer of *waka* poems in the *Kokindenju* tradition, as of *kyōka* and *haikai* verse, and the retired Emperor Go-Mizunoo (1596–1680), who is said to have directed the construction of his Shūkaguin detached palace personally, a task in which he employed his many artistic talents. Distinguished artistic *samurai* included the *daimyō* Kobori Nasakazu (Enshū) (1579–1647) who was a first-rate tea master (and taught the third *Shōgun*, Iemitsu) as well as an architect, garden designer (of the Kohō-an garden of Daitokuji temple among others), *waka* poet and painter. From the ranks of the priesthood came Shōkadō Shōjō, acknowledged as one of the three great calligraphers of the Kan'ei period (1624–44), a talented painter of *suiboku-ga* and *yamato-e*, a *waka* poet and a tea master. And from the *chōnin* (or *machishū* as they were more commonly known at the time) came Hon'ami Kōetsu, the great judge and restorer of swords who also produced masterpieces of calligraphy, ceramics and lacquerware.

The centre to which all these accomplishments contributed was undoubtedly the tea ceremony. Architecture, garden design, calligraphy, painting and ceramics were particularly influenced by the conventions and taste of the tea ceremony and the artists themselves seem to have met most often at tea gatherings in Kyōto where, or near where, they all lived. Their coterie life and their interest in *waka* bore a closer resemblance to the life of the Heian aristocracy, who would gather for poetry parties, than to that of the *samurai* intellectuals of the Muromachi period, who were involved in the popular culture of *sarugaku* and *renga*. The tea ceremony originated in the upper classes and, during this period at least, stayed there. (Later in the Tokugawa period groups of intellectuals gathered to paint, compose poems and practise calligraphy but they were quite different from the tea ceremony group – they were Confucianist, their verse was Chinese and their intellectual centre had moved to Edo and, to some extent, been diffused into the provinces.)

The loosely knit group of artists and men of culture in Kyōto seems to have found its social centre in Kōetsu, whose acquaintanceship ranged far and wide. Coming from a family of swordsmiths and connoisseurs, Kōetsu had close connections with the families of several higher *samurai* (especially Maeda of Kaga) and the *Shōgun*. He was close to the governor of Kyōto, Itakura Shigemune (who in turn was a friend of Hayashi Razan and Ishikawa Jōzan), and through him several *daimyō*. And he also had strong links with wealthy Kyōto merchant families, including two of the three greatest. He worked with one wealthy merchant, Suminokura Soan, on the production of the printed editions of Nō plays, Ise monogatari and other Heian works that were named Sagabon (Saga edition) after the Kyōto suburb where they were made. In his later years Kōetsu set up an artists' community in Takagamine, north Kyōto, on land granted to him by Iemitsu, and there still exists a plan of the 'village' with the names of the residents. Among the fifty-five householders there was a merchant, Chaya Shirōjirō, and, next door to him, Ogata Sōhaku, the grandfather of Kōrin and Kenzan and himself a chōnin.

The nature and extent of Kōetsu's relationship with Sōtatsu are not known definitely. Kōetsu was acquainted with the aristocrat Karasumaru Mitsuhiro and Mitsuhiro knew Sōtatsu. Kōetsu's calligraphy is found on paintings attributed to Sōtatsu. These facts alone do not prove that Kōetsu and Sōtatsu knew each other or worked together but they go some way towards supporting the proposition. Similarly Kōetsu's connection with the tea masters Shōkadō Shōjō, Kobori Enshū and Senno Sōtan (1578–1658) are by no means clearly established. All that is definitely known, from an extant letter, is that Senno Sōjun, Sōtan's father, knew Sōtatsu. However, in the group of highly cultured, versatile and like-minded people which was the world of the tea ceremony in the seventeenth century, we can imagine that it would be almost inevitable that these people would know each other. Certainly there were enough intellectuals and craftsmen who felt themselves to be part of this cultural community for Kōetsu's artists' village to flourish for many years.

We can glimpse something of Kōetsu's life in the collection of letters, sayings and anecdotes of the Hon'ami family entitled Hon'ami gyōjōki, of which the first volume, apparently put together by Kōetsu's grandson Kōho (1601–82), is concerned with Kōetsu and his parents. (Subsequent volumes, apparently of different editorship, are fragmentary and obscure.) It mentions Kōetsu's involvement with swords but not his calligraphy or ceramics; of his character we learn that he was frugal ('when he was ill Lord Itakura and his son often visited him and were concerned that he lay in cotton bedclothes'), disliked flattery and believed fervently in the Nichiren Sect. Two parts of the volume stand out. One comprises Kōetsu's letters to Matsudaira Nobutsuna, in which he gives his opinions on various topics, and the other is the set of anecdotes about Kōetsu's mother, Myōshū.

Kōetsu's views on politics were level-headed and practical. He thought that attempts to exert strict control over the country were futile, quoting Ieyasu's words, 'Ruling a country is like washing a nest of boxes using a pestle' (that is, remarkably imprecise). As for economics he thought that even if *daimyō* 'did not borrow gold and silver from *chōnin* things would probably work out one way or another'. This, it may be added, was at a time when such borrowing was well established. On higher matters, in that statesmen 'bring peace to society' they were 'following the will of the gods and the Buddha' and need have no belief in them apart from that. All that they needed to do was show them a 'distant respect'. Scholars were of no use to government, nor were Neo-Confucianist thinkers: 'Evil men become more evil through scholarship, fools merely become glib; men who make the essence of learning their own and use it in the affairs of the day are rare indeed.' Even in China, 'while I accept that in the writings that have come to us from the Song dynasty there are some lofty arguments, these are essentially just verbal formulations and I cannot say that they add anything to the ability to rule the state in harmony.' Kōetsu's dismissal of 'lofty arguments' speaks for his faith in the fundamentalist Nichiren Sect and his practical, craftsman's outlook. And of course his frequent visits to the mansions of *daimyō* must have given him some taste of the realities of power.

THE MASSES: TEARS AND LAUGHTER

In the late sixteenth and early seventeenth centuries there were two developments that were to have considerable effect on the world of the popular arts, the development of printing and the creation of officially approved brothel quarters. Both of these were to be of great significance throughout the Tokugawa period.

By the turn of the century the Jesuits at Nagasaki were producing Christian literature in printed form, and in Kyōto printing with movable wood or copper type (said to have been brought from Korea by Hideyoshi) was making progress. In the 1620s, however, the technique in which an entire page was printed from one wood block appeared, and almost everything printed after 1650 was done in this way. These years marked the beginning of a new relationship between the mass of the population and its literary arts; to a tradition which had until then been oral was added a growing body of written and printed works. In the first half of the seventeenth century there were more than a hundred publishers, and one book, a catechetic exposition of Confucianism written in *kana*, *Kiyomizu monogatari*, is said to have sold two thousand copies. Works in *kana*, including the popular stories known as *kanazōshi*, met with increasing success through the latter part of the seventeenth century. In 1670, for instance, 1,025 books were sold and by 1692 the figure had risen to more than twice that, 2,456.

During the same period the Tokugawa authorities adopted a policy of gathering together in designated areas the prostitutes who worked in the major cities. These areas, known as *kuruwa*, were established in Shimabara in Kyōto, Shinmachi and Sonezaki in Ōsaka, and Yoshiwara in Edo. They quickly flourished and later expanded enormously; at the beginning of the eighteenth century, for instance, there were said to be 8,400 licensed prostitutes in Ōsaka and 3,000 in Yoshiwara. Prostitutes usually came from the lower classes of society but within the *kuruwa* they established an independent system of rank and status, the highest of the several ranks being the *tayū* and *tenjin*.

Clients for their part left social status behind when they entered the *kuruwa*; inside, money alone was important. Thus these areas became in a way separate worlds within society and no doubt served as safety valves for the pressures created by the rigid social stratification imposed by the authorities. For *chōnin* with money there was more liberty to be had within the walls of the brothel quarter than outside them. Moreover, according to *Naniwa monogatari* (published 1655, author unknown), there were some among the higher-class courtesans who could not only sing popular songs (*kouta*) and dance but also play the *koto* and 'write an excellent hand in a style that can be relished' (*fumi ni aji o kaku*). The *kuruwa* and the culture which developed within it was a rich mine of material for the Tokugawa writers of fiction and drama dealing with the *chōnin*.

There was of course also a considerable cultural legacy from the Muromachi period. Above all, there was a concern for the arts on the part of the common man, the same concern which had been shown for the 'popular culture' of the Muromachi period, with its universally popular *sarugaku* and *renga*. By the beginning of the seventeenth century, however, *Nō* and *Kyōgen* had become the pastimes of the ruling class, and the masses who had watched them in the fifteenth century now watched women's *Kabuki* (*onna Kabuki*) and, after its prohibition in 1629, young men's *Kabuki* (*wakashū Kabuki*). Another popular traditional form, *katarimono*, or narratives chanted to a simple accompaniment, was combined with puppet plays during the early seventeenth century to produce the forms known as *jōruri* and *sekkyōbushi*. There were other debts to tradition, among them the iconoclastic tone and explicit sexual descriptions of *haikai*, descendants of the linked-verse *renga* of the collection *Inu tsukubashū* and the secularism of the verse of the *Kanginshū*.

The writers who picked up these traditions in this new age of printing and a *chōnin* readership were for the most part intellectuals. Among them were doctors like Hata Sōha (1550–1607), who wrote *Inumakura*, and Isoda Dōji (1585–1634), author of *Chikusai*; priests like Anrakuan Sakuden (1554?–1642), who wrote *Seisui-shō*, *samurai* like Asai Ryōi (1612?–91); and scholars like Kitamura Kigin (1624–1705). All of them wrote in a style which mixed Chinese characters with *kana* and, to a greater or lesser extent, included elements from popular speech.

Some wrote in a literary manner, some in a manner close to the colloquial. Content was equally varied, ranging from *Kiyomizu monogatari* and *Ninin bikuni*, which are expositions in dialogue form of, respectively, Confucianism and Buddhism, through *Uraminosuke*, a romantic novel, *Chikusai*, a comically illustrated diary of a journey to famous places, *Otogi bōko*, ghost stories based on the Chinese collection *Jian deng xin hua* (New Tales for Lamplight), *Seisui-shō*, a collection of comic stories, and *Meijo nasake kurabe*, instructive folklore stories, to *Naniwa monogatari*, a guide to courtesans and the art of love and a direct product of the *kuruwa* society. There were also parodies of famous Heian works, which did in prose what parts of *Inu tsukubashū* had done in verse. *Inumakura*, for example, parodies the 'lists of things' (*mono wa zukushi*) of Sei Shōnagon's *Makura no sōshi*, and *Nise monogatari* (author unknown, probably written about 1640) is a parody – the word *nise* means 'copy' or 'fake' – of *Ise monogatari*.

The 'lists of things' given in *Inumakura* include such 'pleasant things' as 'writings that pass an idle hour' (a reference to

Kenko's *Tsurezuregusa*); 'unpleasant things' include 'rats that eat books and likewise bookworms', and 'things that alleviate tedium' include 'times when one takes out ancient writings'. The writer seems to have led the life of an intellectual and the *kyōka* or comic *tanka* at the end of the volume are reminiscent of *Inu tsukubashū*:

> Wide things: the enlightened spirit
> The sky over all,
> A mother's thing,
> Musashino plain.

The writer's insights into everyday thoughts and feelings are acute. There are, for example, 'things that don't seem to succeed but succeed': 'a catamite with a patron, an intellectual woman, practice in the performing arts and a grafted fruit tree'. On human life generally he comments that life 'full though it be of shame' is one of the 'things better for being longer' and that the years after fifty are among the 'things better for being shorter'. It seems that he was not an orthodox follower of the teachings of either Buddhism or Confucianism but had a *carpe diem* view of life tinged with pessimism.

Nise monogatari, unlike *Inumakura*, follows the work it parodies word by word and phrase by phrase, changing it for comic effect. The opening sentences of the respective works are:

ISE MONOGATARI	NISE MONOGATARI
Mukashi	*Okashi*
long ago	a strange
otoko	*otoko*
a man	man
uikōburi shite	*hōkaburi shite*
who had donned his first hat [of manhood]	covering his face with cloth
Nara no kyō Kasuga no sato ni	*Nara no kyō Kasuga no sato ni*
and in the village of Kasuga in the capital Nara	to the village of Kasuga in the capital Nara
shiru yoshi shite	
had an estate	
Kari ni inikeri	*sakenomi ni ikikeri*
he went hawking.	he went to drink *sake*.
Sono sato ni	*Sono sato ni*
in that village	in that village

ito namameitaru onna	*ito namaguusaki sakana*
some very fresh and graceful girls,	very fresh fish
harakara suminikeri	*haraka to iu arikeri*
two sisters, lived.	there was, called *haraka* [salmon trout].
Kono otoko	*Kono otoko*
the man	the man
Kaima mitekeri	*Kaute minikeri*
spied them through a chink.	bought some to see [what it was like].

In the case of *mukashi/okashi uikōburi/hōkaburi* and *harakara/ haraka*, the parody takes the form of a simple echoing of the sound of the original word. But when 'hawking' is transformed to 'to drink *sake*' and 'fresh and graceful girls' become 'fresh and sweet fish' we notice the strong contrast between the life of the aristocracy and that of the masses. To appreciate the ingenious detail with which the author of *Nise monogatari* adapts all of *Ise monogatari* one must know the original virtually by heart. There were no doubt people who had this kind of detailed knowledge, as *Ise monogatari* had been much read from Muromachi times, but such a level of education was far beyond the common man. *Nise monogatari* is mainly about relationships between men and women but it also touches on a variety of things that were part of everyday *chōnin* life, including *sumō*, *go*, gambling, foxes and racoon-dogs or *tanuki* (both creatures with supernatural abilities), brothels, all kinds of food and, most frequently, *sake*. Its attitude is generally life-affirming and optimistic.

The *waka* in *Nise monogatari* are naturally parodies of those in the earlier work. For example, Ariwarano Narihira's original 'Spring' reads:

> If there were no more cherry blossoms in this world of ours
> How free and easy our feelings in spring!
>
> (*Ise monogatari* 82)

This becomes in *Nise monogatari*:

> If there were no more wives and children in this world of ours
> How free and easy our feelings now!

This new verse anticipates the *senryū* of the *Haifū yanagidaru* collection compiled from 1765 to 1838. Narihira's 'Elegy' reads:

> I had long heard of the final journey
> But did not think yesterday
> It would be today.
>
> (*Ise monogatari* 125)

This becomes:

> I'd heard I'd need no money on the final journey
> So I gave it yesterday
> To that sutra-chanting priest.

The latter parody is a good example of the attitude of the people at that time to death, an attitude not unlike the 'gallows humour' of the West. A man deals with what is within his power and jokes away the things – death, the government – which are beyond it. The author of *Nise monogatari* shared with his contemporaries this clearheaded and practical view of life and the concomitant distrust of absolute values that might confuse and complicate it.

The sense of humour of the ordinary man and woman of the time is felt most clearly in the *shōwa* or 'funny stories' such as those in the collection *Kinō wa kyō no monogatari* (Yesterday's Happenings Are Today's Tales, editor unknown, published probably around 1620). This collection of 230 humorous anecdotes, some apparently from a previous oral tradition, was widely read at a time when popular colloquial books, *kanazōshi*, of which of course it was one, sold in large numbers. Many of the stories are about priests and their breaking of dietary prohibitions or sexual peccadillos. Frank sexual jokes, about both priest and layman, and jokes which depend on the quick-wittedness of one of the characters are both common. To take one example: A man goes to a temple, asks for the priest and is told he is out. The man, who has come a long way, rests for a while and, peering through some bushes, sees the priest plucking a goose. The priest, in some confusion, explains that he is plucking it because he has heard that if he puts goose feathers in his pillow it will help his gout but, not being used to it, he is finding the plucking difficult. Saying, 'Oh that's easy, give it to me,' the man plucks the feathers and gives them to the priest. Then with a quick 'Well, you won't be needing this carcass then,' he takes it home and happily eats it.

In another story a couple want to have a 'midday session' but are inhibited by their two children. They think up the plan of sending the boys to the stream to wash pans, but just as the couple have started and 'are far away', the children return. When the somewhat flustered parents demand to know why they have come back without washing the pans, the older boy answers, 'Well, there's a lot of lunchtime hanky-panky going on so a lot of kids have been sent down to the stream to wash pans. There was no room for us to wash ours so we came home.'

The layman is more quick-witted than the priest, the children quicker than their parents; this is reminiscent of *kyōgen* in which the servant Tarōkaja exercises his quick wits on his master. There is a difference however. The comedy of *kyōgen*, which typically has a slow-witted provincial lord as the butt of the jokes, arises from the disparity between social position and ability. The humour of *Yesterday's Happenings Are Today's Tales* springs from the abrupt overturning of expectations and the thwarting of the desire for food or sex. The two types of comedy were for different audiences. *Kyōgen* developed as an entertainment for all classes whereas *Yesterday's Happenings Are Today's Tales* was read by only one class of a rigidly stratified society.

It was not only laughter that the ordinary citizen wanted from literature; the affecting and touching were also in demand. And grief was something that *sekkyōbushi*, for example, had in full measure. *Sekkyōbushi* was developed from *katarimono*, narratives recited to the accompaniment of *shamisen*, *sasara* (a simple percussion instrument of split bamboo) and *kokyū* (a bowed string instrument resembling the *shamisen*), by itinerant beggars known as *Ise kojiki* who would go from door to door. Later, in the early seventeenth century, these narratives were set to puppet plays and became extremely popular. Extant works from this period include such relatively well known pieces as *Sanshō dayū*, *Karukaya*, *Shuntoku-maru* and *Oguri hangan*. They are written largely in a 7–5 syllabic pattern and recount episodes of ineffable hardship in the lives of the principal characters, the aim being to bring tears to the eyes of the listener. The passage 'He drew her close and wailed with grief, pushed her from him and wailed, he shed burning tears, weeping as if he would pass away' is from *Karukaya* and describes the grief of a young man at the death of his mother. It continues with the stock phrase *ara itawashiya Ishidō-maru* ('Ah, what grief, Ishidō-maru!'); such conventional phrases of lamentation (*ara itawashi, itawashiya* etc.) were a common feature of *sekkyōbushi*. The hero usually escapes from these hardships, eventually achieving worldly success and avenging himself on his tormentor, in a story which follows a fixed pattern. Both Zushiō, the hero of *Sanshō dayū*, and Oguri, of *Oguri hangan*, are appointed by the Emperor as provincial governors and ask to be sent to the province where their enemy is, even though this means exchanging a great province for a small one. Once installed as governor, the hero uses his power to exact a thorough revenge. Zushiō buries his enemy up to the shoulders in the ground and forces his son to decapitate him using a bamboo saw. Oguri has his enemy bound in a reed mat and cast into the sea. The audiences of *sekkyōbushi* seem to have thought it only fair that the hero should mete out punishment as cruel as that which he had suffered. The idealization of the *Sekkyōbushi* heroes does not feature magnanimity, and this sets them apart from the forgiving heroes of the tales written for the Heian court, such as *Ochikubo monogatari*.

The way the heroines of *sekkyōbushi* are idealized also distinguishes them from their counterparts in the earlier tales. They are proud and strong-willed, two qualities not greatly prized in the refined Heian court. Terute, the heroine of *Oguri hangan*, is forced by circumstances to change her name and take the lowly position of water-carrier in the household of the governor's steward. Oguri, whose betrothal to Terute had started the series of disasters that befell them, comes to the province as governor and instructs the steward to send Terute to serve him. At first she refuses, but relents when her master and mistress convince her that they will be punished for her recalcitrance. The couple, now delighted, tell her to put on an elaborate *jūnihitoe* court dress but she refuses curtly. If she were an exiled princess such clothes would be proper, but as she is no more than a serving woman she will go as she is. With these crushing words she goes to serve *sake* to Oguri. When he asks her real name, she bangs down the *sake* bottle and answers, 'As for me, I have come at your command to serve you *sake*. I have not come here, sir, to tell you about my life and misfortunes. If you don't want the *sake*, shall I take it away?'

This particular heroine is the daughter of a rich and powerful provincial family, but the type can be seen as representing the spirit of Japanese womanhood, not yet resigned to the restraints being imposed on it by the Tokugawa social system. Indeed, Japanese women never wholly accepted the image of them dictated by Tokugawa society, but the other image, that of pride and independence, was to be found increasingly in the world of the *kuruwa* and less and less in society at large.

The Buddhism of *sekkyōbushi* (the word means literally 'chanted sermons') is chiefly a matter of miracles and communication between this world and the supernatural world below (*jigoku*). The heroes of *Karukaya*, who are father and son, both become priests, unknown to one another, and die at the same time, one in Zenkōji temple, in the province of Shinano, and the other on Mt. Kōya, south of Nara. Auspicious violet clouds form in the north (the direction of Shinano) and west (that of Mt. Kōya) and then merge. Father and son, who were unaware of each other's identity when alive, are now finally and joyfully united in the Pure Land. In *Oguri hangan*, the eponymous hero and ten of his men are killed; Enma Daiō, the Great Judge of Hell, attempts to restore them to life. He orders his servants 'to go and see if they still have bodies in Japan' but they find that the remains of the followers have been cremated and only Oguri's body, which has been buried, is left. Saying, 'If there are no bodies there is nothing that can be done,' Enma returns the hero alone to the world. His appearance when he returns, thin and like a 'hungry ghost', is described in detail.

There had been many stories of miracles and people returning from the nether world in Buddhist tales, such as those in the collections *Nihon ryōiki* and *Shasekishū*, and *sekkyōbushi*'s use of them marked one more step in the religion's secularization. These stories are, however, very far from being endorsed by Buddhist priests such as Suzuki Shōsan, who in *A Refutation of Christianity* says, 'The fox and racoon-dog spirits of this country perform wonders' but 'people who follow the practices of Buddhism have nothing at all to do with wonders.' By the early seventeenth century the common man had already assigned to Buddhism a position outside the concerns of everyday life.

Laughter was to be found in such as *Yesterday's Happenings Are Today's Tales*, tears in *sekkyōbushi*, and it was by their response to these that the people expressed their feelings most naturally.

In verse there were continuations of two traditions, the *kouta* and *Yamato-bushi* of the types found in the Muromachi collection *Kanginshū* and *renga*. A late seventeenth-century anthology, *Matsu no ha*, of whose compiler, Shūshō Ken, we know nothing except the name, contains a large number of anonymous verses which cannot be dated accurately but are almost certainly from the seventeenth century. Many were written to be sung to the *shamisen*, a three-stringed instrument introduced to Japan from the Ryūkyū Islands only at the end of the sixteenth century.

In some songs, there is an echo of the hedonism of *Kanginshū* but the scene is now the *kuruwa* and the feeling more of the transience of existence and the courtesan's sadness at the brevity of her time of popularity and prosperity.

> Gallantry and love affairs,
> Are only while we live.
> We will die at last, will die.
> Come let us drink our fill, carouse,
> Who know no tomorrow.

Also:

> It matters not at all.
> Charms are but the colours
> Of the morning glory
> That stay only until
> The sun is high.
> Resented and resenting
> Go to nothing together,
> All dew on the fields.

Not all the songs bewail the courtesan's lot. Some are finely observed moments, crystallizations of points on the psychological switchback of a love affair.

> It's because of you
> My hair's awry.
> You've undone my clothes
> So many times
> And forced me, made me
> Love you.

And:

> What time is it?
> Late? Must go.
> Your words tell me
> To hurry up.
> Unsympathetic
> Time.

The Tokugawa period began with the division of the rulers and the ruled. With this division came the dual value system of 'duty' (*giri*) and 'feeling' (*ninjō*), and the dual mode of behaviour of the official, formal and rigorous (*omote*), and the unoffical, informal and loose (*ura*). The effects of these became clear in the latter part of the seventeenth century, the period which culminated in what is known as Genroku culture.

GENROKU CULTURE

The era name Genroku (for the years from 1688 to 1704) has come to be used for the cultural renaissance which took place in the major cities of Ōsaka, Kyōto and Edo in the decades around the turn of the century. This period produced an impressive range of distinguished works of both literature and scholarship.

In the field of scholarship, Ogyū Sorai (1666–1728) created a new and positivistic philological method in his studies of the Chinese classics, and Arai Hakuseki (1657–1725) made a major contribution to the history of Japanese thought in his examination of subjects which ranged, as did those of his European contemporary, Leibnitz, over a wide spectrum, from history and studies of political policy to linguistics and his own verse and prose. In literature, Chikamatsu Monzaemon (1653–1724), working with Takemoto Gidayū, created a puppet theatre without parallel in the world; Matsuo Bashō (1644–94) and his followers took the *haikai* verse from the linked form *haikai renga* and developed it as a separate and new form of lyric verse, and Ihara Saikaku (1642–93) wrote realistic tales of *chōnin* life, faithfully describing its various aspects, especially the economic ones, at a time when such realism was virtually unknown in either China or the West. In the fine arts, the painting of Ogata

Kōrin (1658–1716), although influenced by that of Sōtatsu, differed from his predecessor's in its subject matter, which was taken from the everyday life of the *chōnin* rather than being a reflection of aristocratic taste; his work represents the final liberation of Japanese painting from the powerful Chinese influence.

The men who achieved these epoch-making advances were all born in the years between 1640 and 1670. Saikaku, Bashō and Chikamatsu were born at the beginning of the period and, some twenty years later, came another influential generation, that of Hakuseki, Sorai, Kōrin, Muro Kyūsō (1658–1734), Yamamoto Jōchō (1659–1719), Takarai Kikaku (1661–1707) and Ogata Kenzan (1663–1743). With the notable exceptions of Kōrin, Kenzan and Saikaku these men were all *samurai*. Hakuseki, Sorai, Kyūsō and Jōchō were clan officials who wrote most of their work as part of their duties. Chikamatsu, Bashō and Kikaku came from *samurai* or physician's families but left the family occupation to become full-time writers whose readership was overwhelmingly *chōnin*. Thus, as in previous times, the products of *samurai* education were directed at a more or less passive group of *chōnin* consumers. There were, however, two major points of difference from earlier ages.

Previous writers of *kanazōshi* stories, for example, had sought to popularize *samurai* values among the *chōnin*. In contrast, some at least of the Genroku writers adopted, or incorporated, *chōnin* values in their works in order to satisfy the *chōnin* reader. Typical of this approach are the 'love-suicide pieces' and other *jōruri* of Chikamatsu; these will be discussed in more detail later. The other new element was the emergence of a number, albeit small, of great *chōnin* writers. Saikaku was the most outstanding of these but with him we can mention the scholar Itō Jinsai (1627–1705). Genroku culture, while by no means a wholly *chōnin* phenomenon, had important *chōnin* elements.

Genroku culture was thoroughly secular, the culmination of the long process of secularization which had started in the Muromachi period. Song Confucianism had attempted to explain this world as a whole from a completely secular viewpoint. But in the latter half of the seventeenth century its metaphysical element was progressively discarded and its conceptual tools were used in the study of the natural sciences, ethics, politics and economics, all subjects with a direct connection with everyday life. This process, which we can call the 'Japanization' of Neo-Confucianism, reached its peak during the Genroku period. There were no new religious movements during this time and no notable religious thinkers. Art did not depict the lotus of the Pure Land but the plum blossom of this world; craftsmen decorated not temples but the homes of wealthy *chōnin*. The tones of the *shamisen* rose not in praise of Buddha but as accompaniment to the last journey of some doomed pair of lovers. The heroes of novels did not find salvation in the next world but sensual pleasure and monetary profit in this one. Like Confucius, the thinkers of the time 'never talked of prodigies, feats of strength, disorders or spirits', preferring the more sensible topics of history, society and ethics.

Another central feature of the Genroku culture came from the security of the government, which was under no threat from any foreign power (for the Ching government was barely established in China and western power was still distant) and insulated from the possibility of threat by its apparently unchallengeable exclusion policy. The government was permanent and so was the social system it imposed; these were facts for the people of the time, not subjects for debate. From this limitation in the range of possible speculation sprang the dual system of values usually referred to as *giri* and *ninjō*. *Giri* ('obligation', 'duty') was an external value and encompassed the ethics of self-denial. *Ninjō* ('feeling') was internal and sensuous. This should not, however, be taken to mean that *giri* represented human ideals, *ninjō* was the reality of the human spirit and there was a gulf between them. The two factors were present in all actual situations, perceptions and ideals. The teachings of Confucianism stressed *giri* and the virtue of self-denial; in drama and fiction *ninjō* was idealized and hedonism openly advocated. On the one hand were the demands of the social order, on the other the emotional needs of the individual, and the two were complementary; external norms of behaviour played a role in life that the internal and personal sense of values could not, and vice versa. The external norms, guaranteed in the last resort by the power of the *samurai* authorities, remained external; they were not internalized by the individual to replace or contend with *ninjō*. Similarly *ninjō* was never externalized as a set of norms for social behaviour. In a sense the two sets of values, answering as they did different needs, were parallel. *Samurai*, however conscious of *giri*, inevitably had feelings; *chōnin* were never free of the bonds of *giri*. The difference lay in which of the two was stressed in the literature in which they defined themselves. *Hagakure*, written by and for *samurai*, is an extreme statement of *giri*; the emotional values of Chikamatsu's *Sonezaki shinjū* are the essence of *ninjō*. Both these works are discussed later.

At the same time as this distinctive parallel ethical system came into being, there emerged a philosophical trend which sought to adapt the philosophical systems of China, with their assumption that China was central, to the different circumstances of Japanese society and history. The first stages in the 'Japanization' of Song Confucianism are to be found in the work of three men, all born around 1620 and active in the second half of the century: Kumazawa Banzan (1619–91), Yamaga Sokō (1622–85) and Yamazaki Ansai (1618–82). All three tended to affirm the self-identity of Japan, which was in the position of receiving rather than originating philosophical thought, in the face of the claims to objectivity and comprehensiveness made by the philosophy which came from China. In other words they stressed their own particularity against the universality of the philosophical system. For Banzan, this particularity took the form of his subjective feelings, the *kokoro*; for Sokō it was the community of which he was part (Japan, or the 'central nation', *chūchō*, as he termed it); for Ansai it was the myths of the community, which he rationalized to accord with Neo-Confucian concepts in the doctrines of the religion *Suika Shintō*.

The last two methods of dealing with and countering a foreign philosophy had already been used in a more limited form to cope with the challenge presented by Christianity in the sixteenth century. With the suppression of Christianity, however, development of intellectual countermeasures ceased. Neo-Confucianism had the endorsement of the temporal powers and this meant that it was impolitic, perhaps impossible, to attack the philosophy itself; rather the attack had to feature an attempt to free Japanese thought from the authority of specifically Chinese thought and, in a broader way, from the authority of tradition. We can say that this opened the way to the coming 'Japanization' of Neo-Confucianism.

Ansai started as a perfectly orthodox follower of the Song Neo-Confucianists but later abruptly began to advocate a form of Shintō known as *Suika Shintō*. This swift conversion to Shintō represented a complete break with Ansai's former ideas. His Neo-Confucian notions, which were Chinese, could not be extended to take account of or accord with the distinctively Japanese ideas of Shintō and his jump from the 'Way open to the whole world' to a Shintō faith which Japan could be seen to have 'as its own' omitted a vital step, a thorough critique of the Neo-Confucian system.

In contrast, Sokō did attempt a critique of Confucianism in his comparative history of the thinkers who succeeded Confucius, *Seikyō yōroku*, published in 1666. This study led him to attempt to refute the Neo-Confucian theories which identified two parts in man's nature, the 'Original Nature' (*honrai no sei*), which was regarded as a part of the universal Principle, and the 'Specific Ether' (*kishitsu no sei*), a part of the universal Ether and the origin of evil in man. Sokō's argument was that the sages of old did not make such distinctions: 'The sages did not distinguish between the Will of Heaven and the Specific Ether.' In turning to the most basic and earliest texts and deriving from them a way of approaching later thought, Sokō's arguments resemble those of his successors Kaibara Ekiken (1630–1714), Jinsai and even Sorai, but he produced no original body of thought to supplement this approach and was prone to self-contradiction. *Yamaga gorui*, completed in 1666, which is in fact a compilation of his sayings by his followers rather than a sustained argument, shows this only too well. Indeed it may be that Sokō, a man whose prose style was notably vague, was himself unclear as to what he meant. This did not diminish his confidence in his views, as his book *Haishozanpitsu* (1675) indicates, but he is not the only thinker, Tokugawa or other, to have this sublime self-confidence. His noted expertise in the military arts, too, would suffer little from a lack of precision in an age when war was a distant prospect.

In another of his important works, *Chūchō jijitsu* (Facts of the Central Nation, completed 1669), Sokō advances the view that Japan, the nation without peer, is the centre of the world. The work favourably compares the reigns of Japanese Emperors with several famous Chinese Emperors. Incidentally he gives several examples of things in which Japan excels – her natural beauty, the unbroken line of Emperors untroubled by revolution, a people who look on the country as they do their parents, the Imperial court which has taken the good parts of mainland culture, a literature which although descended from foreign origins is not inferior to them (i.e. verse and prose in Chinese) and incomparable arts and crafts. On religion he holds that Buddhism, Confucianism and Shintō are essentially the same, being distinguished merely by differences in local custom.

In none of the writings of Sokō or Ansai are there developed arguments or tenets of belief which could effectively confront the foreign ideology. Kumazawa Banzan's approach was more consistent. Unlike Ansai and Sokō he did not reject Neo-Confucianism's claims to universality in favour of the particular claims of Japan. In his major work, *Shūgiwasho* (second printing, 1676), a collection of short pieces including letters, his historical method is subjective, more so than that of Sokō, and he gives an impressionistic account of the differences between the classical Confucianism and the later Neo-Confucian schools of the Song dynasty and Ming dynasty (Wang Yangming's *Studies of the Heart*). In this respect his work is closer to the methods of Ekiken, Jinsai and Sorai than to Sokō, but whereas Ekiken was sceptical of Neo-Confucianism, Jinsai eventually rejected it and Sorai subjected it to rigorous criticism, Banzan, clearly under the influence of Wang Yangming, attempted to subsume the various schools, including Neo-Confucianism, in his own comprehensive historical account: 'The name *Studies of the Heart* is wrong. The Way is the Way, learning is learning. It was because there had been Confucian exegesis in the Han dynasty that the Neo-Confucianism of the Song dynasty came about. And the *Studies of the Heart* of the Ming dynasty are dependent in turn on the advance made by Song Neo-Confucianism. It is as a consequence of the thought of the Ming dynasty that countless people like us have taken up the pursuit of virtue,' he says. Later in the same volume: 'When it [i.e. Confucianism] is mainly concerned with the refutation of error we call it Neo-Confucianism; when it is mainly concerned with controlling the heart we call it "the laws of the heart". In the Jin dynasty the thread was lost. Therefore exegesis was the strong point of the Han dynasty. After that many incorrect theories arose and there were many errors abroad and so the studies of Song Confucianism were rational. Once error had been refuted we returned to the feelings of the heart, and thus the theories of the Ming dynasty are of the laws of the heart.'

Banzan's metaphysics for the most part followed that of Song Confucianism. The concepts of Principle, Ether and Human Nature however, were not clearly defined, although they did not achieve the vagueness of those offered by Sokō. In *Shūgi-washo*, Principle, for example, is both 'the individual's true heart' and 'eternal'. Banzan also says that 'the spiritual part of Ether is the heart' and that Ether 'circulates' within the body. These bear a resemblance, albeit confused, to the Neo-Confucian theory that the universal Principle is immanent in man's nature and that Ether is both universal and specific to individuals (as the Specific Ether). He also comes close to Zhu Xi's concept of the Supreme Ultimate as a universal standard that is both normative and ontological in the concept he terms *tada ikki*, 'the single Ether', and *riki*, 'Principle-Ether'. Banzan was not, however, profoundly concerned with questions of metaphysics or objectively defined ethical norms. He kept his gaze firmly fixed on the subjective truth (*makoto*) within himself: 'What is visible from the outside is behaviour. What we perceive inside is the heart and the feelings. Heaven and the gods bless those whose hearts are good even though their behaviour may not be good.' Thus the essential element in his ethics is not what is done but the motives or 'state of heart' of the doer. Banzan calls the virtuous state of heart *makoto* ('sincerity', 'subjective truth'). His opinions about behaviour are unoriginal ('human life should be carried on as a day-to-day affair') but the notion of *makoto*, which resembles *ninjō* in some ways, is distinctive. As a statesman he would no doubt have valued both benevolence and rectitude but have much preferred the warm humanity of the former to the punctilious correctness of the latter. His way of thought placed human feelings above social order.

In *Shūgiwasho* Banzan does assert that 'Japan is the country of the Gods' but it does not seem to be an assertion of the identity of Japan as an absolute but rather an attempt to find a position from which to examine the foreign ideology. The position he eventually adopted was founded on subjectivity in ethics – *ninjō* given a rationale – and deeply connected with the popular culture of dual values. What this position did not give him was the possibility of making objective ethical judgements about society, a feature that the rigorous Sorai had no hesitation in exposing.

THE 'JAPANIZATION' OF CONFUCIANISM

Kaibara Ekiken was born in 1630 in Fukuoka castle where his father was secretary to the head of the Kuroda clan. Ekiken himself entered the service of the clan and received a stipend of 150 *koku* in 1664. He was employed as a Confucian scholar and his works fall into four types. One was the study of natural history and hygiene. He wrote a major work on each of these, *Yamato honsō* (The Plants of Japan, twenty-five volumes of text, two of illustration, 1708) and *Yojōkun* (Advice on Health, 1713). Secondly, he wrote commentaries and popularizing accounts of Zhu Xi philosophy. These included *Kinshiroku bikō* (Notes on Recent Thought, 1668), *Gojōkun* (Lessons on the Five Constants, 1711) and *Taigiroku* (Records of a Great Doubt, 1714). Thirdly, at the behest of the head of the clan, he spent seven years in the preparation of a genealogy of the house of Kuroda (*Kuroda kafu*, 1678) and later prepared a variety of genealogies and topographies. Fourthly, he wrote travel journals recording his twenty-four visits to Kyōto, twelve visits to Edo and five visits to Nagasaki. In all he produced eighteen of these records and in them described the scenes and customs he encountered.

For his descriptive catalogue *The Plants of Japan*, Ekiken used information from the Ming catalogue *Mu-cao gang-mu* prepared by Li Shizhen (published 1590) and supplemented it when a plant was not common to both countries with the results of his own field surveys. He gives the name, history, description and medical use of more than 1,300 trees and plants to make up a survey that is regarded as marking a new era in Japanese studies of natural history.

Ekiken thought of knowledge derived from books and knowledge derived from practical experience as having complementary roles; there was no need to use one to verify the other but neither should be ignored. This approach is evident in his preparation of *The Plants of Japan*; and in *Advice on Health* he says, 'When studying medicine you should find out about the methods of old, study widely and think about many of the old ways' and balances this with advice on the necessity of being 'mindful of the movement of the times in the world of today, estimating people's strengths and weaknesses and knowing the conditions and customs of Japan'. The ideal was to blend the two. 'To try to suit things to present circumstances without knowing the traditional way' and 'to follow the old way without suiting things to present circumstances' are 'similarly mistaken'. The question of what should be done when the traditional way is clearly contradictory to modern practice is not one that Ekiken addressed. Perhaps he felt no need to do this because of his long and successful life (he wrote *Advice on Health* at the age of 83) during which he occasionally relied on traditional methods and occasionally did what seemed best at the time. Long experience of the efficacy of this eclectic approach would no doubt add to his confidence in it as well as to his optimism about the basic rightness of the world as he saw it.

In the first volume of *Advice on Health* Ekiken states that there are three pleasures in human life: 'to avoid error and enjoy good', 'to enjoy long life' and 'to enjoy the pleasure of good health' and explains how to achieve a long and healthy life. Firstly, one should leave to 'the will of heaven' those things that are beyond one's power to influence: concentrate instead on those things one can do. 'In all things, what comes from heaven is beyond the power of man. Only those things that fall within your sphere are possible to do by your own strength.' The causes of disease are 'inner desires' and 'external evils'. Of these the 'inner desires' are the more likely to be affected by human effort, and the basis of ensuring good health is the restraint of these desires – for food and drink, for sex, for sleep, for unrestrained speech and for the appetites stemming from the emotions. Ekiken explains the need to restrain these desires using the Neo-Confucian terms Principle and Ether but puts little or no stress on the role of Principle. Generally the message is: 'Restrain the inner desires and cultivate the Fundamental Ether (*genki*).' Specifically, it is bad to eat too much, overindulgence in sex damages the Fundamental Ether and violent emotions are bad for the health. This advice seems unexceptionable even in the light of modern medical knowledge but there are passages derived from traditional sources (such as the Chinese

Suwen and *Qianjinfang*) which are more than a little obscure –
'the technique of cultivating the Ether [is] to hold the waist and
hips correctly and concentrate the True Ether in the belly' – or
simply superstitious – 'in the spring months when thunder first
is heard, avoid connection between man and woman.' There is,
on the other hand, much that is accurate and seems to bear the
mark of personal observation. Ekiken advises not to drink
standing water or water from a well contaminated by seepage,
both pieces of very practical and sound advice on hygiene.

Ekiken's concern to collect an exhaustive body of knowledge,
his respect for the fruits of everyday experience, his eclecticism,
his belief in the rightness of the World order and this belief's
attendant optimism all are features of his approach to Song
Confucianism, especially that of Zhu Xi. His ideas are most
clearly set out in *Records of a Great Doubt*, which he wrote
towards the end of his life.

As Yamaga Sokō had done before him, Ekiken begins by
directing attention in his first volume to the inconsistencies in
the canon of Confucian and Neo-Confucian thought, especially
the differences between classical Confucianism and Confucianism of the Song period: 'The theories of Sóng Confucianism are
not the same as those advanced by the sages of old.' One should
accordingly 'trust what one can trust and doubt what one can
doubt'. Doubt is important because 'studying sceptically makes
things clear, but credulity creates obscurity.' Song Confucianism
differed from classical Confucianism in possessing a metaphysical system which incorporated many Buddhistic elements
and had in fact been created in response to the Buddhist
challenge. Ekiken, a natural scientist who valued the tangible
and effective, stressed such aspects of Confucian thought: 'Our
Confucianism is the Way of Government, the Great Way that
governs society and succours the people. Its learning, being
useful learning, first governs the self, then governs the people
and causes the Way of Human Ethics to be followed; it is
scholarship which is of use to the state and to the entire
universe. It is not a useless thing of empty words.' By 'useless
. . . empty words' Ekiken means the metaphysical elements of
Neo-Confucian thought which had developed under the influence of Buddhism and the Taoist classics *Lao Zi* and *Zhuang Zi*.

Ekiken disagreed with Zhu Xi on the question of how far

Principle (or Supreme Ultimate) and Ether can be distinguished, asserting that 'Principle is the principle of the Ether; Principle and Ether cannot be differentiated' and 'Principle and Ether are one thing' and that 'I would say that the Supreme Ultimate is a term for the Ether when it was still in an inchoate state, when *yin* and *yang* were not yet differentiated and the universe had not been created.'

This view of Ether as central and Principle being an insubstantial regulatory force has ethical implications. Zhu Xi had viewed humanity as being composed of the Principle (or Ideal Form) and of Ether (or Physical Endowment). As nothing physical can be perfect, by definition, man was more or less imperfect, the degree of his imperfection being decided by the kind of Ether with which he had been endowed. In Ekiken's view however Ether is all; Principle depends on it when alive, and on death the Principle disappears as the Ether disperses. Thus there exists no duality between the Principle and man's endowment and it follows that man is not imperfect, in that there is no perfect Principle against which his imperfections can be judged. If man is not imperfect then he is perfect, at least ethically. This leaves the problem of evil. It is difficult to deny the existence of evil completely and Ekiken did not try to do so. He maintained, like Mencius, that man was fundamentally good and went on from this basic assertion to say: 'Good is the constant of nature and evil is an aberration. These aberrations are extremely few and cannot become the constant.' This argument is social, statistical and optimistic. The rarity of really evil men does not, however, explain why those people who are more or less good do bad things, and in fact Ekiken never acknowledged the need to address this problem. He preferred to accept the people and society of his age as they were and this and his eclecticism led him to doubt Neo-Confucianist thought in his later years, although he continued to regard himself (and is still regarded) as a scholar of Zhu Xi.

Itō Jinsai (1627–1705) was born into a Kyōto merchant family, never gained an official post and spent his life teaching privately. His philosophical standpoint is not far from that of Ekiken in that he is critical of the metaphysics of Zhu Xi, but unlike Ekiken he based his criticism on a thorough study of the Confucian classics, especially the *Analects* of Confucius and the *Mencius*.

His works include a commentary on the *Analects* (*Rongo kogi*) and one on the *Mencius* (*Mōshi kogi*) and a work which gives his own formulation of what he takes to be the main points of the two classics (*Gomō jigi*). He gave an account of his own thought in the dialogue *Dōjimon*, a work that underwent frequent revision but seems to have reached its definitive form in 1693. It was published posthumously at the same time as *Gomō jigi*, another work that Jinsai revised throughout his life, by his son Itō Tōgai (1670–1738). The arguments of these works are consistent and give a clear idea of Jinsai's thought.

Jinsai was not alone in pointing out the differences between Neo- and classical Confucianism and criticizing the later schools on this basis; his originality lay in his ability to go beyond commentaries to a deep understanding of the original works, and from them extract the 'basic meaning'. Once he had understood the 'basic meaning' of Confucian thought (and he regarded the *Mencius* as a commentary on the *Analects*) he was then able to go through the two works again and comment on them in detail. The understanding he gained seems to have been in the nature of a revelation, as he expressed in *Dōjimon*: 'Put aside all commentaries and concentrate on the text itself. By careful reading and thorough understanding, calm study and absorption of the contents, you will find in them the true meaning of Confucius and Mencius. And this great and instantaneous enlightenment comes as if awakening from a deep sleep.' Jinsai was the first thinker, either in Japan or China, to absorb himself in the classics to this extent.

He understood the teachings of the two classics as essentially centred on man – the Way that man should follow, human morality, and, as politics was an extension of individual morality, the Way of governing the state; in short 'there is no Way without man and no man without the Way.' 'When you teach about things not connected with this world or this time you give no support to human morality and no benefit to the governing of the state.' These errors were to be found in the thought of Lao zi and the *Zhuang zi* and in the metaphysics of Neo-Confucianism.

Morality consisted in the proper understanding of the relationships between master and servant, father and son, and husband and wife and in the four virtues of benevolence, righteousness, propriety and wisdom. Of these four the two former were the most important. 'Benevolence' was much as we would understand the word today while 'righteousness' was a matter of 'doing what ought to be done and not doing what ought not to be done'. Thus benevolence is an internal virtue and righteousness is external, a matter of behaviour; they are complementary. For Jinsai their natures were as described in the *Analects* and the *Mencius* and were eternally the same. It was possible to find analogies for these virtues in cosmology – 'The Way of Heaven consists of *yin* and *yang*, the Way of Earth of hardness and softness and the Way of Man of benevolence and righteousness' (*Dōjimon*) – but for Jinsai, as for Mencius and Confucius, there was no close connection between human morality and the cosmic order. For the Neo-Confucianists of course the opposite was true; the Principle was both universal and specific to individuals. Jinsai considers human nature to be Ether granted by Heaven, with no connection with the Principle. Similarly, the ultimate source of the Universe is Ether and the creation of things is brought about by the action of *yinyang*; no transcendent or ideal Supreme Ultimate exists, and there is no duality of Principle and Ether. Principle is only the basis of *yinyang*, the internal 'order' of the Ether. These views are not very different from those of Ekiken. Where Ekiken concentrated on the natural sciences, however, Jinsai turned his attention to ethics.

Jinsai's grasp of the dual nature of human ethics – the internal virtue of benevolence complemented by the external virtue of righteousness – was one which displayed his originality at its greatest. Thus he was able to attack Buddhism for its lack of righteousness and Neo-Confucianism for a lack of benevolence: 'Both Buddhism and Lao zi are different from my Confucianism; the difference lies in righteousness, and the later Confucianists differ from the sages; this difference lies in benevolence' (*Gomō jigi*).

Jinsai apparently regarded prose as more important than verse. As he says in *Dōjimon*: 'It is necessary to write prose; without words it is impossible to express your ideas; without prose it is impossible to transmit the Way.' This comment also shows that he understood ideas and the words in which they are expressed to be indivisible. The Chinese prose in which

Jinsai wrote remained a model of style throughout the Edo period. *Gomō jigi* is concise and pointed and the lines of the argument are clear. In *Dōjimon*, however, the argument is somewhat badly organized although individual points and analogies are striking. Among Jinsai's most famous short pieces is one which he sent to a priest who had attended his lectures. He starts by mentioning his own love of learning and praising the priest's scholarship and goes on to expound the relationship between Confucianism and Buddhism, which may be different from a scholar's point of view but 'in the sight of heaven there is no Buddhism and no Confucianism, only the one Way'. He concludes with the thought that although Buddhists and Confucianists usually were at loggerheads they had talked profitably, a thing that would delight Buddha himself. Within a few lines he encompasses a whole cultural critique, which in any language would be a minor masterpiece; that this is written in Chinese by a man who had never been to China makes it all the more impressive.

Ekiken removed Neo-Confucian notions from the confines of the Neo-Confucian system to use in a study of the natural sciences; Jinsai rejected Neo-Confucian metaphysics completely in his examination of ethics. They both used selected Confucianist conceptual tools in their studies of man and nature. These two contemporaries sought to create studies of natural science and humanity. The process of 'Japanization' of the professedly universal intellectual system of the foreign metaphysics and the ideology which sought to transcend the demands of practical living is clear. Banzan turned it inward to psychological subjectivity; Ekiken dismantled it for his natural science, Jinsai for his ethics.

OGYŪ SORAI AND HIS METHOD

Sorai was the pen-name of Ogyū Nabematsu (1666–1728) the son of Ogyū Hōan, a doctor who was the physician to Tokugawa Tsunayoshi before he became *Shōgun*. Sorai says that at the age of seven or eight he was capable of taking down his father's diary from dictation in Chinese prose and at the age of twelve or thirteen could read Chinese classics without the aid of Japanese punctuation marks. This precocious ability and the direction it took were perhaps a precursor of his later studies. Hōan was dismissed by Tsunayoshi and banished to Kazusa (present-day Chiba Prefecture) in 1679, only being allowed to return to Edo in 1692. Thus Sorai, who accompanied his father to Kazusa, spent much of his youth in the country. This period had great influence on his subsequent work – he read widely and was able to see the conditions of the peasantry, which represented of course the overwhelming majority of the working population of the time. Upon his return to Edo Sorai opened a private school, at which he taught Confucianism, and began to prepare *Yakubun sentei* (A Guide to Translation), a kind of Chinese-Japanese dictionary in which the meanings of more than two thousand Chinese verbs and adjectives are explained in Japanese. This, as the introduction to the first edition of 1711 makes clear, was designed to make the reading of Chinese easier without recourse to the usual practice of rearranging the Chinese word order to conform more closely to Japanese.

After less than five years at his school Sorai was engaged as a Confucianist by Yanagisawa Yoshiyasu, one of Tsunayoshi's advisers and the lord of Kōfu. He became a teacher at the fief Confucian school in 1703. Until Tsunayoshi died and Yoshiyasu went into retirement in 1709 Sorai lived in the Yanagisawa mansion, a sojourn that may have had considerable influence on him. In the first place Yoshiyasu was a convert to the Ōbaku Sect of Zen which had recently been imported from China and retained considerable connections with the mainland. Yoshiyasu, thus came into contact with Chinese priests and interpreters and is said to have spoken Chinese. This was no doubt of some assistance to Sorai as he practised Chinese conversation in the Yanagisawa mansion. Even after he left, in 1711, to live in his own house in Edo he and several colleagues practised their Chinese under Okajima Kanzan, a former interpreter, four or five times a month. Also during his time at the mansion he obtained two collections of verse and prose prepared by the Ming scholars Li Panlong and Wang Shizhen. Impressed favourably by the fact that they had limited the prose they included to that from the Chin and Han dynasties and the verse to Han, Wei and high Tang, Sorai studied only writing up to the Song dynasty. To this extent he was doing no more than follow a fashion of the Chinese Ming dynasty many years after it had been popular on the continent. He still followed and taught the philosophy of the Cheng brothers – but his later extension of this literary classicism into a method of interpreting Confucian doctrines was to make him a unique figure in both countries.

Another important event was when Sorai, much impressed by Itō Jinsai's classicist approach in *Gomōjigi* (The Words and Meanings of Confucius and Mencius), wrote to him asking for instruction. Jinsai did not reply and it can be supposed that this had something to do with Sorai's subsequent harsh attacks on Jinsai's thought. The other important aspect of Sorai's time in Yoshiyasu's service was that, being engaged as a Confucianist, he was conscious of and anxious to stress his position's essential difference from that of the 'common minions' who engaged in the execution of policy; he was a literatus, a man of 'good taste'. When he was sent to Kōfu to inspect the site of a new temple and a memorial stone to Yoshiyasu – a mission that was not to be confused with the usual business of government – he was amused at his train which, with its halberdiers, soldiers and attendants, and him and his companion Tanaka in palanquins, resembled that of a 'common minion'. His trip is recorded in *Kyōchū kikō* (A Record of Travels through Valleys, 1706), itself a revised version of the original version, 'Travels of an Elegant Emissary'. He mentions his feelings of relief and freedom on being sent on a mountain trip after more than ten years in the city and remembers the constrictions of official life in the mansion surrounded by men of power and influence. At the same time, however, he says that his position as a literatus spares him some of the restrictions: 'In general to be a literatus is not a specialized job; it has no fixed offices; by necessity it involves much free time; there are few restrictions; one is sufficiently on one's own.'

This 'literatus' is not the Confucianist as Sorai would later define him. It is clear however that Sorai was interested in and closely observed the country through which he passed. He notes the economic state of the towns such as Fuchū, finds one source of the capital's water in the Tamagawa and observes the silkworm raising and gold mining at Kobotoke Pass, details that Bashō did not record in his travel journals. Both men were poets but in Sorai's case we can already see the author of *Seidan*

(Political Discussions) in the writer of this elegant travel journal.

After Yoshiyasu's death in 1714 Sorai was at a distance from the centres of power although he continued to live on his Yanagisawa stipend. At this time it was Arai Hakuseki who was the thinker closest to the Bakufu and in a position to make suggestions about state policy. Sorai, who was at odds with Hakuseki, established his own original method during this period and set it out in three works written in Chinese: *Bendō* (Defining the Way), *Benmei* (Defining Terms) and *Gakusoku* (Discourse on Method). All of these were completed around 1717 and subsequently revised; only *Discourse on Method* was published during Sorai's lifetime, in 1727. There is also a summary of Sorai's methodology in Japanese, *Sorai-sensei mondōsho* (Dialogues with Master Sorai, 1727). His letters, occasional writings and verse were published posthumously in 1740. Most of them are difficult to date. Sorai's political views are to be found in *Taiheisaku* (Policy for Great Peace, completed between 1719 and 1723) and *Political Discussions* (1727?).

Sorai's influence was great. Direct successors in the Sorai school of philosophy included Dazai Shundai (1680–1747) and in the Sorai school of poetry Hattori Nankaku (1683–1759). But in a wider sense we can say that but for Sorai's work the view of philosophy as a history of ideas propounded by the early eighteenth-century thinker Tominaga Nakamoto would not have been possible and neither would the positivistic philology of the late eighteenth-century Motoori Norinaga. Even the thinkers of the nineteenth-century Mito school who opposed the conventional Confucianists with the argument that Confucianism was basically and originally a political philosophy, owe much to Sorai.

The first distinctive feature of Sorai's method was his refusal to follow the practice of most Japanese Confucianists and render Chinese into Japanese word order. His translations into Japanese were free and in the language of the day. 'I established my methods when I first began to study: first I apply the colloquial Chinese I learned from Nagasaki; and when I read something aloud I use Chinese readings of the characters; I translate into contemporary Japanese, without rendering each separate character into Japanese'. Chinese being, of course, a language which differs from Japanese in grammar and vocabulary, any attempt to reorder a Chinese text into a form which can be read as Japanese is sure to be attended with a considerable number of errors. The next stage of this process is to render it into a special form of elegant literary Japanese, a step which is in effect translation with the important qualification that it is translation into a language that the translator would not speak or write under any other circumstances. As Sorai points out this does not aid understanding of the text; rather, 'When Chinese is examined using modern Japanese ... for the first time it is possible to understand and express Chinese adequately.' This is the translation method that Sorai advocated. He says of Chinese itself that there were both ancient and modern languages: 'Ancient words and phrases are of pristine purity and well-ordered.... Modern writing is long-winded and has many redundancies and moreover is vulgar.' Therefore the scholar who wishes to overcome the differences between Japanese and Chinese and understand the thought should study ancient rather than modern Chinese; and this is the substance of the 'study of ancient words and phrases' that he advocates in the introduction to *A Guide to Translation*.

However, the advocacy of the 'study of ancient words and phrases' in *Discourse on Method* is based not on the attraction of the pristine purity and well-ordered nature of the style but on the fact that pre-Han texts are inseparably connected with classical Confucianism and 'the Way of the Former Kings'; and it was mistaken attempts to understand these early texts as modern language that had created the errors of later Confucianists. 'Language is dependent on the age and changes with it; the Way is dependent on language and changes with it. That the Way is [now] obscure is basically because of this.' A prerequisite of any attempt to rectify the Way is therefore 'the study of ancient words and phrases'. Details of how to go about this are given in *Defining the Way*. *Defining Terms* is a kind of dictionary of Confucian philosophy in which Sorai gives his own definitions of the (less than a hundred) basic concepts of Confucianism and a critique of the errors of other Confucianists' definitions, from the Cheng brothers to Jinsai. It is a good example of Sorai's method; he examines and compares the usage of each term in classical texts in an attempt to ascertain its meaning at the time the texts were written. But he does not consider that complete comprehension of the texts will come from comparison of various usages of terms. One should also become familiar with classical texts and write imitations of them so that one becomes completely identified with them; 'Do not employ your mouth and ears [i.e. senses], your heart will direct your eyes. Think about it again and again and the gods will take you through [to the real meaning].' Another thing that was necessary was to investigate the historical background; in order 'to see things of a thousand years ago as if they were today' one must 'investigate widely'. The second of these clearly leads to the conclusion that 'scholarship finds its ultimate expression in history.'

Thus Sorai's second characteristic was his approach to history. One aspect of this approach involved the belief that the legendary kings of ancient China had demonstrated universal principles of government. These principles appeared in a concrete political system and method of rule ('the rites, music, punishment and government') and it was possible to learn of these through the Six Classics (*The Book of Odes, Book of History, Book of Rites, Book of Music, Book of Changes, Spring and Autumn Annals*). One had to depend on 'the study of ancient words and phrases' to understand the Six Classics: 'The Six Classics are now incomplete and even if they were complete they are in an ancient language.... If one wishes to understand ancient language, it is impossible to do so without studying ancient works and syntax.'

The basis of Sorai's intellectual methodology was the application of philological methods to the systems of the Chinese classical age. He believed that the principles that lay beneath these systems were universal and were above geographical considerations. This belief was not the fruit of his scholarship; it was its point of departure. He believed the early Chinese kings to have been historical figures and thus his belief in the principles of their rule differed considerably from the Neo-Confucianists' assertions that the Principle was a natural, metaphysical law: 'The Way of the Former Kings is something created by the Former Kings. It is not a universal Way of nature.' However, the Way of the Former Kings functioned as a transcendent standard *vis-à-vis* the rest of the Confucian tradition and could be employed in the critical examination of any theory. This meant that Sorai's position differed greatly from that of Jinsai's in his 'ancient studies', to say nothing of the thinkers who followed an orthodox Neo-Confucian line. 'The Cheng brothers and Zhu Xi were great men but did not understand ancient syntax. In recent years, Master Itō was a great man but was very like them in this. Even Mencius, when he interpreted the *Analects*, looked at old language as if it were modern language, and how much more so did the Song Confucianists.' Japanese thinkers of the late seventeenth century, such as Banzan, Sokō, Ansai, Ekiken and Jinsai, had drawn attention to the discrepancies between classical Confucianism and Neo-Confucianism and criticized the latter on this account, but Sorai was the first to establish a method of ascertaining the meaning of classical Confucianism. The Way of the Former Kings was established as an absolute to which all subsequent Confucianism related and through which it could be comprehended.

This did not mean that Sorai subsumed all the particular characteristics of each age indiscriminately under this transcendent principle. A second aspect of his approach to history was a respect for the concrete facts and the special techniques of government of each age. His account of this in *Discourse on Method* reveals the freshness of both his thought and his style:

There were sages in antiquity; there are none now. It is therefore necessary to study antiquity so that there is no 'antiquity' and no 'present'. How, though, if there is no 'antiquity' and no 'present' are we to dispose of the present? The ages reflect upon each other; none is 'antiquity', none the present. The age [can be understood] from its customs and institutions, the customs and institutions from the age.

Find the particular characteristics of customs and institutions by examining the records. Then compare these particular characteristics. Having done this fully, then discuss each age. It is facile to discuss all ages according to fixed criteria.

The third characteristic of Sorai's method was to distinguish between personal and political ethics, attempting to establish the true nature of the latter by an objective historical method. The Way of the Former Kings was a political value, an ideal form of rule. 'The Way of the Former Kings is The Way to rule the world.' This was distinguished from individual ethics: 'The theory that if men control themselves the state will be ruled of itself is, in my opinion, something which comes from Buddhism and Taoism.' This approach was a sharp challenge to Neo-Confucianism which considered 'self-mastery' and 'peace in the world' to be connected, a view which had influenced the majority of the Japanese Confucianists of Sorai's time. In Neo-Confucianism individual and political morality are linked by the Principle, which means that any explanation of the abstract Principle in concrete examples is inevitably subjective. The 'Studies of the Heart' popular in the Ming dynasty, which sought in effect to rule the heart by means of the heart, was also inevitably subjective. In Sorai's view the Way of the Former Kings was both a value and a historical fact, whose substance could be found in the Six Classics. Their interpretation was not subjective but a matter of objective scholarship and knowledge. The last sentence of *Discourse on Method* is as follows: 'How far a man may increase his intelligence and improve his ability is a matter of the character given to him by heaven and so one should study the thought and art of the ancients rather than hoping for anything from moralizing scholars.' If the universal applicability of the Way of the Former Kings was a problem of faith (in the religious sense), its applicability to one actual society, Tokugawa Japan, could be objectively supported by historical fact. In *Dialogues with Master Sorai* he says that the historical background of the Way was ancient China before the Han dynasty, a time when the country was divided into autonomous regions. As power became more centralized this regional autonomy was lost in China and with it the Way of The Former Kings. But in Japan the process was in the opposite direction, with centralized power giving way to regional autonomy. Thus, since the social system of Japan is now the same as when the Way was established it is obvious that it can be applied.

Through his use of these methods Sorai achieved an almost complete dismantling of Neo-Confucian metaphysics and constructed his own system of political philosophy. As it appears in *Defining the Way*, *Defining Terms* and *Dialogues with Master Sorai* the system is far less comprehensive than that of Zhu Xi but the consistency of its argument is by no means inferior, and it is, of course, far superior to that of any Japanese thinker of the time. It concerns only the Way of the ruler and has little to say of the ruled, being in effect almost a discourse on monarchy. Naturally Sorai's influence was strongest on such original thinkers as Tominaga Nakamoto and Motoori Norinaga and scarcely felt by such popular teachers as Ishida Baigan.

The Way of the Former Kings is an ideal method of ruling the state, not a Way of nature and the universe. Nature and the universe were beyond the comprehension of man: 'All the marvels of the universe, not only wind, clouds, lightning and rain, are things beyond human understanding.' The Way of the Former Kings was the actuality of rule and historical fact: 'The teachings of the Former Kings are material, not theoretical.' The actuality of rule, as recorded in the Six Classics, consists of rites, music, punishment and policy: 'The teachings of the Former Kings are all how to do things.' The ancients employed these techniques with a great virtue, humaneness: 'Humaneness is the virtue with which the superior man rules the people; it is the great virtue of the sages.' Thus humaneness is a virtue of the ruler, not of the ruled, and Itō Jinsai is wrong in interpreting it as universal love. Because humanity is 'active' and cannot be ruled simply by laws and punishment the ancients ruled with 'rites and music' too. Men must be brought to wisdom without realizing it by the ritualization of behaviour ('the rites') and the actions that follow from this: 'They knew that laws and punishments were not enough to rule people so they created rites and music.... Rites and music do not use language and in this are superior to what language teaches men. They change fundamental things. When one trains the people through practice they are aware of this; when the change takes place throughout their heart, mind and body it is in the end imperceptible.'

This is a universal policy; the 'rites' will always be capable of ruling men's hearts and minds. There is however an infinite range of actual circumstances, and righteousness is necessary to deal with each of these in the way appropriate to its particular needs. Individual personality, and what the Neo-Confucianists call 'Specific Ether', are given by heaven and are unchangeable; thus the Neo-Confucian belief in the perfectibility of human nature through the refinement of the Specific Ether to permit the Principle within to 'shine through' is mistaken. Human nature is variable and thus it is the duty of the individual to follow the will of heaven and develop his personality in the direction of virtue.

These are all of Sorai's basic concepts and it is notable that only extremely rarely does he introduce the metaphysical notions of the Neo-Confucianists such as Principle and Ether. One can say that he has almost completely 'demetaphyzed' Neo-Confucianism.

The concrete political proposals that Sorai made to the *Shōgun* Yoshimune can be found in *Political Discussions* and there is some mention of the advice he gave to the senior counsellors of the Sakai domain in *Dialogues with Master Sorai*. These do not always have a close connection to the theoretical arguments outlined above. However, his theoretical identification of the Tokugawa social system with early Chinese feudalism is obviously connected with his argument in *Political Discussions* that the concentration of population in the cities was the source of all social evils: 'The vital things are the existence of inns open to any traveller and a lack of regulation in these matters; everything comes back to these two. Accordingly a register of households should be prepared and everyone should remain where they live.' This idea is also to be found in *Policy for Great Peace*, where the necessity of returning people from the cities to their home villages is linked with the classical ideal of the peasant living on his own plot (to be found in the *Mencius* and elsewhere).

Sorai's prose is lucid and well ordered and is notable for, among other features, the high incidence of the vocabulary of logic. His poetry was usually traditional in theme – the moon, the north wind, drinking, parting, the reunion of friends, old age and so on – but he also wrote on subjects unusual for the time such as agriculture, the price of rice and the ways in which provincial ladies imitate the ways of the capital, which may have something to do with his having spent his youth in the country. He also wrote a few fine humorous poems. In a different mood is his poem about 'feelings in a wood in autumn':

> Old trees, the west wind cold
> A scattered wood, lonely in the evening glow.

This is as fine and sensitive as Matsuo Bashō's

> Bright bright
> The sun shines on
> Autumn wind.

ARAI HAKUSEKI

Arai Hakuseki (1657–1725), the son of a *rōnin*, entered the service of Tokugawa Tsunatoyo of the Kōfu clan and, when Tsunatoyo became *Shōgun* in 1709 (under the name Ienobu), Hakuseki was in a position to influence Bakufu policies, a position he retained for some four years after the death of his lord in 1712. Comparison with the career and character of Ogyū Sorai reveals many differences. Hakuseki had a substantial influence on Bakufu policies; in his later years, Sorai's influence on Shōgun Yoshimune was extremely limited. Hakuseki wrote little on Neo-Confucianism and what he wrote was conventional and unoriginal; Sorai was both prolific and original. Hakuseki wrote in Japanese, Sorai in Chinese. (Both, it should be said, made great advances in the prose style of the respective languages. Hakuseki's prose, with that of Saikaku, marked a new age in Japanese writing.) Sorai concentrated on the Chinese classics whereas Hakuseki covered a wide range of subjects, from Japanese history and studies of the Japanese language to comparative cultural studies and human geography. Sorai's character seems to have been that of a poet, Hakuseki's that of a prose writer. These two contemporaries, who treated each other with indifference or hostility, were neither of the general current of the times. They were exceptional by virtue of their rationalism and respect for facts, their lucid prose, their opposition to all kinds of 'mystification' and indeed by their intellectual courage as autonomous human beings.

The first of the three volumes of Hakuseki's *Oritaku shiba no ki* (Told Round a Brushwood Fire, 1716, later revised) gives a detailed account of his life before he took a role in national government. He was a studious child, copying each day three thousand Chinese characters (followed each night by another one thousand) and, at the age of seventeen, embarking on a study of the Confucian classics (and Confucianism in general) and Chinese literature, armed only with a dictionary and what must have been considerable determination. This autobiographical first volume is followed by two volumes of political reminiscences concerning the period 1709–16 when Hakuseki was a policy-maker for the *Shōgun* Ienobu and Ietsugu. In these volumes the stress is on Hakuseki the public figure to the exclusion of the private man, and he chooses six events as the most important of the period.

First was the repeal of the law which required the people to show respect and affection to animals, the *Shōrui awaremi no rei*. This had been promulgated by the previous *Shōgun*, Tsunayoshi, and its repeal in 1709 was greeted with some relief, not least among the 9,000 or so who had been imprisoned under its provisions.

Second was an incident in 1710 in which the peasants of Echigo (present-day Niigata Prefecture) protested to the central government at the excessive tax levied by a local official. Although this kind of direct appeal was illegal the peasants were not punished, government displeasure being directed instead at the corrupt official.

Third was the problem of how to receive the envoy from the Korean court. At the examination in 1711, two decisions were made: that when the envoy came to pay his respects to the new *Shōgun* he should be afforded a less sumptuous reception than previously and that he should be required to address the *Shōgun* as the King of Japan, as had been the custom under the Ashikaga *Shōgun* and Ieyasu. Here economic considerations were mixed with a desire for formal equality.

The fourth incident, the dismissal of the minister Ogiwara Shigehide in 1712, represented a victory for Hakuseki after a hard political campaign. Shigehide had been a minister under Tsunayoshi and had retained his position and considerable entrenched power under Ienobu. He also had the support of the powerful minister Yanagisawa Yoshiyasu. The dispute between him and Hakuseki arose over what should be done about the currency. Shigehide had followed a policy of debasing it in order to provide some relief for the hard-pressed government finances but Hakuseki was strongly against this, advocating its restoration to the value it had had before the Genroku era. His grounds for this were that 'the sages of old' having used gold, silver and copper in their unadulterated forms it was wrong for man to interfere with treasures 'born from the earth' and that 'the gold and silver that is circulated through all countries' had a high degree of purity. The second point no doubt refers to the role of precious metals in the settlement of international debts. Shigehide had powerful allies, the guilds of gold- and silver-smiths, the *ito wappu* merchants who had a monopoly of imported yarn, the exchange houses and several important members of the Bakufu cabinet. Hakuseki, however had the *Shōgun's* ear; Shigehide was eventually dismissed after what was, if *Told Round a Brushwood Fire* is to be believed, a consider-able struggle. Shigehide was not without justification for his policies. The production of gold and silver was declining and the economy had expanded since the Genroku era and was continuing to do so. Not enough is known about the economic conditions of the period to say which of the two policies was in fact more appropriate.

Having succeeded in gaining the chance to implement his policy of increasing the purity of the gold in circulation, Hakuseki went on to deal with an attendant problem, that of how to prevent Japanese gold reserves from leaking away as the result of foreign trade. He did this by limiting the number of Chinese and Dutch trading vessels allowed to use the port of Nagasaki, and in 1715 he put a limit on the amount of trade permitted in a year. His own estimate was that a quarter of Japan's gold had left the country since the beginning of the Tokugawa period, and three-quarters of the silver. This policy was complementary to the others outlined above. Corrupt officials were purged to increase government income from taxes; unnecessary government expenditure (such as elaborate recep-tions for foreign envoys) was curbed; and an effort was made to restore the currency to its former value and prevent it from leaving the country. These formed a coherent strategy, whether or not this was ideal for the times.

The sixth important event that Hakuseki mentions is his interrogation of the Italian missionary Giovanni Battista Sidotti (1668–1714) who had come to Japan in defiance of the ban on Christianity. The recommendations that Hakuseki made to the Bakufu in 1709 were: it would be the best to return the missionary to his own country without delay; failing that he could be imprisoned; and, least advisable of all, he could be executed. Hakuseki reasoned that it was against Confucian principles to kill a man who had come such a long way at the prompting of his personal beliefs. To hold him without executing him, however, would be against the law of Japan. Also if he was sent back possible future missionaries and their governments could be warned of the complete ban on Christianity in Japan. The Bakufu chose in fact to imprison Sidotti.

Hakuseki lost his influence with the *Shōgun*, and hence his power, when Ietsugu was succeeded by Yoshimune in 1716. He was dismissed and retired into the country, recommending in his place the Wang Yangming scholar Muro Kyūsō (1658–1734) who became one of Yoshimune's trusted ministers and was, unlike Hakuseki, by no means an organization man. As his policies demonstrated, Hakuseki was practical, rational and concerned with international affairs, but he nevertheless often followed Neo-Confucian modes of argument. (The only exception is in the case of the Korean envoy.) He prevented any clash between Neo-Confucianist theory and the rational solution of problems by using only such theoretical arguments as were appropriate and keeping them within limits that did not interfere with practicality. Unlike Sorai, he did not reject Zhu Xi's thought; he domesticated it.

The main points of Hakuseki's Neo-Confucian thought are to be found in *Kishiron* (On Demons and Gods, publication date unknown). They are centred on the concept of Ether. Human life is explained in terms of the condensing and dispersing of Ether (or the two Ethers of *yin* and *yang*): 'The birth and death of a person is [a matter of] the condensation and dispersion of *yin* and *yang*; when they are condensed a person is formed and when dispersed they go to be *oni* (demon) and *kami* (god). That part which returns to the earth becomes an *oni*; that which ascends to heaven becomes a *kami*. The Ethers that are condensed were originally the Ethers of heaven and earth and so when they disperse they return again to heaven and earth.' The two separate spirits of a person – the *kon* and the *haku* – which are respectively consciousness and *yang*, and form and *yin* – separate on death. The former expands and rises to heaven while the latter contracts and sinks to the earth. This process is neither swift nor smooth and there are spirits which linger between heaven and earth in a state of incomplete dissolution (what Hakuseki calls 'sunken *kon* and delayed *haku*'). Principle, in the sense that Zhu Xi used the term, is unnecessary to this mechanistic process of condensation and dispersion of the Ether, a process which is described in an almost wholly materialistic and rationalistic way in a kind of materialistic schema.

The Ether of this theory, and the two elements of the spirit that are part of it, are homogeneous and do not vary from person to person. Once the Ether is dispersed it reverts to anonymity. Thus ancestor worship is somewhat futile for 'It is difficult to believe that it will necessarily be the *kami* of their ancestors that receive the ceremonies offered up by descendants.' Again the Buddhist doctrine of reincarnation is impossible to believe because it implies that the first people in the world are still individually alive today: 'Each and every person in the world would be the product of individuals of the most ancient days being born and dying over and over until they reached the world of today.' And, like Confucius, he thought it unnecessary and wrong to talk of miracles and marvels. For Hakuseki 'the teachings of the sages' were to do with everyday life and involved the virtues of filial piety, love between brothers, loyalty and faith. There was no need to challenge the metaphysics of Zhu Xi; they were simply irrelevant.

The physical world of course provided Hakuseki with considerable scope for investigation and he was always eager to find out as much as he could. His interest in foreign cultures was deep and he found opportunities to ask about them in his repeated meetings with the Korean envoy, in his visits to the Dutch when they came to stay in Edo and in his interrogation of Sidotti. One result of his studies was the first Japanese world geography, *Sairan igen* (1713, revised 1725) the five volumes of which deal, respectively, with Europe, Africa, Asia, South America and North America. They consist mainly of a summary, in Chinese, of the information he had gained from foreign maps, and even give such details as the foreign names for China and Japan, but the information is inevitably quite limited. He assembled the information he had obtained from Sidotti into the three-volume work *Seiyō kibun* (Information on the West, 1715).

The first volume gives an account of his interrogation of the Italian, which of course took place through an interpreter. The second volume is a geography and (fragmentary) history of the world. The third volume is on Christianity and includes Hakuseki's views on the subject. Hakuseki seems to have been especially struck by three aspects of Sidotti's character: his courage as shown in leaving his parents and travelling so far for his faith; his knowledge of maps, calendars and geography; and his political theories, which included the opinions that the importance of a nation did not depend on its size or geographical position and a nation's misfortunes came not from religion but from man. Hakuseki agreed with these views: 'On consideration, talking of nations, to say that the size of territory and whether it is near or far are not crucial seems the best theory; and it seems to be reasonable to say that when a country errs it is not because of [religious] doctrine but because of its people.' On the second of these points it is not surprising that Hakuseki, who shared with the majority of the Japanese the view that humanity and the concrete world outweighed abstract doctrinal questions, found himself in agreement with Sidotti.

There was never any possibility of Hakuseki being converted to Christianity. First there were the political problems it posed. Christianity was illegal and furthermore, with its doctrine of a Lord who was above the lords of the world, it demanded that its followers should serve two masters, a thing that any Japanese Confucianist knew to be impossible and an incitement to disaffection and rebellion. Theologically, Hakuseki found Christian doctrine inconsistent. If God had created the universe what had created God? If He had come about spontaneously did not that mean that the creation of the universe was actually spontaneous? God was concerned with man's sins; He had punished the generation of Noah with the flood and later had come into the world to take man's burden of sin. Why had He not simply created man without sin? These arguments were common to several of the anti-Christian works of the late sixteenth and early seventeenth centuries but Hakuseki, unlike the other polemicists, did not adopt a Buddhist standpoint. Indeed he was critical of Buddhism and found Christianity to be similar to Buddhism, except shallower. 'I have now heard the teachings of Jesus; in them there are images, commandments, sprinkling with holy water, the reading of holy works, the telling of beads, theories of heaven and hell and reincarnation and retribution. There is nothing in them that does not resemble the teachings of Buddha. But, in that they are extremely shallow, they cannot be taken as ideas worthy of comparison.'

In *Information on the West* Hakuseki examines what the West, in the person of Sidotti, has to say and analyses it from his own rationalist and secular standpoint. He is impressed by the knowledge he finds and by the person of Sidotti himself (and he accordingly recommended his release), but he is unimpressed with the world-view of the seventeenth-century Catholic church, as he was with the metaphysics of the Neo-Confucianists. His interest was in the present state of the world rather than its origins; he investigated its geography and recorded its history. He collected information on the areas which lay close to Japan. In *Ezoshi* (Records of Ezo, 1720) he investigates the customs of the Ainu of the north. In *Nantōshi* 'Records of the Southern Islands, 1719) he gives an account of the history, geography and culture of Okinawa, mentioning among other details that its literature was distinguished for its ballads.

Hakuseki's studies of language produced the twenty volumes of *Tōga* (1719), a kind of historical dictionary of Japanese in which the most important nouns of the language are put into categories, such as astrology, morality, fauna, and divided into twenty types. There are explanations of the etymology of each word – how its meaning differed in each historical period and what words were derived from it. The general argument includes a description of his methodology: differentiation between 'ancient word' and 'modern word' based on historical differences in usage, a consideration of dialect (regional differences in usage) and the existence of 'elegant' and 'vulgar' language (social differences in usage). He also considers the influence of foreign languages on Japanese, instancing classical Chinese, Sanskrit, the various versions of Song- and Yuan-dynasty Chinese, and comments, on the subject of pronunciation, that 'There is no language with fewer sounds than ours of the East and there is no language with as many sounds as the languages of the West. Chinese is in the middle.' The West was advanced in the study of phonemics and China had a superior writing system, but neither of these was much respected in Japan.

Hakuseki puts forward a detailed method for ascertaining the changes in pronunciation of Japanese, involving the examination of 'the names of gods, the names of people and the words of songs', and uses as literary sources (in order of importance) *Kojiki*, *Kogo shūi*, *Shokoku fudoki*, *Nihon shoki* and *Manyōshū*, which he looks at in scrupulous detail. *Tōga* is not only a masterpiece of scholarship but a triumph of rationalism, respect for facts and broad international vision, and it required Hakuseki not just to shake himself free from the bounds of Zhu Xi thought and the mystifications of Shintō but actively to oppose them on many points.

Hakuseki's most important work was in the field of Japanese history. He wrote two books, *Koshitsū* (Knowing Ancient History) and *Koshitsū wakumon* (Dialogues on Knowing Ancient History, both 1716), on ancient history and another volume, *Tokushi yoron* (On Reading History; completed in manuscript 1712?, revised and supplemented 1724), on the history of the warrior families from Fujiwara times to the beginning of the Tokugawa period. In ancient history Hakuseki is careful to distinguish between legend and fact and holds to the latter: 'History records events according to the facts and thus provides examples for the world.' Therefore it is necessary to examine materials comparatively: 'It is wrong to follow the accounts of *Nihon shoki* only and pass over such works as *Kyūjiki* and *Kojiki*. Good scholarly practice should be to follow those accounts which seem to be strong in reason and justice and which do not stray at all from the facts, whatever the work they appear in.' Japanese sources alone were inadequate for the study of ancient history and classical Chinese histories should also be consulted (in the third volume of *Dialogues on Knowing Ancient History* he mentions specifically the history of the Han dynasty, *Houhanshu*, and the Wei dynasty history, *Weizhi*) as should Korean histories: 'In the Korean history [*Hagdong Cheguk-ki* (Overseas Eastern Countries)] there appear the era names of the Japanese court and [other] details from the earliest times. Of course these things do not appear in our histories.' The phrase 'of course', although apparently casual, is an indication of how much Hakuseki valued the material from foreign sources and how he resisted the trend of the times which was to reject these in favour of the 'pure' sources of Japan. This led him to some

devasting conclusions on the subject of, the creation myths of
Nihon shoki as for example in *Dialogues on Knowing Ancient
History*: 'In short this work has been put together from such as
Huainanze and *San-wu-li-chi* [*Records of the Emperors*; both these
books are Chinese histories]. In other countries there is no lack
of accounts of the beginning of heaven and earth. Is there,
however, anyone who really knows about the beginning of
heaven and earth? How much less satisfactory then are things
found in a foreign work and made to apply to Japan.'

On Reading History describes history in terms of the rise and
fall of families who had grasped or inherited power. Broadly this
means the transfer of power from the Imperial family and the
aristocracy to the *samurai* families. The reasons that Hakuseki
gives for the fall of individual potentates and the transfer of
power vary considerably. They include the failure of the inheri-
tors of power to hold onto it (as in the case of the Fujiwara
family), moral shortcomings and consequent heavenly punishment (Minamotono Yoritomo), 'the Will of Heaven' (the Hōjō
family), failure to reward troops for military success (Emperor
Go-Daigo) and arrogance of the rulers coupled with financial
troubles (the Ashikaga family). Unlike Sorai, Hakuseki did not
always distinguish between a man's personal ethics and his
effectiveness as a statesman, and there are some signs of the
influence of Zhu Xi thought in his use of the idea of the 'Will of
Heaven'. (Sorai, it should be said, did not reject the concept of
'the Will of Heaven' but regarded it as unknowable. The notion
of fortuity can never be kept out of historical studies entirely; the
problem is whether, like Hakuseki, to link it with 'the Will of
Heaven'.) Usually, however, Hakuseki attempted to explain the
historical process in pragmatic terms and looked for political,
economic and sometimes systematic factors. It is this feature
that makes *On Reading History* superior as history to both
Kitabatake Chikafusa's *Jinnō shōtōki* and to Jien's *Gukanshō*
(*Gukanshō* often introduces an extrahistorical force) although it
owes something to each of these Kamakura-period works. Most
modern historians agree that it surpassed its predecessors in its
handling of materials and became the model for its successors,
including Rai San'yo's *Nihon gaishi* (Popular History of Japan). It
is true that Hakuseki's historical works show the influence of
Zhu Xi thought to a greater degree than his other works but his
central attitude was always positivistic.

Hakuseki's prose style is best displayed in the genealogical work *Hankanpu* (in twelve volumes, with a separate volume of remarks and catalogue, 1702, later revised), which he prepared at the request of the head of his clan. It consists of a genealogy of every *daimyō* with a stipend of 10,000 *koku* or more, and each family's history is chronicled from 1600 to 1680, with special reference to their military exploits and their relationship to Hideyoshi and Ieyasu. In the preparation of this Hakuseki used a wide range of material – ten or more historical biographies, more than a hundred reference works, contemporary letters and the evidence of living people – and 'sought and strove to arrive at the facts' and 'make the beginning and end of the family plain to see, without going into unnecessary detail'. His descriptions are in fact lucid and uncluttered; they usually do not mention the man's physical appearance, describe particular episodes, give direct quotations or attempt psychological insight. The events described are usually battles, the characters are military leaders. There are of course exceptions: incidents which took place off the battlefield, examples of the behaviour of *samurai* as administrators and judges (Itakura Shigemune, for example), instances of the decisiveness and willpower of men and women in mortal danger (Asano Nagamasa, and the wife of Hosokawa Tadaoki), and the plotting and opportunism of the civil war *daimyō* as they tried to advance or protect their positions (Date Masamune). Surprisingly this spare and objective record, despite its avoidance of details of the emotional life of its subjects, often, if not always, manages to give the reader a sharp picture of their personalities. When these vivid evocations come they stand out from the ascetic and restrained prose which surrounds them. A good example is the description of Date Masamune as he arrived to meet Hideyoshi at his base in Hakone. Masamune was a successful general who had met his match in Hideyoshi and did not know whether the outcome of their meeting would be his execution as a troublesome potential rival. Hakuseki says in Volume 7: 'Masamune, a man of more than twenty, with one eye and his hair cropped short, was extremely strange in appearance.' The fact that there are so few physical descriptions only adds to the impact of this one. Similarly the quoting of Asano Nagamasa's speech criticizing Hideyoshi's personal obsession with the conquest of Korea is immediate in its effect. The reader can feel what it meant to Nagamasa to make these cutting remarks in face of the considerable risk of the dictator's displeasure and his own death. Overall *Hankanpu* is a masterwork of Japanese prose, one that stands above its contemporaries and above most of the writing of the Tokugawa period.

Hakuseki's achievement was to extend the historical objectivity and rational thought to the limits of what was possible within the twin restrictions of a military dictatorship and the orthodoxy of Zhu Xi philosophy. In doing this he opened the way for two subsequent schools, National Learning (*kokugaku*) which concentrated on the study of Japanese language and literature, and Western Learning (*yōgaku*) which studied the culture of other countries.

GLORIOUS DEATHS

Ogyū Sorai said that there was no such thing as *Bushidō*, 'the Way of the Warrior'; there was only *Bugei*, 'the martial arts': 'Within the Way there is no [separate] "Way of Letters" nor "Way of Arms".' Elsewhere: 'It is said that as well as the Way of the Sages there is another Way, that of the warrior, which suits our country. This is, basically, an error of the uneducated springing from the workings of minds too imbued with modern ways.' And again: 'The ignorant believe that the warrior families have handed down a way of smashing down [opposition] through force of arms and valuing the simple direct course in everything and that this is the "Way of the Warrior" handed down from the earliest days of Japan.' This 'ignorant' belief seems in fact to have been 'modern' in Sorai's time, in the early years of the eighteenth century. The idealization of behaviour appropriate to a period of civil war took place a long time after the civil war itself had finished; it was only from the latter part of the seventeenth century, the Genroku era, that 'the Way of the Warrior' was proclaimed. The *samurai* of the actual struggles and battles, although undoubtedly warriors, acknowledged no formal 'Way'; only when the need for combat had long passed did the phenomenon arise among the administrator-*samurai* of the Tokugawa system.

There were aspects of the 'Way of the Warrior' which helped to support the system. The most important of these was its stress on fidelity of the followers to the lord. The Bakufu of course encouraged loyalty and in 1682, for example, issued a Prescript on Fidelity (*chūkōsatsu*) which incorporates some characteristically *Bushidō* phraseology. But problems arose over the matter of the object of a warrior's loyalty. The Bakufu obviously required that the ultimate and overriding loyalty should be to the central government whereas *Bushidō* advocated a warrior's absolute and unconditional loyalty to his lord. When two lords came into conflict the loyalty of their followers would be to them rather than to the government authorities which might try to stop the conflict. To avenge the death of the lord was the duty of the *samurai* (according to *Bushidō*) and some, like the famous forty-seven *rōnin* who eventually achieved their vengeance in 1702, accepted this in deadly earnest. At the same time the government could not permit prolonged vendettas. Thus there were two kinds of loyalty, one which was used by the Bakufu as a tool of government, and another which was adopted by individual *samurai*, who, feeling unable to become merely a small part of a huge system, used it as a way of justifying their position.

The *Bushidō* of this period was summarized most clearly in *Hagakure*, the thoughts of the Saga clan *samurai* Yamamoto Jōchō (1659–1719) recorded by a *samurai* of the same clan, Tashiro Tsuramoto, between 1710 and 1716. It was circulated at the time in manuscript and seems not to have been published. Jōchō, the page of the clan head Nabeshima Mitsushige from the age of eight, tried unsuccessfully to commit suicide on the death of his lord in 1700. (He was not permitted to do so as this kind of suicide, *junshi*, had been forbidden by the Saga clan in 1661 and by the Bakufu in 1663.) He became a hermit priest and dictated *Hagakure* during this time, in his later years. *Hagakure* is written for any *samurai* 'who would be of service to his lord', from the point of view of the 'servant'. This point of view and mental attitude are in sharp contrast to those of Sorai, who takes the standpoint of the lord and discusses how best to rule the country.

On the other hand, Jōchō's experience of life and his social background were markedly different from Miyamoto Musashi's; he had no experience of combat and did not write on the practical problems of defeating and killing an opponent. He wrote instead on how to kill oneself. In the hundred years from Miyamoto Musashi's *The Five Circles* to Jōchō's *Hagakure* the emotional focus of the *samurai* had moved from the battlefield to ritual suicide, or *seppuku*.

There are many repetitions in *Hagakure* but the main theme is clear and simple. It is that Jōchō owes loyalty to the Nabeshima family and will put aside any thoughts of self or of life in order to serve them; other than that, 'nothing is needed'. This loyalty is absolute; he acknowledges no values which transcend the group to which he belongs: 'Neither Sakyamuni, Confucius nor [the great warriors] Kusunoki Masashige and Takeda Shingen were, after all, in the service of the Ryūzōji or Nabeshima [families], and so they do not accord exactly with the ways of this house' (Ryūzōji is the name of the family which preceded the Nabeshima as the lords of the Saga domain). Even if Sakyamuni, Confucius and Amaterasu were to appear on earth, even if Jōchō were cast into hell to endure divine punishment, 'for my part, I need nothing other than to obey my lord's will'. The relationship between the Nabeshima clan and the wider community, and its place within that community, are left out of consideration. Jōchō does not mention Japan or the Tokugawa family, and the Emperor and the rest of the population, the peasants, artisans and merchants, are even further from his thoughts. Thus there is no possibility of questioning the aims of this closed community; to do so would imply a need to refer to a value or values that transcend it, and these he denies *a priori*. The focus of his attention is the unity of the group, the intense fellowship of its members.

The structure of the group is founded on 'the pledge between lord and follower', an obligation which is not reciprocal. When the lord is obviously in error the follower should attempt to correct him through remonstrance: 'The greatest loyalty is that of he who turns his lord's mind to the good, and serves him so that he makes no mistakes.' In *Hagakure* there are repeated and detailed descriptions of how to remonstrate with one's lord (perceive the right moment, start the conversation from a subject the lord is fond of, etc.) and these include, as a final measure, admonitory suicide. There is no mention of the possibility of the follower breaking off the relationship; that can only be done by the lord.

The absolute value given to the master-servant relationship implies that no such value can be given to scholarship: 'Scholarship,' *Hagakure* says in Part 1, 'is a good thing but quite liable to error.' Again this view is contrary to that of Sorai. The martial arts too are only of relative value: 'In the martial arts one should learn just what is absolutely necessary', a view that Miyamoto Musashi, for one, would not have agreed with. The central ideal of a follower should be to be ready to die for his lord; the most glorious fate was actually to do so: 'I offer myself humbly to my lord and die instantly, then when a ghost, grieve the day through for my lord' and 'There is no death so good as to die fighting.' This cast of mind is expressed most forcefully in the famous statement: 'I have realized that the Way of the Warrior is to die.'

The philosophy of *Hagakure* begins with the unconditional master-servant relationship but does not end there. Eventually death itself is glorified without consideration of the possible purposes of dying or what effect it might have. Death, aimless and meaningless, is made sublime; death is the supreme emotional experience, the ultimate 'mad' mental state as the descriptions of it in Part 1 clearly show: 'meaningless death with a rapt heart', 'let your heart be rapt and die as one possessed' and 'in *Bushidō*, you die as one possessed'. But this is not an aesthetic of death. Jōchō does not say that death is beautiful.

Why did Yamamoto Jōchō glorify death in this way? Firstly, his own relationship with his lord was precious to him and the death of his lord robbed his life of purpose. (There is no evidence that this relationship was overtly homosexual.) After failing to follow his lord by committing suicide, Jōchō's life must have seemed a bleak waste. These feelings would have been compounded by his commitment to the arts of war in an age when they were unnecessary and unwanted. The skills of the administrator were what the hateful age demanded but they were far from what Jōchō admired. His comments on his contemporaries are scathing: they are merely self-interested, they are like women, they lack spirit because they are safe, the world is coming to an end and, in Part 2, 'though we may wish to recover the good ways of a hundred years ago it will not be possible.' These 'good ways' are the same 'customs of the civil wars' that Sorai dismissed with contempt. They belong to a condition of society of which Jōchō had not the slightest experience.

Hagakure stands as a great memorial to an anachronistic illusion. At a time when they were irrelevant, the mores of a previous violent age were idealized and glorified by a man who spent his entire life without any prospect of battle and glorious death. Moreover his image of the world of the civil-war society was influenced strongly by the society in which he lived. The master-servant relationship that he was devoted to was projected back into the previous age. The result was a heady mixture of devotion and death. And of course in a time when death in battle was impossible the only way of following the 'Way of the Warrior' was to find some private quarrel and die a meaningless death, and it is precisely this kind of death that was glorified. For Jōchō the purity of the death is more important than any other factor. He criticizes the famous forty-seven *rōnin* who in 1702 avenged their master's death for failing to commit suicide immediately after their deed and for spending such a long time in planning the attack. Would it, he queries, not have been a matter for infinite regret if their enemy had meanwhile died of natural causes? 'The people of the Kyōto region are intelligent and clever and so are good in the art of flattery but they never act without forethought, as [men did] in the Nagasaki quarrel.' The 'Nagasaki quarrel' started when a *samurai*'s raincoat was splashed with mud from a road where snow was melting. This led to a quarrel involving four *samurai* and their retainers in which many men were killed. In its meaninglessness and the promptness with which the warriors engaged in mortal combat it was more in tune with the spirit of *Hagakure* than the cautious, methodical and effective plotting of the forty-seven *rōnin*.

Elements of fantasy and illusion apart, *Hagakure* is also an assertion of the primacy of the emotional unity of the group and the importance of discarding personal considerations. The group is all; no universal value, whether Confucian, Buddhist or Shintō, can transcend it. It is this aspect that makes *Hagakure* one of the major expressions of the thought indigenous to Japan. Jōchō was a Japanese and a retainer first and a Buddhist second as his account of his prayers in Part 1 shows: 'In my morning prayers I first humbly address my lord, then my parents, and next the *ujigami* [tutelary god of the clan] and the guardian Buddha.' This intense involvement of the individual with the group of which he is a member is a permanent feature of Japanese society and this expression of it cannot be regarded as anything other than completely valid. Modern Japanese society retains this characteristic. What has changed is the social structure; the master-servant relationship is much weaker than formerly.

The suicides and battlefield deaths of *Hagakure* were not the only way in which death was glorified during this period. There was also the consummation of the love between man and woman in double suicide, evoked sublimely in the puppet theatre (*ningyō jōruri*) of Chikamatsu Monzaemon (1653–1724), notably in plays like *Sonezaki shinjū* (Love-suicide at Sonezaki). The lovers kill themselves in order to achieve perfect union in the next world. They will become 'Buddhas' together: 'They are a model of love, sure to become Buddhas in the future'. This however is not Buddhism in any basic sense; the lovers go to their death with the assurance that they will be together – 'on one lotus leaf' – not that they will achieve enlightenment but be freed from the pains of earthly existence. The exalted suicides of such pieces as *Love-suicide at Sonezaki* involve the glorification of death but are by no means of the type to be found in *Hagakure*, where death is the ultimate negation of self. For a follower of *Bushidō* the essentially personal and private feeling of love was best expressed by devoted and completely undemanding service unto death: 'Love that is announced as such during life is not deep love; love that goes to death kept within the heart is beyond measure ... to die with love in your heart is the ultimate' (*Hagakure*, Part 2). Love in the warrior society of the time often meant homosexual love and in the case of *Hagakure* this kind of emotion was expressed as the devotion that a close retainer felt towards his lord. The love between the hero and heroine of *Love-suicide at Sonezaki* is in complete contrast to this. Their love is intense and personal, and their suicide is its ultimate expression; in it the self finds consummation. For them the 'love that is announced as such during life' *is* 'deep love'; it is only because they are prevented from realizing it fully in life that they turn their hopes to the next world. In *Hagakure* death is deliberately sought in circumstances in which it is possible to avoid it. Courage and strong will are necessary (if not intelligence) and it is these two qualities that are stressed. In *Love-suicide at Sonezaki* death can only be avoided by abandoning love. Behind the lovers' predicament is the pressure of social obligation (*giri*), which in turn is a part of the regulation of society in which the positions of the various classes and of men and women are strictly defined. Like the love between parent and child, sexual love is one of the 'human feelings'(*ninjō*) which are spontaneous. When *giri* and *ninjō* clash, when internal feelings cannot be reconciled with external regulations, the protagonists have no avenue of escape. They do not choose death; they choose love even though it means death. What is glorified here is not a meaningless death but love taken to its limit.

The last significant contrast between *Hagakure* and *Love-suicide at Sonezaki* derives from the difference in the social class of their authors and audience. Jōchō wrote for professional warriors with no wars to fight. He himself was lost in the fantasy of combat and death in which these alienated middle- and low-grade *samurai* of the Genroku era steeped themselves as an escape from their roles as petty administrators. He thought that the world was coming to an end, and in one sense this was true – the age of the warrior had ended. Unable to find a *raison d'être* the *samurai* turned to the search for a rationalization of their non-existence. *Love-suicide at Sonezaki* was written about and for *chōnin* – although Chikamatsu was the son of a *rōnin* he was much more of a *chōnin* than a *samurai* – and the merchant classes were certainly not facing any kind of apocalypse. In the late seventeenth century the Bakufu and many *daimyō* were in financial straits and the great merchant houses were gaining ever greater financial power; in the Genroku era the large merchants of Edo and Ōsaka not only lent money to *daimyō* but also exchanged the rice in which the lords received their income into currency. Smaller merchants were also doing relatively well (as Saikaku's novels show) but the culture was not, as is often supposed, a *chōnin* culture.

Chōnin did not usually receive a great deal of formal education (and it was not until the eighteenth century that there was a marked growth in higher education available to merchants generally) and thus did not develop a distinct and articulate body of values. What formal values they had were imposed upon them by the *samurai*; but these were never truly accepted, remaining as external obligations (*giri*) rather than being internalized. This did not of course mean that this rising class did not seek some kind of self-recognition at least in terms of that part of them that was unreachable by the dictates of duty – their emotions, or *ninjō*. The values of *ninjō* were not, could not be, externalized; they never became a way of regulating behaviour. When *giri* and *ninjō* came into collision *giri* would always dictate what the individual would do (if not how he would feel about it). Nevertheless, within the narrow confines of their class, in the arts that they created for their own consumption, the *chōnin* affirmed their emotional life and achieved a balance between *giri* and *ninjō*. It is *giri* that forces the lovers to die but their death becomes a triumph of their love for each other, for *ninjō*. And it is this that lies behind their journey to an exalted death, accompanied by the plaintive notes of the *shamisen*.

Comparatively little is known of the life of Chikamatsu Monzaemon, born in Kyōto as Sugimori Nobumori, the son of a *rōnin*. He seems to have studied *haikai* verse in his youth and his name appears as the author of *Kabuki* plays and *jōruri* pieces from the 1680s. *Jōruri* is a form of chanted rhythmic accompaniment to the actions of the puppets; in it the narrator acts the dialogue, comments and heightens the emotional effect. Chikamatsu's early work was mainly for the Kyōto *Kabuki* troupe of Sakata Tōjūrō (1647–1709) but after 1686 he concentrated on writing *jōruri* for the puppet theatre of Takemoto Gidayū (1651–1714) in Osaka, and it was in this later period that he produced his best work.

The histories of *Kabuki* and *jōruri* are closely linked, both beginning as public performances at the beginning of the seventeenth century. The earliest form of *Kabuki*, known as *onna* (women's) *Kabuki* was, as the name suggests, all-female. After this was banned in 1629 its place was taken by a version performed by youths between the ages of thirteen and fifteen which consisted mostly of mime, music and dance; this was called *wakashu* (young men's) *Kabuki*. When this in its turn was suppressed (generally from 1652 but not until 1661 in Kyōto) there sprang up other all-male troupes, somewhat older, who performed another form, again largely mime, known as *yarō* (men's) *Kabuki*. In the latter part of the century (perhaps from 1664) the *Kabuki* repertoire began to include pieces with several scenes, known as *tsuzuki kyōgen* ('serial plays'), and slowly changed from being a spectacle of dance and mime to a dramatic form relying more on the spoken word and acting techniques. The two most prominent actors and leaders of troupes at the time were, in Kyōto, Sakata Tōjūrō, who was famous for his performance as an effeminate habitué of the licensed quarters, and, in Edo, Ichikawa Danjūrō (1660–1702), originator of the bravura *aragoto* style of acting.

The best puppet plays of the time were probably the *kinpira jōruri*, a name derived from that of the protagonist, Sakata Kinpira. These usually had as their highlight scenes of super-human valour, and their popularity seems to have been one factor that influenced Danjūrō in his adoption of the exagger-ated heroics of the *aragoto* style. But influence was not just from *jōruri* to *Kabuki*: there are traces of the influence of the style of Tōjūrō's *Kabuki* in Chikamatsu's early *jōruri*.

From the time of Chikamatsu, however, the puppet theatre began to move ahead in popularity and *Kabuki* came to depend more and more on adapting its rival's repertoire. It was not until the second half of the eighteenth century that *Kabuki* again became the dominant force of *chōnin* theatre. Chikamatsu was centrally involved with this rise in the fortunes of the puppet theatre. Indeed his work brought *jōruri* to its fullest flowering and changed the course of theatre history.

Chikamatsu's originality is expressed in his choice of subjects and in his style. Previously all *jōruri* had been to do with the adventures of historical personages of aristocratic or warrior families. Chikamatsu did not abandon this kind of subject matter; two-thirds of his *jōruri* were of this type (called *jidaimono* or historical pieces). But the other third, beginning with *Love-suicide at Sonezaki*, was about the townspeople, principally the *chōnin*. Thus the characters on the stage were of the same social background as the vast majority of the audience (as in the modern European theatre). These 'domestic pieces' (*sewamono*) opened a new horizon for the puppet theatre. Not only did people of the contemporary world appear but contemporary events were dramatized and with astonishing promptness; *Love-suicide at Sonezaki* (first performance 1703) and *Hakata*

Kojorō nami makura (The Wavepillow of Kojorō of Hakata, 1718) were both staged only one month after the events they portray; in the case of *Shinjū ten no Amijima* (Love-suicide at Amijima, 1720) the gap was less than two months and for *Onnakoroshi abura no jigoku* (The Hell of Oil: Murder of a Woman, 1721) inside two and a half months. In an age when there were no mass media to report news widely and quickly some of the popularity of these plays must have been due to the curiosity of people who wanted to know 'exactly what happened'. Not all domestic pieces were staged with this in mind as is clear in the case of the commemorative piece *Gojūnen ki uta nebutsu* (In Memory of the Fiftieth Anniversary of the Deaths of O-natsu and Seijūrō), staged in 1709, but based on events which took place in 1660. Chikamatsu's historical pieces were quite unlike his domestic pieces. They transmitted without noticeable alteration the values of the *samurai* and were replete with scenes of high drama and battle.

All these distinctive features are to be found in his most commercially successful *jōruri*, *Kokusen'ya kassen* (The Battles of Coxinga, 1715), which ran for seventeen months. In it, for example, the wife of a Chinese general commits suicide to ensure the success of a plan she has made with her half-Japanese younger brother to restore the Ming dynasty, and her husband, to power. This act of self-sacrifice is one of the conventions of these historical plays, and there are several other parts of the plot which likewise follow convention. For example, many historical pieces have a scene in which a loyal retainer substitutes his own child for his lord's in order to preserve the continuity of the family to whom he owes allegiance although this very often means the death of his son. In *The Battles of Coxinga* a minister of the Ming court cuts the Emperor's heir from the womb of the dead mother (killed by the enemy) and replaces him with his own son, whom he kills. Such acts of sacrifice of self and family (including admonitory suicide) are the chief constituents of the historical pieces. The glorification of this kind of heroism indicates that neither Chikamatsu nor his audience dissented appreciably from the ethical values of the *samurai* as they are expressed in *Hagakure*. In his historical pieces, in fact, Chikamatsu is acting as a propagandist for the values of the class into which he was born.

The Battles of Coxinga begins from the collapse of the Ming dynasty in the face of invasion by the Tartars. The hero is born in Kyūshū the son of an ex-minister of the Ming who has fled his enemies after the defeat. Although he grows up in Japan Coxinga is determined to restore the dynasty and take revenge on the general who betrayed it. This character is based on the real-life figure of Zheng Sen or 'Coxinga', of whose exploits there were many tales. The battle scenes are magnificent and spectacular, if somewhat exaggerated, and contribute much to the undoubted success of the piece. The elements of exoticism in the play were no doubt another factor in its popular success; few other puppet theatre or *Kabuki* pieces were set in a foreign country, and such lines as Act 2's 'You who sneer at us for coming from a small country, do you understand now the strength of the Japanese, that frightens even a tiger!' would no doubt have been received with applause. But although the hero is half-Chinese and can speak the language, the behaviour of the 'Chinese' characters and the nature of the heroes and villains are no different from those of any other historical piece. This 'China' is no more than an extension of Japanese society; only Tartars are beyond the pale, 'northern barbarians, the same as animals'. Elsewhere Arai Hakuseki was making great efforts to understand the culture of foreign lands as revealed to him by Sidotti, but for Chikamatsu and his audience only 'beastly countries' lay outside the Sino-Japanese cultural sphere and there was no culture of any worth there, with the possible exception of Indian Buddhism.

Domestic pieces were generally not concerned with the *samurai* values of loyalty and sacrifice but with sexual love between man and woman, a subject that *samurai* writing barely touched upon. The plots of these *sewamono* varied little from the pattern established by *Love-suicide at Sonezaki* and the main features can be summarized as follows: the hero is usually not a rich merchant but an assistant or apprentice in a *chōnin* family business (examples include an assistant to a soy sauce maker or a calendar maker, a young man married into the family of a dyer or an express agency, an apprentice to a rice wholesaler or a paper merchant); the woman is usually a licensed prostitute. Very few domestic pieces deal with adultery. There are some, such as *Horikawa nami no tsuzumi* (Revenge on the Drummer,

1707) and *Yari no Gonza kasane katabira*, (Spearman Gonza's Illicit Love, 1717), which are about adultery by the wives of *samurai*. But whether these should properly be called *sewamono* is a matter of definition. In the typical plot the couple's feelings (*ninjō*) come into conflict with some social obligation or pressure (*giri*). This latter may involve a rival for the favours of the woman, financial complications, the machinations of a villain or some combination of these. There are two ways of resolving the contradictions between *giri* and *ninjō*. One is double suicide, as in *Love-suicide at Sonezaki*. The other is to live – to flee; to be caught, as in *Meido no hikyaku* (The Courier of Hell, 1711); for the man to kill himself and the woman to be forgiven; or for both to be saved by the intervention of a priest, as in *Daikyōji mukashi-goyomi* (The Ancient Calendar, 1715). In all plays that take this second solution, the couple do not choose to die together but try to resolve the problem, however despairingly, in this world.

Of course not all *jōruri* follow this pattern. In the commemorative piece *In Memory of the Fiftieth Anniversary of the Deaths of O-natsu and Seijūrō*, the heroine is the daughter of a rice wholesaler, and the man flees and kills himself when discovered. The woman goes violently mad but later recovers and performs religious services to comfort the man's soul. The play *Yūgiri awa no naruto* is even more exceptional: the hero is the son of a wealthy family, the plot involves a *samurai* couple and the two lovers eventually marry. The work in which Chikamatsu moves furthest from his usual *sewamono* themes, however, is *The Hell of Oil* in which the dissolute son of a *chōnin* family cruelly kills a woman for money to spend on his amusements.

The deaths of the lovers in Chikamatsu's *jōruri* are made beautiful by the author's use of two devices. Firstly the setting and action of the play are all chosen for their familiarity to the audience; this helps the playgoers sympathize with the lovers' plight. The couple's only fault is their love, and it is this that brings them into tragic conflict with the inflexible set of social circumstances and obligations which, compounded by bad luck, drives them to their unhappy end. They can change neither their own feelings (*ninjō*) nor the social pressures which control their lives (*giri*). The act of double suicide is unusual but the other circumstances are familiar and everyday; it 'could happen to anyone'. Chikamatsu's other device, very distinctive, is the *michiyuki*. This is the passage that describes the lovers' flight from their predicament, often, although not always, to the place where they will kill themselves; the description is not strictly psychological but elegiac, pathetic and allusive. Stylistically the *michiyuki* is distinct from the rest of the *jōruri*. The *michiyuki* of *Love-suicide at Sonezaki* begins:

> Farewell to this world.
> Farewell to the night.
> Sadness is
> The dream of a dream.
> Dew on the road
> To the graveyard
> As we go to death
> Vanishing step by step.
> Count them –
> Of the seven dawn chimes
> Six have rung.
> One remains, the last
> Echo of our life.

The lovers' last journey passes as swiftly as a dream, as slowly as a lifetime. Between each exquisite instant, a step, the sound of the temple bell, their life flows ineluctably away. To achieve this compression of time and the heightened perception of its passage Chikamatsu uses two stylistic devices, *kakekotoba* and *engo*. *Kakekotoba* resemble puns with the important difference that the two meanings of the word are those in which it is used in the preceding and succeeding phrases. Thus in the passage quoted above the verb 'vanish' can be understood as applying to both 'dew' and 'dream'; a more literal rendering shows how: 'dew step by step *vanishing* dream of a dream is sadness'. One vivid image holds and focuses the attention of the listener; then, before he perceives the transition, the crystalline moment has vanished, and in its place is another equally vivid image. It is, one could say, wrenched away from the listener just as the moments are wrenched from the lovers. In this effort are the lovers' lives and their awareness of their impending death; time is transcended. *Engo* are fixed epithets which serve to expand the referential frame of the passage and at the same time fix it within a tradition familiar to the listener. These two devices are intensified by the use of an insistent 7–5 syllabic pattern and by the other important factor in the impact of *jōruri*, the plangent tones of the *shamisen*.

Seventeen years after *Love-suicide at Sonezaki*, Chikamatsu wrote *Love-suicide at Amijima*, and its *michiyuki* passage shows his increasing mastery of the form. The couple go to kill themselves from bridge to bridge.

> I shall kill you, then myself.
> Our fault a foresight not enough
> To fill the tiny shell of the
> Shijimi Bridge.
> Short our life here
> As the autumn day....
> Although in this world we could not be together
> In the next and every one to come
> We shall be man and wife.

Here 'Shijimi', both the name of a tiny shell and the bridge they are crossing, serves as a *kakekotoba*.

No Japanese treatment of the *liebestod* has surpassed that of Chikamatsu, whose words with *shamisen* accompaniment expressed in the eighteenth century what the composers of Germany expressed in music a century later – love impossible of earthly fulfilment which soars into eternity, ardent passion all-transcendent in death, things both historical and timeless. If he did in fact practise *haikai* in his early years Chikamatsu's style may well be directly influenced by linked verse *renga*. Linked verse, like the *michiyuki*, flows from phrase to phrase, but also concentrates the reader's attention on the single instant and on the movement from one instant to the next. If this supposition is correct all three of the major writers who opened the new age of Japanese writing in the late seventeenth century – Chikamatsu Monzaemon, Matsuo Bashō and Ihara Saikaku – came from the world of linked verse. And linked verse was one of the most important traditions to be passed on from the feudal society that had preceded the Tokugawa system. It had been widely popular before and was still extremely influential.

HAIKAI: THE ART OF BASHŌ

The literary form known as *haikai* began with the practice of using the *renga* linked-verse form to express not the elegant sentiments and sensibility of the Heian aristocracy but the comedy or satire of the ordinary people using language appropriate to the everyday life on which it commented. This became so popular in the sixteenth century that there appeared a number of *haikai* specialists and teachers known as *haikaishi*. In the seventeenth century these specialists concentrated on development of technique, concerning themselves with literary precedent and reference, figures of speech and originality in the links between phrases. Their work was often teasingly obscure. A poet whose work typifies this trend is Nishiyama Sōin (1605–82), a former *rōnin* from Kumamoto whose style, and that of the school he founded, is known as *danrinfū* ('temple study-hall style'). The use of words in this style was very playful, and this was encouraged by competitions in which contestants had to compose as many *renga* as they could within a fixed time. (These competitions were called *yakazu haikai* or 'counting arrows *haikai*', a name inspired by the traditional archery contest at the Sanjūsangendō in Kyōto in which archers vie to shoot the most arrows within twenty-four hours.)

The most noted exponent of this marathon verse-making was an Ōsaka writer, later to be better known for his novels, Ihara Saikaku (1642–93), who achieved fame in 1677 by composing 1,600 *haikai* in twenty-four hours. These were later published under the title *Haikai ōyakazu* (A Great Number of *Haikai*). Two years later his record was broken by a Sendai poet who composed 3,000 within the same time, but the following year Saikaku regained the top spot by composing 4,000 (published in 1681 as *Saikaku ōyakazu* [A Great Number of Arrows by Saikaku]. Four years after that he is said to have composed 23,000 as part of a religious service at Sumiyoshi Shrine in Ōsaka. The *haikai* of this last astonishing effort are not recorded apparently because his speed of composition – an average of sixteen *haikai* a minute – was too great for them to be written down. Naturally the *haikai* in *Saikaku ōyakazu* are not great lyric verse, although there are some of interest including these:

Tonight will my bed rock
Or not rock.

> Money is the enemy
> Of wedlock
> In this world of ours.

In the subjects of these verses there is a foreshadowing of the concerns of Saikaku's later work, his brilliant novels of the brothel quarters and the economic life of the *chōnin*.

In contrast to these verbal acrobatics and the world of dalliance and money, Matsuo Bashō (1644–94) wrote of an old pond, the rough sea of Sado and summer grasses growing on an old battlefield. He established a personal style known as the *shōfu*. The particular characteristics of this style are the use of the *haikai* form not simply for verbal play but as a mode of lyric poetry and the shaping of the first three 5–7–5 syllable lines of the *renga* (the *hokku*) into an independent verse form. This would later be called *haiku*.

Very little is known of Bashō's life before he began to compose *haikai*. He was born in Iga Province (present-day Mie Prefecture) and was in the service of a local *samurai*, Tōdō Shinshichirō, but it is not clear whether he himself was a *samurai*. He composed *haikai* with the eldest son of the family, Tōdō Yoshitada (whose *haikai* pen name was Sengin), and after his death in 1672 went to Edo. It is said that during Bashō's time in Iga he also had a common-law wife.

On leaving Iga he composed the *haikai*:

> A friend 'on the far side of the clouds'
> The wild geese on their way.

His life in Edo seems to have been one of continuous success as a *haikai* poet. During this period he contributed to the *haikai* collection made to celebrate the visit by Nishiyama Sōin and had the poet Takarai Kikaku among others as his pupil. Little else is known of his life during this time but what is certain is that Bashō, like his contemporary Chikamatsu Monzaemon, had dropped out of *samurai* society. He was by no means the only *haikai* poet to have done this; many of his more prominent pupils came from *samurai* backgrounds. Among these were Hattori Ransetsu (1654–1707), Mukai Kyorai (1651–1704), Naitō Jōsō (1662–1704), Kawai Sora (1649–1710) and Hattori Dohō

(1657–1730). Chikamatsu left *samurai* society for the life of a *chōnin* and this move involved not only his own acceptance of the *chōnin* values of *ninjō* but also the *chōnin* acceptance of the *samurai* values of *giri*. Bashō and his pupils, however, did not move from *samurai* society to *chōnin* but kept their distance from both, attempting to create their own world on the fringes of society. This group included people from various backgrounds – for example, Takarai Kikaku (1661–1707) and Nozawa Bonchō (?–1714) were from medical families and Sugiyama Sanpū (1647–1732) was from a *chōnin* family. These poets were committed neither to the values of the *chōnin* nor to those of the *samurai*, and this is one of the major points of difference between Bashō and Chikamatsu. The poets tried to leave the 'vulgar world' of both the *chōnin* and the *samurai*, and this escape was seen almost as a religious act. This does not mean however that they retreated into religion; Bashō's record of his retirement to his cottage Bashōan has no mention of Buddhism, only of retreat from the world. Indeed it is difficult to find any strong Buddhist influence in his writing. His attitude is rather one that advocated literature as a means of escaping from the turmoil and coarseness of daily life; it was, in a sense, art for art's sake. This was what Bashō called 'the Way of Elegance' (*fūga no michi*); his life was 'run through by the single thread' of art; he spent it 'following no religious law, observing no popular customs'.

This kind of 'art for art's sake', or something like it, is evident in the poets of the twelfth and thirteenth centuries whose work is to be found mainly in the collection *Shin Kokinshū*. It was thus perhaps no coincidence that Bashō had a high opinion of these poets, especially Saigyō and Minamotono Sanetomo. But there are significant differences between the aestheticism of *Shin Kokinshū* and that of Bashō. The earlier poets were part of the declining aristocratic society whereas Bashō identified himself with no social group, regarding isolation from the 'vulgar world' as the (self-chosen) fate of the artist. In *Zayū no mei* (1691?) there is the *haikai*:

> Things spoken
> Turn lips cold.
> The autumn wind.

This typifies his attitude of non-involvement. This does not imply criticism of one aspect of society or any specific social system but rather of society *per se*. (Of course in the Genroku era the Tokugawa system must have seemed permanent and unchangeable and to reject it would have been in effect to reject society completely.) Another difference between the two attitudes is that, unlike Bashō, most of the *Shin kokinshū* poets, including Saigyō, made a distinction between poetry and life, although there were exceptions to this, notably Kamono Chōmei in his later years. The general attitude might have been one of 'art for art's sake' but it was not 'life for art's sake'. Bashō did not learn to devote his life to art and to make his life itself a work of art from aristocratic poets such as Fujiwara Teika; if he learned it from anyone it was the great arbiter of taste of the late sixteenth century, Senno Rikyū. It had been economically possible to live as a professional *haikai* poet since the time of the priest Sōgi in the 1400s and this made it possible for Bashō, who was famous in his own time, to devote his life to his art.

Bashō did not spend all his life travelling. He remained in the province of his birth, Iga (near the city of Nara), until he was almost thirty and after his move to Edo did not leave it until his house was burned down in the great fire of 1682, when he was nearly forty. He then spent about five months in a mountain village in the province of Kai (present-day Yamanashi Prefecture). Subsequently he could afford to leave the literary scene for some time as his reputation was by then secure. The travels for which he is so well known began when he was in his forties and continued over the remaining ten years of his life. This period produced the most important of his works and made the journey inseparable from the figure of Bashō.

On his first great journey (1684–85), which for eight months took him from Edo through Iga and Yamato to Kyōto and thence back to Edo, he wrote *Nozarashi kikō*, (Exposure in the Field: A Travel Account, also known as *Kasshi ginkō*). After his next, shorter journey, which lasted about one month in 1687 and took him to Kajima, he set out on a ten-month journey (1687–88) through Iga, Ise, Suma, Akashi, Shinano and back to Edo; this provided the material for the travel sketches *Oi no kobumi* (The Records of a Travel-worn Satchel) and *Sarashina kikō* (A Visit to Sarashina Village). These are both prose descriptions of the places through which he passed interspersed with *haikai*. His last major journey lasted a year from 1689 to 1690 when he went from Edo to Rikuzen, Rikuchū and Dewa in the north and then back to Iga through Echigo, Ōgaki and Ōmi. He then went back and forth between Ōmi and Iga before stopping eventually in the latter. This journey is the basis of the work *Oku no hosomichi* (The Narrow Road to Oku). All of Bashō's major journeys pass through his home province of Iga and, with the exception of his last journey to the north, all of his journeys were limited to the area between Edo and the Kyōto-Ōsaka region.

Compared with the wanderings of his near-contemporary, the priest Enkū who travelled throughout the country and, if the evidence is to be believed, reached Hokkaidō, Bashō cannot really be said to have been a great traveller. Furthermore Bashō observed and described places traditionally celebrated in verse, famous places and famous remains and spent very little time in considering the life of the people of the areas through which he passed. If we compare his attitude with that shown by Sorai in his travel journal, *A Record of Travels through Valleys*, it is clear that Bashō's range of observation is narrower. Of course the two journeys were different in nature. Sorai was part of an official party whereas Bashō, 'beckoned by Dōsojin [the guardian spirit of travellers], unable to put my hand to anything, mending a tear in my pants, fixing the cords of my hat', went off 'on the journey down the long road to Oku', a journey whose essential aimlessness was unlike the purposeful progress of the clan official, if not as random as Bashō himself suggested.

During the year or so of his last major journey Bashō was probably not alone for a single day. At first he was accompanied by Kawai Sora and towards the end of the journey when this companion fell ill and left him, by another of his pupils. Bashō rarely stayed at inns; he was almost always entertained by local *haikai* poets or a wealthy family. Indeed the special note he makes of a night when he stayed at a poor house and was kept awake by fleas and mosquitoes indicates what a rare event this was. Although in *The Narrow Road to Oku* Bashō describes himself as travelling alone with only 'one set of *kamiko* [paper clothes]', this was not actually the case. He was accompanied by at least one pupil, sometimes many, from one warm reception to another. But the factual reality and the artistic significance of these journeys are radically different. To travel at all was outside the tradition of Japanese lyric verse which, since the time of *Kokinshū*, had used a fixed vocabulary of place-names chosen initially for their literary and historical associations but seldom if ever visited by the poet who used them. Bashō saw with his own eyes the green-sprouting leaves of Nikkō, the swollen stream of the Mogami River, and heard with his own ears the sound of a distant waterfall and how 'the voices of cicadas/ penetrate the rocks'. This rediscovery of nature was revolutionary. Bashō did not write about nature because the Japanese of the time (or any time) were generally fond of it; rather it is because Bashō wrote of it that the Japanese have come to believe that they were, and are, fond of nature.

Bashō's prose works include another form apart from the travel journals; these are the *haibun*, a kind of prose equivalent of the *haikai*. In them he bids farewell to friends, talks of pictures and describes his home in a style which, though polished Japanese, follows classical Chinese rhetorical conventions. Probably the best work in this style is *Genjūan no ki* (A Record of Genjūan) included in the collection *Sarumino* (The Monkey's Raincoat, 1691). Bashō also presided over meetings at which linked verse (*haikai renga*, or *renku* as it is known now) was composed. The verse from these was published, and the best-known of these collections are *Fuyu no hi* (A Winter Day, published 1684), *Arano* (published 1689), *The Monkey's Raincoat* (published 1691), *Sumidawara* (A Bag of Charcoal, published 1694) and *Zoku-sarumino* (Sequel to the Monkey's Raincoat, published 1698). After Bashō's death these five works were grouped together with *Haru no hi* (A Spring Day) and *Hisago* as *Haikai shichibushū* (The Seven Part *Haikai* Collection). Several poets would attend the meetings and take turns composing the first part of the *renga* (which was of the 5–7–5 *haikai* form) or completing it with two seven-syllable lines. There were sometimes a hundred verses in a volume, sometimes fifty but most often thirty-six, a number chosen out of respect for the thirty-six famous *waka* poets of the late Heian period, the *kasen*, or 'immortals of song'. *Fuyu no hi*, for example, is made up of five volumes each of thirty-six verses. Bashō's own verse was not published until after his death when his pupils made anthologies. The two major anthologies, *Hakusenshū* (published 1698)

made by Kasakuni and the *Shōō kushū* (1709) of Dohō, each
contain more than five hundred *haikai*. A total of more than a
thousand of Bashō's verses are extant. The *haikai* and the verses
Bashō contributed to the *haikai renga* collections are rather
different. The latter sometimes refer to sexual love, a topic never
touched upon in the *haikai*. In one of the sequences in *Arano*, for
example, there is the following first verse:

> As we dressed in the morning
> How slender she was
> How elegant.
>
> (*Kasen*, 1689)

In fact eight of Bashō's *haikai renga* begin with the phrase
kinuginu, which means literally 'clothes and clothes' and is a
conventional phrase indicating the time when two lovers must
disentangle their clothes and put on their separate lives for the
new day. This phrase never occurs in his *haikai*. Again, in a
thirty-six verse collection of 1689 the following verse appears:

> Dressed for bed
> Her make-up was beautiful.

This kind of verse was not common in the lines Bashō composed
as the second part of the *renga* but at the least it shows that he
did not completely ignore the long tradition of erotic Japanese
lyric verse.

It is Bashō's *haikai*, however, that were his great achievement
and which influenced Japanese literature immeasurably. They
have several distinguishing characteristics. Firstly, they represent a personal discovery of nature; the vision is acute and
personal in such lines as 'Rough seas/and stretching over Sado
Island/the milky way' and 'Between the waves/small shells/are
mixed with bush-clover dust'. Secondly, the subtlety of his
perceptions required a new and vividly realistic prosody with a
range of striking onomatopoeic effects. Onomatopoeia is impossible to translate adequately but perhaps the following *haikai*
will give some idea of the effect it can create:

> *Akaakato*   Bright bright
> *hi wa tsurenakumo* The sun shines on

aki no kaze   Autumn wind.

(1689)

Here the repeated *k* sounds, especially in *akaaka*, evoke the cold brightness of the autumn sun.

Horohoroto   Scattering
yamabuki chiruka The globe flowers fall.
taki no oto   The sound of the waterfall.

(1688)

As in the preceding *haikai* the first phrase is an onomatopoeic evocation of the scene; the sound in this case is a soft fluttering of the falling blossom. Bashō also used surrealistic images to express his subtle perceptions:

Stillness
Penetrating the rocks.
The sounds of cicada.

(1689)

And:

Whiter
Than the stones of Stone Mountain.
The autumn wind.

(1689)

Thirdly, Bashō was capable of self-irony and sharp self-mockery as in the verses:

Not yet dead
And the end of a journey.
Autumn evening.

(1684)

And:

Muttering satirical verse
Out in the biting wind
Like that odd man Chikusai.

(1684)

He was also capable of distancing himself intellectually from his own life as in these *haikai*:

> This autumn
> Why do I feel my years?
> A bird in the clouds.
>
> (1694)

> The road
> And no-one going on it.
> Autumn evening.
>
> (1694)

Fourthly, Bashō's *haikai*, even though their form is derived from linked verse, are complete lyric verses in their own right. In this sense Bashō can be said to have created a new form of Japanese lyric verse to add to the only forms available to poets before him, the *tanka* and the *chōka*. (And of these two forms the *tanka* was the only one much used.) From the *tanka* was born the *renga*, and this was popular until after Bashō's time. But it was the *haikai* – later called *haiku* – that came to be the central form of Japanese poetry, and although *renga* slowly declined, the form that Bashō pioneered remains popular today.

The *haikai* form, a mere seventeen syllables, is not one in which the poet can describe a process or a train of thought; the focus is usually on the impressions of an instant. Bashō says about the composition of *haikai* that 'you should put into words the light in which you see something before it vanishes from your mind' (in the collection *Sanzōshi*, edited by Dohō, published between 1702 and 1704). To do this Bashō trained his sensibility and focused his attention on the strength of the instantaneous impressions outside objects gave him. In his own words: 'In the making of *haikai*, there are those that become and those that are made. When you concentrate on the inner sensibilities and put them in harmony with things the essence of your mind and heart becomes the *haikai*. When you do not work on your inner sensibilities then a *haikai* will not happen and then you make one from your own thoughts.' To make a *haikai* 'from your own thoughts' is to write it not from direct experience but to create it consciously. It is clear that it is direct experience and its expression that Bashō valued.

Bashō's achievement, in sum, was to encapsulate the tradition of Japanese poetry and to advance it significantly. In this he also advanced the sensibility of the Japanese people. His concern was with this world, his attachment to the subtlest of details and his aesthetic sensitivity extremely refined. These qualities were enough to support Bashō in his solitary life, from 'A friend "on the far side of clouds"/The wild geese on their way.' to 'On a journey and sick./Dreams of roaming./A withered moor.'

For this poet, uncommitted to the values of the *samurai* or the *chōnin*, unconcerned with the other-worldly doctrines of Buddhism, the 'Way of Elegance' came inevitably to be the only value in which he believed and by which he lived. There were few if any examples of such a thorough commitment in the secularized culture of the seventeenth century.

Bashō's pupils were active into the eighteenth century. Of these Takarai Kikaku was perhaps the most accomplished. Although the son of an Edo doctor he eschewed medicine to become a professional *haikai* poet and wrote of city life and the ways of the *chōnin*, which Bashō of course did not. In *Gogenshū* (published 1740s), one of his *haikai* collections, there appear these *haikai*:

> In the rays of the setting sun
> Flying along a city street
> A butterfly.

> The heat haze continues to rise
> And my heart
> Reels.

He writes of the brothels, of *Kabuki* and, often, of *sake*; in his verses appear 'the women of a spring evening', carpenters, priests, acolytes, maidservants, runny noses, urination, beancurd and chestnuts in their shells. In this Kikaku follows more closely than did Bashō the tradition of *haikai* since the Muromachi period, and he is closer to the life of the *chōnin* than his master. Bashō thought little of Saikaku's 'flippant efforts' but in *Gogenshū* Kikaku records the poem he wrote when, taking part in one of the Sumiyoshi *yakazu haikai* meetings, he 'was asked to supply some assistance' to Saikaku:

As the horse rushes on
Two myriad verses
Of flies sing together.

Haikai continued in the style of Kikaku until the time of Yosa Buson in the mid- to late eighteenth century.

Bashō described verse as being composed of two elements, the permanent (*fueki*) and the fashionable (*ryūkō*), and this combination of characteristics can also be said to apply to the position of *haikai* in this period. In that it could as art transcend the age in which it was written it was permanent and in that it changed with the times it was fashionable. Bashō's art was 'permanent' for it encapsulated the indigenous sensibility; it was also fashionable, for it provided a form of expression for a significant group of writers who had left *samurai* society and were not connected with *chōnin* culture.

CHŌNIN IDEALS AND REALITY: IHARA SAIKAKU

The *chōnin* of the late seventeenth century, particularly the merchants of the large cities, devoted themselves to the pursuit of two things – monetary profit and sexual pleasure. Sex could be either heterosexual or homosexual; the former was available in the organized and licensed brothel areas (such as Yoshiwara in Edo, Shimabara in Kyōto and Sonezaki in Ōsaka) and the latter in association with male prostitutes, *wakashū*. During this period many guides to the licensed quarters and directories to prostitutes were published, often under a slight fictional cover. Among the many works of this type we can mention *Nanba monogatari* (Tales of Nanba, 1655) and *Naniwa dora* (The Gong of Naniwa, 1680), and a general description of the *kuruwa, Shikidō ōkagami* (The Great Mirror of the Way of Venery), was written by Fujimoto Kizan and published in 1678.

Homosexuality had long been common in monasteries (since the fourteenth century at least) and is mentioned in the poetry of the five great Zen temples, for example in the early fifteenth-century *Shinden shikō*, the late fifteenth-century *Ryūsuishū* by Tōshō Shūgen and the early sixteenth-century *San'eki enshi*. It had also been the subject of Japanese fiction for some time.

There is, for example, the fourteenth-century work *Aki no yonaga monogatari* (Tales of Long Autumn Nights). The attachment of *samurai* to good-looking young men was a theme dealt with by not a few of the colloquial books, *kanazōshi*, of the early part of the seventeenth century, one example of which is *Shin'yū ki* (The Record of a Friendship of the Heart, 1643). In contrast there is almost no literature on lesbianism.

Novels about making money and related activities did not appear until the work of Ihara Saikaku, the first writer to deal with both of the two great quests of *chōnin* life. Little is known of the life of Saikaku other than his activities as a *haikai* versifier. It is commonly believed that he came from a *chōnin* family, lost his wife and children when he was thirty-four or -five and subsequently entrusted the family business to a manager and became a *haikai* poet and travelled widely. His journeys, which included several to Edo and one to Naruto in Shikoku were perhaps more extensive than those of Bashō, although it is impossible to be certain. In his later years he wrote short novels in Japanese, his first popular success being *Kōshoku ichidai otoko* (The Life of an Amorous Man, 1682). There are doubts as to whether some of the works attributed to Saikaku are in fact his, but there is no doubt in this case. His works fall into three types. There are those dealing with sexual relationships, either between man and woman or man and man – such as *The Life of an Amorous Man*, *Kōshoku gonin onna* (Five Amorous Woman, 1686), *Kōshoku ichidai onna* (The Life of an Amorous Woman, 1686), *Nanshoku ōkagami* (The Great Mirror of Love between Men, 1687) and *Saikaku okimiyage* (Mementos of Saikaku, posthumously published 1693). The other group of major importance is made up of those novels which deal with the economic life of the *chōnin*, such as *Nippon eitaigura* (The Japanese Family Storehouse, 1688), *Seken munezan'yō* (Reckonings That Carry Men through the World, 1692) and *Saikaku oridome* (Saikaku's Last Weaving, posthumously published 1694). The remainder of his works are on various themes and include *Saikaku shokokubanashi* (Saikaku's Provincial Tales, 1685), *Budō denraiki* (Traditions of the Way of Arms, 1687), *Buke giri monogatari* (Tales of the *Giri of Samurai* Families, 1688) and *Honchō ōin hiji* (The Japanese *Tangyin bishi*, 1689) based on a Chinese collection of stories of judgements. Saikaku's importance in the history of the Japanese novel is derived from the works in the first two groups in which he proves himself to be uniquely capable of describing *chōnin* life realistically from a *chōnin* standpoint.

Not all the readers of *chōnin* novels were members of the urban commercial classes. Indeed only a few *chōnin* read books, as most of them had no more than the basic education supplied by the temple schools, the *terakoya*. (It was not until the early eighteenth century that a higher standard of education became common among the *chōnin*.) The sales figures of Saikaku's books are not known but it is reasonable to suppose that they were in the thousands (this estimate being supported by the fact that the earlier *Kiyomizu monogatari* is known to have sold between two and three thousand copies).

In his time Saikaku seems to have had a high reputation as a writer. Bashō, although contemptuous of Saikaku's verse, says nothing against his prose. Later, in the eighteenth century, Yamamoto Jōchō quotes a 'famous line' from Saikaku in *Hagakure*. This kind of reputation suggests that Saikaku's readership included intellectuals and *samurai* as well as upper- and middle-class merchants; although Saikaku described the life of the *chōnin* the great majority or them did not read his novels.

The literature that the *chōnin* did come into contact with was in the form of stories told by professional raconteurs, especially the type known as *shōwa* or 'laughing stories'. These were short humorous stories, told with appropriate gestures and usually ending with some form of 'punch line' (*ochi*). (This type of story-telling later came to be known as *rakugo* and remains popular today.) Sometimes the raconteur (*hanashika*) would be invited to perform at a *samurai*'s mansion, but more often he would find an audience in well-frequented places like a street or a bath-house. The three most well-known *hanashika* of the time were Shikano Buzaemon (1649–99) of Edo, Tsuyuno Gorobei (1644?–1703?) of Kyōto and Yonezawa Hikohachi (dates unknown). Eleven out of thirty-nine stories of Buzaemon which were published in 1686 as *Shikano makifude* are anecdotes of the world of *Kabuki*. Gorobei's best stories appear in the collection *Karukuchi tsuyugahanashi* and Hikohachi's in *Karukuchi gozen otoko* (publication dates unknown); in both cases puns and verbal jokes are prominent and many of the jokes hinge on illiteracy or differences in dialect. There are fewer sexual jokes than in

Yesterday's Happenings Are Today's Tales and they are less explicit. A wide range of characters appear, especially in *Karukuchi gozen otoko*, and they are from all social classes – doctors, Confucianists, priests, merchants, artisans, maidservants, ineffectual *rōnin*, dithering *samurai*, illiterate rustics, *Nō* players, packhorse men, fortune tellers, Buddhist nuns, ladys's maids, *chōnin* matrons, teahouse women addicted to gambling and so no. One example, from *Karukuchi gozen otoko*: A man has a fit on getting into the bathtub and the uproar he creates attracts a local doctor, who comes, takes the man's pulse and calmly says, 'Take out the plug and let the water drain.' When the tub is empty he says, 'Fine. Now just put on the lid and take it down to the graveyard.'

Although the customs of the time, or at least some of them, come across with considerable vividness, these simple stories, without the skill of the performer to project them with gestures, expression and verbal mannerism, lack the strong comic appeal of *Yesterday's Happenings Are Today's Tales* and, to an even greater extent, the incisive criticism of *Kyōgen*. No challenge, criticism or satire is directed towards any authority, be it political, religious or moral. The development of *chōnin* culture in the Genroku era seems to have been towards the refined jest about the trivialities of daily life, safely within the existent frameworks of values and social hierarchy. For the *chōnin* the 'laughing stories' were a diversion; they did not touch upon the essential part of their life. It was Saikaku who perceived and described the central concerns of *chōnin* society and produced a realistic account of the values, aims and behaviour of ordinary people.

The unprecedented commercial success of *Life of an Amorous Man* can be attributed to three factors. Firstly, Saikaku's style is precise, undeclamatory and concrete, capable of depicting the smallest details of a scene. Secondly, the story is erotic and also involves the hero in journeys through the various provinces, thus combining the two features which had been central to popular literature since the Muromachi period. Thirdly, the inimitable hero, Yonosuke, is a great creation and has become a figure of popular legend. Yonosuke is said to have 'dallied with 3,742 women and frolicked with 725 boys'; as the title suggests, *The Life of an Amorous Man* tells of the sexual experiences of the hero between the ages of seven and sixty. If the 'Shining Prince' of the *Tale of Genji* is a master of romantic love, Yonosuke is a master of sexual experience. The Heian work depicts the psychological nuances of Genji's relationship with a variety of ladies whereas Saikaku's book deals only with circumstances and actions, avoiding psychological complexities. But this lack of psychological detail brings into prominence the thought behind the novel. Its philosophy of life is thoroughly hedonistic and involves a pursuit of sexual pleasure with complete disregard for Confucian and Buddhist morality. The completeness of this hedonism is unique in the novels of the Tokugawa period. (The *kanazōshi* of the early seventeenth century contain elements derived from popular Confucian ethics, and the early nineteenth-century 'gay quarter' novels have a certain amount of 'editorial comment' from the standpoint of everyday morality.) After a long active life during which he has 'known all the courtesans, dancing girls and strumpets of the floating world' the hero sets off for the Island of Women, taking with him a few friends and a range of aphrodisiacs. Thus the hero of the Genroku *chōnin* is not punished for his worldly pleasures by an after-life in hell as is his equivalent in Christian culture, Don Juan; instead he sets off unrepentant to carry on in the same way in some foreign place.

The plots of the five stories that make up *Five Amorous Women* are very different from this. They are set not in the pleasure quarters but in the *chōnin* households and describe not the uncomplicated joys of sex but tragic love. Each story has a different heroine and is based on fact; the real-life incidents occurred not long before the publication of the book. They concern the love affairs of the *chōnin* girls O-natsu, Yaoya O-shichi and O-man and the adulteries of the married women Taruya O-sen and O-san. The same stories were subsequently used in *jōruri* by Chikamatsu Monzaemon.

The construction of these short stories is superb and the characterization of the heroines more convincing than that achieved by Chikamatsu; with *Reckonings That Carry Men through the World* they stand as Saikaku's finest short stories and the greatest in the entire Tokugawa period. The third story concerns the fate of O-san, the wife of a Kyōto picture mounter. The real-life O-san became close to the assistant Mohee and ran off with him only to be caught and executed (1683). Their intimacy was accidentally connived at by the maid, Tama. Chikamatsu tells his version of the story in the *jōruri Daikyōshi mukashi Koizumi* (The Ancient Calendar). In both his and Saikaku's stories the two come together without realizing what they are doing but after the elopement the behaviour of the couple in the two versions is markedly different. In Saikaku's version the two, realizing that though their fault might have been unwitting the punishment (death) will be the same, try to cling to life and to each other. The man thinks of deceiving their pursuers by pretending to drown himself; the woman has the good sense to bring five hundred *ryō*, a vast sum, with her for their future needs. When they spend a night in the mountain temple dedicated to the Buddhist Bodhisattva Monju he appears to them in a dream to tell them that if they part and enter holy orders they can be saved. They reply that they do not care what happens in the future, that nothing could induce them to part, a response to be expected from characters created by the author of *Life of an Amorous Man*. Mohee says, 'Whatever may happen I don't care. I had an affair because I like it [sex with women]. You, Lord Monju, follow only the way of men and don't know anything about the way of women.'

In Chikamatsu's *jōruri* on the other hand the stress is on the wretched fortune of the pair: O-san and Mohee 'did not want in the slightest to stray into infidelity; it was just the workings of *karma*.' They have no money with them at all and no schemes for staying alive. They are saved eventually by the intercession of a priest who is impressed by their concern for their parents and her husband. This difference in treatment illustrates the differences between Saikaku and Chikamatsu in their attitudes to contemporary values. There are differences too between the Saikaku who wrote these stories and the creator of Yonosuke. In the earlier work the hero and his hedonistic approach to life are idealized at the expense of conventional morality; in the later there is no idealization and the characters are treated realistically. There are inconsistencies within Saikaku's plot of the story of O-san and Mohee – the maid is referred to both as Tama and Rin, for example, and the hero at one point does not have a sword and later does – and these show a certain amount of carelessness on the part of the author, but do not diminish his skill as a novelist. Rather they testify to a genius which could produce flawless and perfectly economical short stories even though failing to pay attention to trivial details.

One of Saikaku's characteristics as a novelist is that he seldom dealt with the same kind of material twice. His first novel was fanciful and philosophical, the next one was topical and realistic. After these came *The Life of an Amorous Woman*, a kind of antithesis to *The Life of an Amorous Man*. The contrast is between the sex life of the man and that of the woman of the time, between the triumphant pursuit of pleasure and an optimistic view of life and the sad decline from high-class courtesan to common drab and a pessimistic view of life. His next work, *The Great Mirror of Love between Men*, is about homosexuality among *samurai* and *chōnin*. His last work *Mementos of Saikaku* describes the desolate lives of men who were rich profligates in the past. In its preface he says, 'All the lies of the world come together to make the elegant pastime of whoring. Knowing this, it is impossible for one who speaks the truth to live in a brothel for a single day.' These ideas are a long way from the spirit of *The Life of an Amorous Man*. If they represent a development in Saikaku's thought it may well be one from simple hedonism to the sad self-awareness that follows pleasure. At the same time the technical aspects of his short-story writing reached something like perfection.

The same kind of development is evident in the novels to do with money and business. *The Japanese Family Storehouse* is a collection of stories about merchants who amass great fortunes by their talent and thrift. The optimism shown in its praise of thrift and diligence is analogous to the optimism of *The Life of an Amorous Man*: 'You should save money. It will be another parent in your life to add to your mother and father.' Money is not something to be inherited but to gain through one's talent, and the same view can be found expressed in *Reckonings*: 'The word "fortunate" is used about people who become rich. The truth is that a family flourishes by working with intelligence and skill, not by Ebisu, the god of wealth.' This is a meritocratic view of society, which at its extreme implies that a rich man is clever and hard-working while a poor man is a stupid idler. *The Japanese Family Storehouse* and *Reckonings* are not only vivid descriptions of the social differentiation within the *chōnin* created by the commercial development of the Genroku era; they also express the philosophy of the class to which Saikaku belonged. In terms of technique, *Reckonings*, which describes the *chōnin* family at the year-end with acute perception, wit, and precision, stands with *Five Amorous Women* as Saikaku's finest fiction.

In *Saikaku's Final Weaving* the attitude to money is far different from that of *The Japanese Family Storehouse*. Wealth is 'not [something] to be celebrated with thousands of cheers'; it 'conceals evil' and with it man 'behaves perversely'. There is a crucial difference between someone with a rich father and someone without such a benefit for 'a [rich] unfilial son remains concealed' whereas for the poor 'even the slightest wrong is impossible to hide'. The conclusion is that 'there is no point living in this world without money.' The contrast between the positive assertion of *The Japanese Family Storehouse* ('You should save money...') and the resigned tone of *Saikaku's Final Weaving* ('As I watch it and hear of it I am repelled by this unsatisfactory world...') is marked. Why was the world 'unsatisfactory'? Saikaku had discovered that ingenuity and effort do not make money; it depends on the use of capital. In Volume 1 he says, 'A merchant without capital, even if he acts with great intelligence and makes a profit, only offers it up to others. A man with a moneyed father is free to do what he likes and often is able to buy up what he fancies and make a profit' and, in Volume 6, 'unlike the old days we have now reached an age in which a man, even of average ability, who already has capital makes the profits rather than a clever able man; a world in which money makes money'. In Volume 3 he asks, 'What predestination divides us into two conditions, wealth and poverty? Riches come to a wealthy man without his asking; even when a poor man pleads, loss piles on loss.' None of the Confucian intellectuals involved in the economic policies of central and provincial government described this aspect of commercial capitalism more clearly. Saikaku had moved from a belief in a meritocratic society to disgust at a society run by the power of money, regardless of individual ingenuity or ability.

Where did Saikaku's revulsion at society lead him? We do not know. From the evidence of *Saikaku's Last Weaving* it was not to Buddhism: 'In the household of a merchant who hopes for wealth, let there be no contemplation of the impermanence of the world, no sympathizing with the sadness of humanity.' The Buddhist view of life was foreign to Saikaku, who was through and through one of the Ōsaka *chōnin* with all their worldliness and their disregard for any supernatural order. The Buddhist-Confucian ideology which came down to the *chōnin* from the *samurai* did not entirely control their emotional life (and thus the *michiyuki* of Chikamatsu's *jōruri* were possible) nor did it shake their firmly rooted interest in sex, materialism and entertainment (hence Saikaku's novels). Again like another great prose writer of the time, Arai Hakuseki, who constantly looked for the facts of history and their rational interpretation, Saikaku, though pessimistic in his later works and repelled by his observations, never satisfied his undying curiosity in the world and people around him. Hakuseki and Saikaku, although one used the vocabulary of Song Confucianism and the other that of the *chōnin* and *haikai*, were alike in trying to grasp the reality of their respective worlds and were thus both excellent observers. Both stood out from their contemporaries. Sorai and Chikamatsu, being poets, were masters of language. Hakuseki and Saikaku produced their incomparable prose not primarily from a concern with language but from a concern with reality.

Chapter 2

Chapter 2

The Age of Wit and Learning

A process that continued unceasingly throughout the eighteenth century was the spread of education, encouraged both by the Bakufu and by the provincial governments which established and maintained new schools, a trend which was especially marked in the latter half of the century. (Of the 278 schools whose dates of foundation are known only 40 were founded before the middle of the century. Thus more schools were founded in the second part of the eighteenth century than had been in the preceding 150 years.) The domain schools were designed to educate the children of *samurai* and the education they gave gradually became more practical; the local governments moreover were increasingly coming to realize the need for effective administrators. The result of this was, as we shall see, increasing specialization within the intelligentsia. Local governments also opened some part of this education to the *chōnin* (unrestricted classes were established at the Shōheizaka Gakumonjo school in Edo in 1718) and encouraged the foundation of private *chōnin* schools such as the Edo Kaiho-dō (1723) and the O'saka Kaitoku-dō (1725). Also, the school which taught the *chōnin*-oriented *Shingaku* ('Studies of the Heart') became increasingly popular and established branches throughout the country. During this century the monopoly on education that the *samurai* and priesthood had previously enjoyed – with only the feeble challenge of the elementary education offered to the other classes by the *terakoya* temple schools – was destroyed. If this century can be called the age of the *chōnin* it is because of these background conditions in which higher education came within the reach of the upper- and middle-class merchants (as well as a few peasants). Not only did there subsequently appear a succession of *chōnin* scholars but their thought was far more original than that of their *samurai* contemporaries.

Occurring continually throughout the eighteenth century was the phenomenon of the peasant rising. There were thirty-five major risings in this period and if we add to these the incidents in which the peasantry backed their demands for justice with a certain show of force or insisted that their claims should be considered by a higher authority, the number reaches seventy. Often thousands of peasants were mobilized in these actions and occasionally several hundreds of thousands of people from several provinces took part. For instance, in the 'Post-horse Disturbances' of the last month of 1764 and the first of 1765, over two hundred thousand people from villages along the Nakasendō highway in the north-central Honshū provinces of Musashi, Kōzuke, Shimotsuke and Shinano are said to have taken part.

The cause of these risings was usually poverty compounded by both the legal obligation to give a part of the crop to the *samurai* authorities and hoarding on the part of merchants. The background to this was one of the development of a commodity economy and violent fluctuations in the rice price on the national market. (When the price fell the Bakufu compelled merchants to support it by buying rice; when it rose it punished merchants who hoarded. This cycle was repeated over periods of several years.) It can further be supposed that involved in the process were the fiscal difficulties of the *samurai* houses; since they were dependent on their part of the peasants' rice for their income their attempts to solve their difficulties would often involve extracting a larger proportion of the crop. (The 'reforms' that successive governments imposed throughout the Tokugawa period invariably featured sumptuary measures as an important element. The concern of individual Confucianists with the problem is shown by the fact that few of the political programmes advanced after Ogyū Sorai's *Political Discussions* failed to mention the fiscal problems faced by provincial or central government.)

Whether the risings resulted in the acceptance or rejection of the peasants' demands (for reduction in the rice tribute and the replacement of local officials) they invariably met with forceful repression and the punishment of their leaders. There are known to have been almost three thousand peasant risings during the Tokugawa period (2,967, an average of 10.6 a year). Not one of these aimed at the reform of the system of military dictatorship; rather they all demanded reform of particular parts of that system. This feature clearly distinguishes Japanese circumstances from those in China and Europe; in Japan there was no equivalent of the Dai Ping rebellion or the Peasant Wars of Germany.

The rising was not the only form of mass movement. There was also the pilgrimage to the Great Shrine of Ise (known as the *okagemairi* or *nukemairi*). Wives, sons, daughters, maids and manservants of *chōnin* or peasant families would join groups to make this pilgrimage, without informing their husbands, parents or employers or obtaining permission to travel from their local lord and often without making any provision for the journey. In some years millions of people took part in these pilgrimages (in 1705 and 1771 between two and three million went; in 1830 the number is said to have been five million). These too were an explosive expression of suppressed popular feeling.

Intellectually the eighteenth century was divided into two parts by the influence of the West. Yoshimune, who as soon as he became *Shōgun* dismissed Arai Hakuseki from his post (in 1716), at least agreed with the author of *Information on the West* in his assessment of the value of western technology (astronomy, calendars and geography) and lifted the ban on the importation of Chinese translations of western works with the exception of those which treated Christianity (in 1720). During this period Aoki Kon'yō (1698–1769) imported the sweet potato into Japan and wrote *Banshokō* (On Growing Sweet Potatoes, 1735) and Yamawaki Tōyō (1705–62) used Dutch dissection manuals in his pioneering examinations of the human body, for which he used the corpses of executed criminals. Twenty years before *Kaitai shinsho*, the first translation of a Dutch dissection manual, he had prepared his own, *Zōshi*, in 1754; in it he wrote, 'We can perhaps overthrow theory but how can we suppress facts?' He maintained that the human body was essentially the same throughout the ages and did not vary according to culture; thus the people of today were essentially the same as those of the classical, and much revered, ages of China. Such an assertion was something of an exception. The influence of western thought on the intellectuals of the first part of the century was limited to a few technical fields and came for the most part in the form of Chinese translation; it thus provided no challenge to their world-view. The major thinkers of the period, including Ishida Baigan, Tominaga Nakamoto and, probably, Andō Shōeki, remained almost completely unaffected by the West.

In the latter part of the century, however, there appeared a group of thinkers who studied Dutch and attempted to absorb western thought directly. They were known as 'Dutch scholars' (*rangakusha*). At the same time western thought began to impinge on the consciousness of most thinkers and press them towards a revision of their traditional attitudes. None of the major thinkers of the period – Yamagata Bantō, Miura Baien and Motoori Norinaga – completely ignored the existence of western culture. Yet the West for them was something remote and exerted almost no influence on the basic framework of their thought. Thus it was possible, for example, for Baien to attempt to incorporate western thought into the traditional framework of Confucianist philosophy. No Westerners, except those few at the trading post in Nagasaki, had appeared in the ports of Japan, and what influenced the Japan of the late eighteenth century was western technology while the West itself was still remote. It was not until the nineteenth century that colonialism and imperialism appeared on the horizon.

The *samurai* intellectuals of the first half of the eighteenth century can be roughly divided into three types. First there were the Confucianists from the previous century, many of whom served a *daimyō* and received an official stipend. Their scholarship was mainly concerned with the Chinese classics, the attitude they took was involved with Confucianist political ethics and their ambition was to advise and influence local or central government. Representative of this type was the Wang Yangming scholar Muro Kyūsō who was born into a medical family and became a retainer of the Bakufu on the recommendation of Arai Hakuseki (in 1711) and later lecturer to the *Shōgun* (from 1722). The *samurai* Dazai Shundai, sometimes in service and sometimes masterless, became a pupil of Ogyū Sorai in 1711 and continued Sorai's thought. Itō Jinsai's eldest son, Tōgai, was not from a *samurai* family and never entered the service of a *samurai* house, continuing instead the private school founded by his father; but the content of his thought was traditionally Confucianist and he can thus be counted as an intellectual of this type.

The second type was that of the technical specialist, which included mathematicians (of 'Japanese mathematics'), calendar makers and doctors. As we have indicated for this type of intellectual, which included Aoki Kon'yō and Yamawaki Tōyō, western thought was strongly, if indirectly, relevant. It was from this type of thinker that there subsequently appeared the 'Dutch scholars' of the latter part of the century. (It is still usual to divide the thinkers of the eighteenth century into followers of Confucianism, National Learning and 'Dutch Studies'. This system of classification, which does not take into account the methodology of the thought but is based half on the subject it addresses and half on the terminology it employs, does not seem helpful.)

The third type of intellectual was the *bunjin* or 'literatus'. Such intellectuals wrote verse and prose in Chinese, painted in a distinctive style (*bunjinga*) and were little concerned with Confucianism, particularly its political and economic aspects. Whether retainers or *rōnin* they felt themselves to be independent both of *samurai* society and of *chōnin* society and had a strong feeling of group identity. Literati first appeared as such a group in the beginning of the eighteenth century. We shall discuss the significance of this later. Here we shall only emphasize the fact that there took place a division into types within – and adjacent to – *samurai* society.

During the first part of the century the priesthood, Buddhist and Shintō, produced such thinkers as Hakuin (1685–1768), Jiunsonja Onkō (1718–1804) and Kamono Mabuchi (1697–1769). Hakuin came from the Kyōto Zen temple of Myōshinji and, like Suzuki Shōsan in the early years of the seventeenth century, devoted himself to the popularization of Zen. His most famous work is *Yasen kanwa* (Idle Tales on a Night Boat, 1757), written in Japanese, which tells of an encounter in the mountains with a mystic who cures him of his spiritual and physical ailments. This is in fact closer to a guide to good health than an exposition of Zen thought. Hakuin was also a painter, well-known for his works in the so-called Zen style. Onkō was an abbot of the Shingon Sect of Buddhism whose major achievement was to introduce the early Sanskrit texts into the study of the Buddhist canon. Kamono Mabuchi's work was the linguistic study of the *Manyōshū*. In the work of all these men there is perceptible the beginning of a tendency towards positivism.

Two of the most original thinkers of the first part of the century were *chōnin*. They were Tominaga Nakamoto (1715–46), who began his short life in a family of Ōsaka *chōnin*, and Andō Shōeki (dates uncertain). Little is known about the latter but it seems probable that he did not come from a *samurai* family and spent most of his life in a farming community. The major works of these two thinkers were all too original to be recognized in their time and remained virtually unread and without influence during their lifetimes. There also appeared a doctrine taught by *chōnin* for *chōnin*. This was the *Shingaku* of Ishida Baigan (1685–1744). This eclectic doctrine came, later in the century, to have a large number of followers including high-ranking *samurai* and courtiers. The entertainments of the *chōnin* included the puppet play with its chanted *jōruri* narrative accompaniment, popular novels in the style of Saikaku, and comical stories. Most of these were however an extension of Genroku culture; there were no notable innovations in this period. As we have mentioned, the chief forms of self-expression for the peasants were riot and enthusiastic pilgrimage.

In the second half of the century, *samurai* Confucianists concentrated their attention more and more on practical problems of economic policy. One such thinker was Kaiho Seiryō (1755–1817). And, as we have mentioned, there appeared specialists, such as Sugita Genpaku (1733–1817) and his successors, who systematically examined the West as it appeared in Dutch-language works. The *bunjin* or literati of the time included Yosa Buson (1716–83), a *haikai* poet and painter of peasant origins whose culture and circle of acquaintances qualified him to be a representative figure of the time. Following on the great *chōnin* thinkers in the earlier part of the century, Tominaga Nakamoto and Andō Chōeki, came Yamagata Bantō (1748–1821) and Miura Baien (1723–1789), the former a *chōnin*, the latter the son of a wealthy peasant. There was also the towering figure of Motoori Norinaga (1730–1801). During this time the centre of *chōnin* theatre shifted from the puppet play to *Kabuki* and at the same time the *ukiyo-e* print was developed, popularized and turned into a sophisticated art, as was the form of humorous verse known as *senryū*. There was one man who embodied the entirety of this urban culture from the technology of the 'Dutch scholars' to the attitudes of the literati, from the economic policies of the Confucianists to *jōruri* and *senryū*, during a life which spanned the middle of the century. He was Hiraga Gennai (1728?–79), a figure one could call the personification of the whole of eighteenth-century culture.

At the end of his life he became insane, killed a pupil and died in prison.

The peasants continued to rise in despairing insurrection and the *samurai* authorities continued, as they had done in the earlier part of the century, to suppress them and kill their leaders.

BUNJIN: THE LITERATI

A central figure in literati circles in the early eighteenth century was Yanagisawa Kien (1704–58), the second son of a counsellor to the *daimyō*, Yanagisawa Yoshiyasu. He was granted a stipend of two thousand *koku* at the age of seven and when his elder brother died succeeded to the post. We have already mentioned the relationship between Yoshiyasu and Ogyū Sorai, and Kien was influenced by the interests that they shared – in his youth he studied Confucianism and Chinese verse and prose and also the Chinese conversation popular in Sorai's circle. His chief talent, though, was for painting and calligraphy and he is regarded, with Gion Nankai (1677–1751), as a founder of the school of Japanese literati painting. He was proficient in many polite accomplishments – such as the drum, *shamisen*, *haikai*, incense appreciation (*kōdō*) and the martial arts – and in the work *Kinsei kijin-den* (Lives of Distinguished Men of Recent Times, five volumes, published 1790) he is described as 'knowing enough of sixteen arts, including literature and the martial arts, to teach others'. His books include *Hitorine* (Sleeping Alone, 1724–25), written when he was twenty and concerned mainly with the pleasure quarters. He was a hospitable and generous man with a wide circle of acquaintances and a penchant for supporting artists, and his friendship with the painter Ikeno Taiga (1723–76) is well known.

In *Sleeping Alone* appear the values that were to be typical of the *bunjin*, and the most important of these is hedonism – life is short so it is best to spend it pleasantly. A man lives 'for less than a hundred years' and cannot waste time living with an ugly woman; in short: 'To live in ignorance of the pleasures of the world only eventually to regret it when your hair is white – would that not be very mortifying?' Enjoyment is to be found in a wide variety of arts and the arts themselves were chosen on the criterion of how much pleasure they afforded. The highest was the art of love: 'In these peaceful times as well as amusing oneself writing one should enjoy the tea ceremony, compose *waka*, enjoy oneself with courtesans and with *yōkyū* archery, *kemari* "football", dance, mime, *handayū-bushi* – in fact all possible kinds of entertainment.' Notable here is that Kien ranks the pleasures afforded by the courtesan alongside those of the tea ceremony and dance and that included in his list is a form of *jōruri*, *handayū-bushi*. To these pleasures he gives the name *fūga*, 'elegance', the same word as that used by Bashō but quite unlike that poetical notion. Nor, obviously, has Kien much in common with the Confucian ethics of Jinsai or the intense classicism of Sorai. In his efforts to employ all kinds of art for his own pleasure can be discerned the first steps in an attempt to transform his whole life into art.

This attempt would have faced little prospect of success within *samurai* society; only the separate world of Yoshiwara made it possible. For Kien, at least in his youth, 'The amusement of whoring is the essence of the pleasures that the world affords; there is no human pleasure truer than this.'

Another feature of the *bunjin* ethic was a keen interest in Chinese. Kien says in *Sleeping Alone*: 'In painting we should learn from the paintings of China. The reason for this is that even in Japan all painters worthy of being called great have studied China.' Kien's opinion was to be echoed, in this case about literature and art, by Nagai Kafū two hundred years later. The concern of the *bunjin* with the classical culture of China was one that they shared with the *samurai* class as a whole and especially with the Confucianists. On the other hand, they also had relatively strong links with the *chōnin* culture through a common interest in *haikai* – not, it should be said, the lyrical nature poetry of Bashō and his school but the urban school of Takarai Kikaku. These *haikai* were in turn part of a range of literature that covered *jōruri*, the popular novel from the time of Saikaku and the pornographic *makurazōshi* ('pillow books'). This combination set the tone of Kien's approach to life. In *Sleeping Alone* he and his associates joked that, 'In the *Analects* Confucius says that "if a friend comes from afar should one not rejoice?" And if it's a womanizing friend then the rejoicing is something else again.' Also: 'I was made by my mum and dad enjoying themselves so it's only natural that I shouldn't go far away from the joys of sex.' This hedonism was not just a feature of Kien's youth; nor indeed was it limited to Kien. On one occasion Kien's stipend was stopped because of his dissipation, and the same punishment was visited on the poet and painter Nankai.

We have already noted that Sorai was part scholar and statesman and part poet. His followers tended to adopt only one of these aspects to the exclusion of the other. Thus his historical and political ideas were carried on by one of his pupils, Dazai Shundai (1680–1747), whose thought is summarized in *Seigaku mondō* (Questions and Answers on the Study of the Sages, written in Japanese, published 1736). Sorai's poetical tradition was carried on by Hattori Nankaku (1683–1759), who had nothing to say on the Way of the Sages but lived as a *littérateur*, writing verse and prose.

Shundai came from a *samurai* family but Nankaku was the second son of a Kyōto merchant, and it was his youthful verse and paintings that attracted the patronage of Yanagisawa Yoshiyasu, probably from 1701. He kept his position in the Yanagisawa household until 1718, four years after Yoshiyasu's death, when he resigned. After this he made his living independently from his writing. In his collected works *Nankaku-sensei bunshū*, there are *shiyagoka* love poems and descriptions of scenes such as the inky waters of the Sumida River at night and the delicate tracery of fireflies imbued with an oblique but distinct erotic feeling, reminiscent of the prints of Suzuki Harunobu (1725–70). In his later years Nankaku painted the walls of his house with *sansui* landscapes and lay gazing at them, wandering through the landscape of his imagination. In a seven-syllable Chinese poem he says:

> In my lifelong easy going
> I lost myself.
> Achievement name wealth respect
> Are not for me.
>
> (*Bunshū*, Vol. 4, Part 1)

Elsewhere he says, 'Wandering up and down in my dreams I am untramelled even when sitting still.' Rather than expound the virtues of righteousness and benevolence (as a Confucianist) or play a role in society (as a retainer or adviser) he preferred to follow his own tastes and seek pleasure. Thus he says: 'A man is not meant not to enjoy himself' and 'Though I may count as nothing in the world, I will carry on to the end, grow old and die like this. Let me live doing what I like.'

Again in his apology for Ariwarano Narihira, *Zaichūjō-ron* (date unknown), Nankaku argues that people accuse Narihira of licentiousness because they do not understand the customs of the times in which he lived, an argument that shows his belief in the relativity of moral values. He also insists that personal behaviour and beauty of literary style are not connected, thus placing literature outside the scope of morality. Moralistic criticism of historical figures is the opposite of the way he believes in, the way of *fūga* ('elegance'): 'The carping schools of later years are pleased to take up [the matter of] his bad morals. They deprive this man of old of his individual standpoint and thus do not appreciate the elegance of his works.' This defence of course can be extended to more than 'men of old'.

The next great *bunjin* painter to appear after Nankai and Kien was Ikeno Taiga. Nothing that he wrote is extant and we know him only through his pictures which are in black *sumi* ink with sometimes a faint wash of colour and show the influence of Song and Yuan styles. They are mostly fanciful landscapes with figures that are almost caricatures; his line (particularly in finger painting) is uninhibited and lively and has a kind of expressionist power. Unlike many *bunjin*, who painted only small works, his paintings range in size from small fans to large screens. They are strikingly individualistic, in contrast to the essentially decorative work of the Kanō school, and indeed Taiga was probably the most individualistic painter of the eighteenth century.

It is by no means easy to define what a *bunjin* painting is. The simplest definition is of course 'a painting by a literatus'. One can also say that in many cases these paintings were influenced by the literati paintings of Song and Yuan China and tend not to use strong colours. Beyond that it is impossible to go; there are too few characteristics common to the work of all *bunjin* painters to talk confidently of a *bunjin* style; each painter must be examined separately. Taiga's individualistic brilliance in painting, like Nankaku's genius in Chinese verse and prose, places him apart from and above the *bunjin* who made up the circle around Yanagisawa Kien.

Kien's place at the centre of the *bunjin* group was taken in the second half of the century by Kimura Kenkadō (1736–1802), the son of a wealthy Ōsaka *sake* brewer and thus from a social background markedly different from Kien's. He was a polymath and his circle included Takebe Ayatari (1719–74) and Ueda Akinari (1734–1809), both novelists; Shiba Kōkan (1738–1818), a painter; and Ōta Shokusanjin (1749–1823), a *Kyōka* poet. By then the study of Chinese culture had become less central to the *bunjin* and the most noteworthy *bunjin* of the time was the peasant-born painter and *haikai* poet Yosa Buson (1716–83).

Buson in his use of the brush is not unlike Taiga, with whom he worked to produce the album *Jūbenzu jūgizu* (The Ten Conveniences and the Ten Pleasures) in 1771. But his landscape painting, whether it is of riverside willows swayed by a breeze or a snowy night, is far more realistic than Taiga's. Buson brings lyricism much closer to the realities of everyday life, and in this his style differs markedly from that of the other great *bunjin* painter of the eighteenth century. His verse is often reminiscent of his painting, as much of the verse sequence *Shunpūbateikyoku* (Songs of the Spring Breeze and the Embankment, composed 1777) illustrates. The sequence, which is unusual in having Chinese poems among the *haikai*, was occasioned by Buson meeting on the embankment of the Nagara River a woman just returned to her home village and, struck by her beauty, imagining himself in her place. Two *haikai* in particular have the same feeling as his painting:

> The spring breeze.
> The embankment is long
> And home far away.

> A tea house
> And beside it
> An old willow.

The Chinese verse has a quiet, understated eroticism:

> Climbing down from the embankment
> To pick a sweet-smelling flower
> The thorn blocks my way.
> Why is the thorn jealous,
> Tearing my hem
> Scratching my calf?

The thorn was a favourite flower of Buson's and he seems to have associated it with nostalgia and thoughts of home, as for instance in the *haikai*:

> The flowering thorn –
> How like the roads of home!

> Sadly I climb the slope
> And there it is
> The flowering thorn.

Nostalgia is an attachment to the past or rather the discovery of the past in the present, as in the *haikai*:

> Slow days build up
> The distant past.

> A kite
> In the place it was
> In yesterday's sky.

In *haikai* Buson tried to 'escape from the vulgar world using vulgar language', in what he called 'a way of escaping the vulgar' (*rizoku no hō*). This meant familiarity with Chinese poetry and the fostering of elegance (in both the Chinese and the Japanese senses) by 'leaving behind the world of town, castle, fame and profit to find recreation in wooded parks, to feast by mountain and lake, to drink, talk and laugh'. In his *haikai* he wished to 'return to antiquity, following the *sabi* [tranquillity] and *shiori* [empathy with nature] of Bashō's prosody'. His understanding of elegance was closer to Bashō's than to Kien's. The ideals of the young prodigal of *Sleeping Alone* and the poet of *Songs of the Spring Breeze* were not dissimilar however. Both sought to 'escape from the vulgar' and both turned to Chinese literature as a means and symbol of doing this. And both wanted to enjoy life outside the societies of *samurai* and *chōnin*, as did Ikeno Taiga, who was known for his almost complete disregard of personal fame. It is difficult to know the precise nature of Buson's thought, for although a painter of genius he wrote almost nothing on painting (and indeed wrote little on *haikai*). But there is no reason to believe that he did not share the hedonistic attitude of his fellow *bunjin*, and his works never treat religious subjects.

It is difficult to arrive at a definition of a *bunjin* as the people so called varied greatly in education, family background and personality. To define the social ambience of the *bunjin* is not difficult, however, as we know a good deal about the relationships between specific figures. These differ noticeably from the normal run of *chōnin* and *samurai* social life; each man was, above all, conscious of belonging to a specific group, the *bunjin*. And there are extant descriptions of various members of the group written by others as well as anecdotes passed on anonymously. (One work already quoted, Kien's *Lives of Distinguished Men*, is a collection of these anecdotes.) The group had a set of shared values which included a rejection of the 'world of town, castle, fame and profit' and a wish to make life itself beautiful, at least insofar as that life was the life of a *bunjin*. The existence of such a community was made possible by the patronage of Kien and Kenkadō and also by an increase in general demand for 'cultural products' such as pictures, *haikai* and calligraphy as standards of education and levels of purchasing power both rose.

As a group on the fringes of society living an aesthetic, hedonistic coterie life the *bunjin* are not unique in Japanese history. In the Heian period, especially in the Imperial court from the tenth to the twelfth centuries, the ladies of the court constituted such a group, and the *chajin* ('tea-people') of the sixteenth and seventeenth centuries were another. Both these groups, however, were completely cut off from the great mass of ordinary people. Their relationships, peripheral and separated though they were, were with the ruling powers of the age, in the capital city, itself cut off and far from the life of the provinces.

The isolated life of the court was undermined by the development of the feudal system but within the ruling classes of this system there developed an aesthetic sensibility as far removed from the masses as the aristocratic one had been. The rusticity of the tea house is not truly rustic; the thatched cottage by the seashore has an appeal for those who live in gilded palaces that it lacks for the fisherman who might actually inhabit it. The *bunjin*, on the other hand, although far from the masses in their taste for Chinese literature, calligraphy and painting, shared with them a liking for *haikai* and this provided a channel of communication, as did a common taste for the life of the pleasure quarters.

As a group, however, the *bunjin* shared many of the characteristics of their two predecessors. All three had some form of organized activity – court life for the ladies, tea ceremony for the *chajin* and drinking and poetry composition parties for the *bunjin* – and all three despised specialization (a characteristic of the artisan) favoured instead the mastery of a wide variety of complementary skills. The court ladies complemented the composition of *waka* with *monogatari*, the playing of musical instruments and the appreciation of the subtleties of incense. The *chajin's* various skills in the design of tea houses and vessels, hanging scrolls and flower arrangement all contributed to the tea ceremony. For the *bunjin* the central skills of literature, painting and calligraphy were complemented by a wide variety of other interests, notably *haikai*. In each group the interests were decided by the group not by the individual; individuals varied only in the degree to which they had mastered these skills (e.g., Kien with his mastery of sixteen skills). Thus these skills became rituals the mastery of which was a condition of membership in the group; the greater the mastery of them the further the individual was seen to be absorbed into the group. This kind of coterie, where cultural interests and ritual fuse, did not start with the *bunjin* nor did it end with them.

The other aspect of the *bunjin* group shared also by the other two was its values, which were firmly rooted in the tradition of the Japanese sensibility. What was valued in all three groups was the immediate, the temporal and the aesthetically pleasing. For Sei Shōnagon, author of *Makura no sōshi*, this was a view at a certain time of day in a certain season; for the *chajin* it was the ideal of performing each ceremony as if it were the only and most important one in his life (*ichigo ichie*); and for the young author of *Sleeping Alone* it was the conviction that one must live for today because tomorrow never comes. The form that the aesthetic hedonism took varied in each group: the court ladies absorbed themselves in love, especially of someone out of their reach; the *chajin* had *wabi*, an astringent form but aesthetic and hedonistic nonetheless; and the *bunjin* had 'the essence of human enjoyment', eroticism. There were no absolute values that transcended the world of the senses. There was perhaps an instant like that in which the aged Buson looked up to find the kite, the sky and the home of his youth reborn. This instant was everything that Buson valued and it could only be expressed in *haikai*.

TOMINAGA NAKAMOTO AND ANDŌ SHŌEKI

Tominaga Nakamoto (1715–46), with his direct criticism of Confucianism, Buddhism and Shintō, more than any other thinker of the Edo period challenged traditional thought. Living in eighteenth-century Japan, cut off from the rest of the world including the philosophy of the West, this young son of an Ōsaka merchant analysed the history of the three systems of belief and pointed the way to a completely new form of scholarship that he even developed to some extent. This new method was an experimental scientific appraisal of the doctrines and how the notions of each were conditioned by the internal logic of the ideas themselves, by changes in language and by cultural influence.

Nakamoto's father Kichizaemon (also known by the pen-name of Hōshun), a wealthy owner of a soy sauce business, was one of the five merchants whose contributions (in his case of land) helped to found the private Confucian school Kaitoku-dō ('The Pavilion of Virtues') where his own sons studied and where Nakamoto was introduced to the thought of Ogyū Sorai by Tanaka Tōkō (1668–1742), a close friend of the master. We do not know when Nakamoto wrote his first important work, *Setsuhei* (Discourse on Errors) – and it is not extant – but we learn in the later *Okina no fumi* (Writings of an Old Man) that it was a critique of Confucianism. It is said that its contents were sufficient to have Nakamoto expelled from Kaitoku-dō and so perhaps it was destroyed at that time. Whether this is in fact true or not it is certain that when his father died in 1739 and his elder brother became head of the house Nakamoto moved elsewhere in Ōsaka to live with his mother, two younger brothers and younger sister. Of this period of his life, too, little is known except that he was afflicted by chronic illness of which he complained in a 1735 poem, and this led to his death at the age of thirty-one. Before he left the family house he published *Writings of an Old Man* (1738); after his departure he wrote *Shutsujō kōgo* (Words after Enlightenment, 1745). The first, in Japanese, is an analysis of the three doctrines; the second, in Chinese, is an analysis of Buddhism alone. These form the body of his extant work although he is said also to have written some Chinese poems and a treatise on ancient Chinese and Japanese musical scales.

Biographical details do not serve to explain how and where Nakamoto acquired the profound knowledge of the Buddhist classics which in later years so impressed Motoori Norinaga ('when I looked at this I felt I had had my eyes opened', he wrote in an essay in *Tamakatsuma*). The great Buddhist scholar and priest Onkō was born in Ōsaka three years after Nakamoto and perhaps his important new studies influenced Nakamoto to some extent, although there is no concrete proof of this. Similarly there is no proof that he had direct contact with Shintō priests or scholars but one cannot imagine that Shintō doctrines, which were in any case largely borrowed from Buddhism and Confucianism, would present many problems to a man of Nakamoto's ability. Nor is there anything to indicate that he had significant contact with western thought. Generally the Japanese of his age were concerned only with the technical aspects of western learning such as medicine, agronomy, calendars, geography and land surveying. Andō Shōeki was interested in the social and political life of Holland but he was exceptional, and in any case his work was almost completely ignored by his contemporaries, including Nakamoto.

In his earlier period Nakamoto addressed the problem of rationally comprehending the differences between the basic doctrines within Buddhism, Confucianism and Shintō. He explained the various doctrines of each religion or philosophy as stages in the historical development of the system of thought. Seen from this point of view the efforts of Neo-Confucianists to construct a system which would include all known doctrines and those of the various Buddhist schools to assign absolute authority to one specific doctrine were futile. On Buddhism, for instance, Nakamoto wrote in *Words after Enlightenment*, 'Since the death of Buddha there has been no generally accepted doctrine, no book of authority to rely on; everything has been arbitrarily modified and thus transferred to posterity. It is only natural that there is no unity at all between all the doctrines expounded in all the different sutras. None of them can be trusted or followed.' Despite this there were Buddhists who tried to explain this doctrinal multiplicity by saying that the same statement made by Gautama Buddha was heard in different ways by different people, that Buddha changed his teaching five times in his life or that the same teaching was interpreted differently according to the 'disposition' of the individual. These explanations Nakamoto dismisses in *Writings of an Old Man* as 'serious misunderstandings and distortions of the truth'.

In his analysis of the history of ideas Nakamoto employed three basic concepts. First and most important was *kajō* ('to put something on another'), which was used to explain the way in which new theories were created in order to go beyond previous theories. This implies an internal logic for the history of ideas. Secondly he pointed to a function of language as a transmitter of ideas which was conditioned by the speaker, his time and linguistic possibilities. Thirdly there was the notion of *kuse* or 'national character', the social and cultural background to systems of thought.

The notion of *kajō* can be applied, for instance, to the succession of Confucian ideas about human nature. The first theory, that of Shizi, was that 'there is both good and bad in human nature' and this was followed by Gaozi's theory that 'there is neither good nor bad in human nature' which 'goes beyond' it. Gaozi's theory was further surpassed by Mencius's

theory that human nature is good and this in its turn by that of
Xunzi that human nature is bad. Even Confucius himself was
no exception. It was because the Way of the Five Nobles (i.e.,
government by power) was popular in his day that he evolved
the notion of the Way of the Former Kings (government by
ethical principle), which was in turn superseded by the later
theory of Mozi. Later the theories of these two men were
followed and surpassed by the theory of the Way of the
Emperor expounded by Yang Chu, and this in turn was superseded by the theories of Xu Xing, Zhuangzi, Liezi and so on.
'Not realizing this,' says Nakamoto in *Writings of an Old Man*,
'the Song Confucianists thought all [of these theories] to be
convergent. Recently Jinsai has argued that only Mencius continued the important line from Confucius and all other teachings
were wrong and Sorai has claimed that the Way of Confucius
went straight back to the Way of the Former Kings and that Zi Si
and Mencius were not in accord with the Way. They are all
wrong, misunderstanding the facts.'

No scholar before Nakamoto, except Sorai, and none for
many years after described the intellectual history of Confucianism from such an objective standpoint. Sorai had held consistently to an objective viewpoint coupled with a historical
method in his explications of classical texts, and he assigned
particular importance to the historical particularity of the
thought and social system of each age. Nakamoto's notion of
kajō may have been influenced by this, but whereas Sorai
assigned an absolute value to Confucius's Way of the Former
Kings and a relative value to all subsequent schools of thought,
thus becoming a 'super-Confucian' sitting in judgement on
other Confucianists, Nakamoto regarded no theory as having
absolute authority or any special claim to be the truth. Unrestricted in any way by Confucian theories, he was the first, and
until recently the only, truly objective Japanese thinker.

The notion of *kajō* was also applied to the history of Buddhist
thought in *Writings of an Old Man* and in more detail in *Words
after Enlightenment*. Thus the 'emptiness of things' theory gives
way to the 'limitless knowledge' theory and this to 'neither
thing nor knowledge' or 'conception of non-existence' which is
in turn superseded by 'neither conception nor non-conception'.
Or the succession is the 'emptiness' of things of the Hinayana

giving way to the 'emptiness' of the Mahaprajnaparamita. Nakamoto could not of course refer to the Sanskrit versions of the sutras but had to rely on the Chinese translations and therefore could not be certain of the chronology of their composition. He was nevertheless the only scholar of his time to explain the contradictions between the various sutra in terms of historical process. The 'old' Buddhist sects (those founded before the end of the twelfth century) had selected the 'best' sutra to be the basis of their faith but the 'best' varied, as of course did the criteria for the choice, from sect to sect. Of the Kamakura Buddhist sects one (Zen) claimed to have no faith at all in the written word and another (the True Pure Land or Jōdo Shinshū) chose the sutra which seemed most suitable for the salvation of its followers. These later approaches are much more subjective than the earlier ones, but all differ fundamentally from Nakamoto's method.

The notion of *kajō* could not be applied with such incisiveness to Shintō as it could to Confucianism and Buddhism, as *Writings of an Old Man* demonstrates. This is of course because Shintō has not had an independent and developing body of doctrine but has adopted and adapted ideas according to the circumstances of the times. Nakamoto, however, did demonstrate his impartiality by treating Shintō in the same way as the two alien faiths and according it no special position as the indigenous faith. In this he was in agreement with Muro Kyūsō who refused to concede that Shintō was in any way outside the system of Neo-Confucian philosophy – 'the Way is not something peculiar to Japan' – and responded to the invocation of 'the Way of Japan, the land of the gods' by members of the Yamazaki Ansai school with 'Ah, those two words "Our Country" again! Please could you talk about this without always having those two words on your mind.' The idea that the basic principles of faith could and did transcend considerations of nationality had been part of the thought of Dōgen in the thirteenth century and of Sorai and Kyūsō. Nakamoto took this further; he made the concept of universality into an intellectual method.

In the eleventh chapter of *Words after Enlightenment* there is a detailed account of Nakamoto's approach to the language of the sutra. One basic element of this is summed up thus: 'As regards language, three things should be generally considered: speaker, time and the different types of sense. It is my way of learning to interpret all language in relation to these three things.' In the first place, different speakers or authors use different words or expressions to indicate the same things, as different sutra designate the ultimate goal of Buddhism by many different words, such as Buddhahood, *dharmata*, *prajna*, etc. The word should be interpreted in relation to the speaker's overall intellectual position. In the second place, the pronunciation of the same word changes in the course of history, as indicated in the different transcriptions of the same Sanskrit word by translators such as Kumarajiva and Xuanzang; thus the word is related to the time in which it is used. In the third place, there are five different types of senses: a word may be used in a figurative sense in an exaggerated way (the *chō* or extended sense); it may be used in a narrow sense limited to the original (the *hen* or one-sided sense); it may be used in a wide sense (the *han* or general sense); it may be loaded with a new sense evoked by the original one (the *ki* or collided, the *ten* or transformed sense); or it may be used in a good sense although it was originally used in a bad sense (the *han* or contrary sense).

Here again the influence of Sorai is very probable. Nakamoto's explication of the three factors that condition our understanding of words and his studies of religion not only opened the way to the systematic study of the relationship between language, history and society but also provided an insight into the possibilities of studying the secondary meaning of words. With only a little exaggeration we can say that Nakamoto's work prefigured the whole field of semantics.

With the same slight degree of exaggeration it can be said that he also prefigured the field of comparative culture in his attempts to link the characteristics peculiar to a culture with the form of its dominant ideology. An example of this in *Writings of an Old Man* (Ch. 14) is: 'The tendency peculiar to Buddhism is magic, which we now call sorcery. Indian people like it.' Later (Ch. 15) he says, 'The tendency peculiar to Confucianism is rhetoric. Rhetoric is what we now call oratory. In preaching a Way, or in guiding the people, if you are not skilled in oratory, no one in China would believe or follow you.' His comments on Shintō (Ch. 16) are more caustic: 'The tendency peculiar to Shintō is secrecy, such as divine secrets or secret arts for private transmission. Secrecy tends to lead to cheating and stealing. Magic and rhetoric are either amusing to watch or stimulating to listen to and have points in their favour but this tendency is of the lowest sort.' Nakamoto had of course no direct knowledge of the society and culture of China let alone those of India and his arguments on peculiar characteristics lack almost all substantive backing, but the point of view expressed was epoch-making.

In the first chapter of *Writings of an Old Man* Nakamoto says, 'Buddhism is the Way of India, Confucianism is the Way of China and since they are of other countries they are not the Way of Japan. Shintō is the Way of Japan but since it is of other times it cannot be the Way of the present-day world.' What then was Nakamoto's Way? There was none. In *Words after Enlightenment* he says that good and evil are self-evidently 'laws of nature' and there is no need to refer to Buddhist or Confucian teachings to understand them. In *Writings of an Old Man* he says, 'to live in present-day houses, to follow present-day customs, to respect present-day rules' is enough.

This son of a wealthy merchant family who lived fully accepting the social system and ethical values of the age, embarked on an unprecedented intellectual adventure with his critique of contemporary learning and ideology. For this sickly youth, who lived only thirty-one years, this intellectual adventure was probably his sole *raison d'être*. As we have said, Nakamoto's influence among his contemporaries was negligible. His work *Discourse on Errors* was lost completely; *Writings of an Old Man* survived but was long ignored in scholarly circles. Only *Words after Enlightenment* brought some reaction from the intelligentsia. Its critique of Buddhism brought attempts at rebuttal from Buddhist priests and provided powerful ammunition to the scholars of National Learning who concentrated their efforts on criticizing the two alien creeds. Indeed, Hirata Atsutane (1776–1843) confessed that he learned much from this book. But during the whole of the Tokugawa period it was Motoori Norinaga who showed the deepest appreciation of the work, perceiving that no other non-Buddhist had analysed the doctrine in such detail and with such coherent and hard-to-refute arguments. When, after a long period of neglect, Nakamoto was rediscovered in the Meiji period, it was by the man who was to be known as the founder of modern Chinese studies in Japan, Naitō Konan (1866–1934).

Andō Shōeki was a doctor in the small north Honshū town of Hachinohe in the early part of the eighteenth century. Little is known about his life. His date of birth is uncertain – perhaps 1703, perhaps 1707 – and his date of death unknown. He probably completed his major work *Shizen shin 'eidō*, (The Way of Nature and True Vocation), in a hundred volumes, in 1755. He had few pupils (perhaps twenty) and they were doctors, *samurai* or *chōnin* and not, despite the nature of his theories, peasants, although in the small rural town of Hachinohe (and in Akita on the north-west coast where he is said to have lived for a short time) he must have been in close contact with peasant life. One of his pupils had previously been in the service of the magistrate of Nagasaki and perhaps provided Shōeki with some knowledge of western thought. The manuscript of *The Way of Nature and True Vocation* was in ninety-three books. One book, *Seishiron* (On Life and Death) was lost completely, but the rest and a general introduction were rediscovered in 1899 by Kanō Kōkichi. Unfortunately they had not been copied completely before the Kantō earthquake of 1923 in which all but twelve books were destroyed. These and the three copied books are all that remain of this work today. Included in these however is the table of contents and from this and the notes made by Kanō Kōkichi it is possible to have some idea of the overall structure. There is also extant a summary version of the work in three volumes and a copy of another major work, *Tōdō shinden* (A True Account of the Complete Way, completed 1752?).

The originality of Andō Shōeki's thought lies in its fundamental critique of Tokugawa structure. Tominaga Nakamoto's thought, although critical of contemporary ideology, did not include any criticism of the social system whereas Shōeki's philosophy involved both the rejection of Confucianism, Buddhism and Japanese mythology and direct opposition to the Tokugawa social system. In Neo-Confucian theory social order was continuous with natural order (both were shaped by the Principle); in contrast, the Japanese thinkers Sorai, Kamono Mabuchi and Shōeki regarded the social system as completely man-made and distinct from the natural world and maintained that there was no principle common to the two. Sorai did not turn his attention to the natural world at all but considered only society and its history. Both Shōeki and the earlier National Learning scholar Mabuchi made the opposite choice and rejected artificial social systems in favour of an ideal 'life of nature'. Mabuchi projected his version of this ideal society into the age of the Japanese classics (*inishie* or 'the ancient of days' as he called it), and Shōeki projected his utopian 'world of nature' into the future. This meant that the attitudes of the two towards contemporary society were markedly different. Mabuchi, although yearning for the past, accepted the present; Shōeki rejected the present and hoped for the realization of his ideals in the future.

Both of Shōeki's major works are in a form of Chinese so obviously designed to be read in Japanese that it is in effect Japanese. Shōeki himself regarded this style as a necessary evil forced on him by the need to express philosophical ideas clearly. In the introduction to *The Way of Nature and True Vocation* he says: 'When one has grasped the idea through the writing, the writing itself is of no further use.... A person who likes writing is one who studies the Way incorrectly and will lead others into great confusion ... so the writing in *The Way of Nature and True Vocation* is undecorated.'

This type of comment would only be possible for a thinker at some distance from the literary circles of Kyōto and Edo, for composition in Chinese was the most important accomplishment of any Tokugawa intellectual. Probably Shōeki did not write in Japanese simply because it was not the custom for doctors to do so. Mabuchi, who wrote in Japanese, did so for the positive reason that it was part of his rejection of the Chinese spirit and demonstrated his respect for the classical Japanese style. Saikaku and other novelists wrote in Japanese for their popular audience. None of these reasons applied in the case of Shōeki.

The table of contents of *The Way of Nature and True Vocation* shows it to have consisted of the following sections: a general argument explaining the basic principles of the philosophy of nature; a section (Vols. 1 to 23) criticizing traditional learning, especially Confucianism and Buddhism; a critique of contemporary society (Vol. 24); a description of the ideal society (Vol. 25); an explanation of the workings of the human body in terms of the philosophy of nature (Vols. 26 to 50); an account of the workings of the ether in various parts of the world (Vols. 51 to 57); a critique of traditional medicine and a medical and pharmacological treatise based on the philosophy of nature (Vols. 58 to 73); and a description of specific diseases classified according to Shōeki's philosophy (Vols. 74 to 100).

It is clear that the author's central concern is medicine and in particular the attempt to construct a comprehensive system that will account for the whole range of phenomena. The comprehensive nature of this system marks Shōeki as an exception among Japanese thinkers who had, as we have said, increasingly tended to separate off parts of the comprehensive Zhu Xi system – natural studies in the case of Ekiken, political history in the case of Sorai and ethics in the case of Jinsai. Only one thinker in the latter part of the eighteenth century, Miura Baien, produced a system comparable in comprehensiveness to Shōeki's. Shōeki's *A True Account of the Complete Way* consists of a critique of Buddhist and Confucian theories, an original explanation of the phenomenon of man and a kind of comparative cultural study including a certain amount of geography. It is in effect a recapitulation of the non-medical parts of *The Way of Nature and True Vocation*.

Shōeki's method was to explain the structure of the world with reference to a schema of deductive reasoning, although many of his propositions are based neither on observed reality nor on literary sources. This for example is part of his argument for the normalization of consanguineous marriage, a practice not allowed by Chinese custom: 'The first man and woman in the world married and their children married each other. Thus for brother and sister to marry is not a thing to be ashamed of but the Way of mankind.' From the deduction that the 'first man and woman in the world' must have married for the human race to have continued he moves directly to the conclusion that marriage between brother and sister is not harmful to mankind without any consideration of the historical variations in the marriage system. The approach of Kamono Mabuchi in his attacks on the ban on consanguineous marriage shows a greater respect for written sources and is more positivistic. He starts from the same point: 'If we speak of origins, people must have come from the union of brother and sister.' But he continues:

'When society was established, however, there was a ban on marriage between children of the same mother' [which did not however prohibit marriage between children of the same father but different mothers]. Mabuchi's conclusion is that 'depending on circumstances and within limits both "good" and "bad" are permissible, providing they cause no trouble.' In other words a ban on consanguineous marriage should not be applied with too much rigour. Shōeki's conclusion is clear but lacks evidence to support it; Mabuchi's argument is positivistic in taking account of the actual taboos of antiquity but comes to no clear conclusion, amounting to an affirmation of prevailing circumstances.

The basis of Shōeki's cosmology was the movements of 'Ether' (*ki*). The centre and origin of the Ether is 'earth' or 'basic substance' which is neither of heaven nor of this world, but is eternal and central to the universe. (This corresponds to the Supreme Ultimate of Neo-Confucianism.) Ether can exist in combinations of four modes, Advance and Retreat (corresponding to *yin* and *yang* in Neo-Confucianism) and Great and Small. The various combinations of these modes (or movements) produce four elements: wood, fire, metal and water (lacking only the element of earth to correspond to the five elements of Neo-Confucianism). Each of these elements has an Advance and a Retreat mode and these are the 'eight Ethers' which make up the universe.

Much of this cosmology derives from Neo-Confucianism but there is one important difference; there is nothing in Shōeki's system which corresponds to the shaping Principle of Neo-Confucianism. His theory is monist; the nature of any part of the universe is an expression simply of the action of the Ether and this action is reciprocal. Examples that Shōeki gives of this reciprocity include start and finish, hard and soft, movement and stasis, and man and woman. This development of the notion of Ether to posit a universe of mutually complementary elements marks Shōeki's major difference from Neo-Confucianism. To stress the reciprocity and the equality of the sexes, for example, he would write the word for *person* as a combination of the characters for *man* and *woman*.

These mutually complementary modes of the Ether are natural and therefore fundamentally different from social distinctions such as rich and poor, high and low. Since people are all made in the same way from the same Ether they are, in a sense 'the same person'. Thus he writes in the introduction to *The Way of Nature and True Vocation*: 'It can be clearly seen that the myriads of humanity are in fact only one person ... Nature furnishes absolutely clear proof that the distinctions between high and low and noble and common do not exist in reality.' In opposition to these artificial distinctions is the Way of spontaneously following nature, and this can be understood in the wide sense of all the movements of the Ether that produce the universe and in the narrow sense of a life for man that is self-sufficient and in harmony with nature. Shōeki says:

> The wonderful workings of eternal nature, the universe and the basic living material are all of the one Way of direct production and there is no other Way.... When the basic living substance is in forward mobile mode people engage in direct production which produces food and clothing. When the basic living substance is in laterally mobile mode the four types of beasts, great and small, come about and feed on each other. This is, in other words, reciprocal direct production. When the basic living substance is in retro-mobile mode vegetable life is produced and to eat the retro-ether of the plant life is also direct production. Therefore the universe, people and things are all included in the Way of material life. There is no other Way but this. Therefore the Way is a matter of direct production and material life.

It is probable that this country doctor arrived at his notion of 'reciprocity' from an intuitive appreciation of the mutual complementarity and natural order of the everyday life around him, the bodies he examined and the peasant life he observed around his small country town. The only intellectual framework available to him in his efforts to develop a system of thought from these intutitive perceptions was that of Neo-Confucianism, and this is what he used to develop his own distinctive theories. The conclusions of his reasoning became the tenets of his faith. They were the existence of *une harmonie préétablie* ('reciprocity') and self-sufficiency in a sense normatively derived from agriculture ('direct production') and opposed to social distinctions, especially those based on position in a hierarchy.

A society in which everybody produces for himself is the utopia he calls the 'world of nature' whereas the society governed by artificial distinctions – in fact the society of his time

– is what he calls the 'world of law'. He satirizes this latter world in the twenty-fourth volume of *The Way of Nature and True Vocation*. In this the world of animals discusses the 'world of law' of mankind. They equate the Emperor with the eagle of the world of birds and with the monkey of the world of beasts; generals are respectively crested eagles and lions, the court nobles cranes and elephants, the feudal lords hawks and tigers, their senior counsellors peregrines and wolves, the minor warriors kites and leopards. In the world of birds the mandarin ducks fall passionately in love with each other so that they cannot live apart and if one dies of passion the other 'covers the corpse with its wings and joins it in death'. Similarly, 'The people of the world of law, when they fall in love and some obstruction comes between them so that they cannot marry commit suicide together.' In the world of beasts the dog 'always barks at suspicious apparitions and thieves thus being a help to its master. It does not work for itself but eats what its master leaves.' In this it is like the great scholars of the human world since the time of Prince Shōtoku, such as Hayashi Razan and Ogyū Sorai. Thus, 'I may be a dog but here in the world of beasts I am the founder of Buddhism and Confucianism and you must worship me.' This volume is not only an original attack on the social system but also one of the few satirical fables in Japanese literature. The animal fable form may have owed something to Aesop's fables which were translated in the sixteenth century and widely read thereafter.

In the utopian world of nature which is described in the twenty-fifth volume of *The Way of Nature and True Vocation* everybody is self-sufficient, feeding and clothing themselves, so neither taxes nor money is necessary. Nor are 'chamberlains, factotums, functionaries and warriors' allowed. Seaside villages are able to extract salt from the sea and trade it for crops from inland villages. Artisans are necessary and permitted but 'gold and silver' are not used for the payment of labour. Scholars and priests who cannot 'produce directly' for themselves have to go to a village and learn how to do so; there is no system to support them. When everybody ploughs his own fields and supports himself there are no distinctions between high and low. This ideal society is in other words agrarian and classless. Consanguineous marriage is permitted but not polygamy. Adultery is punished, subject to the agreement of the community, by death. (No reason is given for this strict insistence on fidelity to a monogamous marriage.)

Shōeki's utopia was less a possible alternative to the Tokugawa system than a conceptual tool which he could use in his attacks on the society of his day. Whether he himself regarded it as an unattainable ideal however is doubtful. In the part of *A True Account of the Complete Way* which deals with foreign countries, Shōeki claims that in Holland social distinctions have been mostly abolished and monogamy is the rule, with the result that there is no civil disturbance or insurrection. What scholars of National Learning found in the ideal realm of an imaginary past, Shōeki imagined in an infinitely distant foreign land.

SHINGAKU: STUDIES OF THE HEART

The scholars of *chōnin* background we have mentioned, from Itō Jinsai to Tominaga Nakamoto, did not necessarily direct their teachings to the class they came from. There was, however, one doctrine of the early eighteenth century expounded by a *chōnin* for *chōnin*; it was *Shingaku* ('Studies of the Heart'), a popular version of Confucian ethics given a religious form by its founder, Ishida Baigan (1685–1744).

Baigan, the second son of a middle-class peasant in a village near Kyōto, became apprenticed to a merchant at an early age and after a short period helping his family with their agricultural work spent twenty years of his life (from 1707 to 1727) as an assistant in a draper's shop. During these years he studied by himself and in 1722 met and became the pupil of a scholar-recluse named Oguri Ryōun (?–1729). It was shortly after this meeting that Baigan experienced the revelation that was to be the beginning of *Shingaku*. (In fact the revelation seems to have occurred in two stages, the first in 1724 and the second in 1726). These revelatory experiences, which Baigan calls *satori*, seem to have been sudden and overwhelming, of the type that is termed *tongo* in Zen: 'Suddenly [the doubts of twenty years] were dispelled, a feeling of indescribable joy.' Leaving his job he devoted himself to *Shingaku* and held his first public meeting in Kyōto in 1728. Most of those who attended were Kyōto *chōnin*, and Baigan himself said, 'My doctrine is that I teach merchants that there is a Way for merchants', an aim not shared by Jinsai, Nakamoto or even Shōeki. In 1739, Baigan published a summary of his beliefs, a simple question-and-answer account written in Japanese, *Tohi mondō*, (Dialogue on Town and Country). Another work is *Seikaron* (On Managing the Family, 1744). A posthumous collection of his sayings, *Ishida-sensei goroku* (A Record of the Sayings of Master Ishida) was published by his followers. The main points of his thought are all to be found in *Dialogue on Town and Country*.

Baigan and his successors used several new methods in their propagation of *Shingaku*. First among these was the public meeting. This was not novel in itself as it was not unusual for Confucian scholars to give public lectures. But in the case of the *Shingaku* meetings the relationship between speaker and audience was very different. Instead of the abstruse and highbrow explications of the traditional Confucianists, the *Shingaku* speakers used examples drawn from the experience of the *chōnin* to explain the meaning of the Confucian classics. Baigan spoke of assistants and apprentices and of the foolishness and reform of the prodigal son of a rich merchant family, things which his audience could easily understand and relate to. This breaking down of the barrier between the teacher and the taught was further encouraged by the question-and-answer form of writing, not much used by conventional Confucianists, in which there is seen to be a two-way relationship between the sides. Next was the meditation that Baigan urged his followers to practise and the behaviour consequent on this. As 'the heart of things can not be transmitted by words', meditation was necessary to achieve one's own revelation but meditation was not an end in itself nor was spiritual awakening. In answer to the question, 'When you come to know the heart of things do you automatically become a sage?' he answers, 'No. If you do not perform actual deeds you are no sage.' The notion that learning should be applied directly was one supported by most Tokugawa Confucianists but Baigan was unusual in his insistence that this learning should not be external but should become part of the very essence of the believer and suffuse his whole being. In

Shingaku spiritual awakening and moral behaviour were inseparable.

Baigan advocated several virtues to his *chōnin* followers. First, there was thrift. This was the supreme virtue for the merchant and peasant classes, not only in Baigan's view but also in that of the authorities. The early years of the eighteenth century had seen the sumptuary edicts of the Kyōhō Reform promulgated by the government of the *Shōgun* Yoshimune – 'the august ban preventing excess in the administration of the state', as Baigan described it – and this provided the *Shingaku* leader with a powerful endorsement for the importance he gave to this virtue. Government authority gave it legitimacy. There were other more particular reasons why it was necessary: 'Money is the treasure of society as a whole' and must therefore be conserved. Families should be prepared for unforeseen expenses. And, in a different vein, thrift shows a knowledge of true propriety (defined as 'to distinguish between high and low') and 'to live a modest and sober life' is an expression of 'knowing one's place' and thus in itself a moral value. As a moral value it is interiorized and not subject to enquiry as to its specific purpose; the virtue of thrift is to be followed for its own sake. Thus, in *A Record of the Sayings of Master Ishida* we have: 'Ultimately thrift is not for the state, for the Way or for oneself. If one questions what its purpose is, finally it has none. Think of thrift as forgetting every other thing and closely following the Law.' Here the original idea of thrift as something social and economic has become involved with the philosophy of 'the heart of things' (*kokoro*). By meditation and practice the believer can achieve a perception of 'the heart of things' and one of the essential qualities of this is thrift. Thrift is an absolute revealed to one who achieves enlightenment.

Another virtue necessary for the merchant is diligence. The realization that this is a duty follows from the basic perception of 'knowing one's place' and 'accepting one's lot': in *Dialogue on Town and Country* Baigan says that 'the task of ruling the four classes is the lord's. It is the task of the four classes to assist the lord. Basically *samurai* are retainers in high positions; peasants are retainers of the fields; merchants and artisans are retainers of the city.' The four classes, in that they are all the lord's 'retainers', are equal and their tasks are of equal importance, and so 'warrior, peasant, artisan and merchant should each be content with his own task'. The usual view of the Confucianists of the time was that the merchant was merely an unproductive profiteer and thus the lowest in society. Baigan's beliefs represent a clear dissent from this orthodoxy. He regards the role of the merchant to be 'to transmit wealth' in the interests of society in general. The profit that the merchant receives by doing this is similar in nature to the *samurai*'s stipend, unless the profit is unfairly high. Merchants therefore must be honest. What then is an honest profit? The answer to this is not very clear, being something like 'whatever profit can be legitimately obtained by buying and selling at current market prices'. Market forces are not controlled by the merchants but are 'the doing of heaven'. Only those things the prices of which are fixed by the government are to be treated differently.

Although Baigan first addressed his teachings to the merchants he did not think of their case as being unique or isolated. Rather he saw it as one in which they fulfilled a role in society analogous to the roles of the other four classes. The general principle of 'being content with one's own task' was central to Baigan's belief and could be applied equally well to any class of society. This allowed the doctrine to attain great popularity throughout the four classes after Baigan's death.

Baigan also advocated the traditional Confucian virtues of loyalty and filial piety. 'Loyalty', he said, is the acknowledgement of the relative position of the secular authorities and oneself, and filial piety is a recognition of the role of the child *vis-à-vis* the parent. The subject must obey his lord and the child his parents, especially his father : 'The way of the subject is not to give the slightest thought to the self but to devote oneself to, and put oneself in the place of, the lord.' 'For wife and child the master of the house is like a lord; thus you [the questioner] are like a retainer.' Baigan here follows the general stream of Tokugawa thought, uncritical of government policy and the patriarchal, hierarchical structure of society. Indeed, the virtues he stresses would tend to strengthen and support the social structure and help the implementation of government policy.

The argument of *Dialogue on Town and Country* has many inconsistencies. Baigan sometimes groups Buddhism, Confucianism and Shintō together as parts of the Way of Heaven

(*tendō*), saying that the three are equal: 'Among the sages of
Shintō, Buddhism and Confucianism there are no teachers and
no pupils.' Elsewhere he maintains that Buddhism and Confucianism are no more than ways of teaching Shintō and not its
equal: 'To supplement the Only One [i.e. Shintō] you should
take and use the doctrines of Confucianism and Buddhism.' On
some questions of morality also there is inconsistency. What, for
example, is a son to do if his father is unrighteous? Baigan
recommends that he should 'struggle to return him to the right'.
But in a specific case, that of a son who obeys his obviously
corrupt and immoral father's order to kill himself, he endorses
and praises the son's action. In effect the question remains
unanswered. Baigan's chief aim, however, is to explain how to
deal with the practical problems of everyday life. It is not his
intention to give internal consistency to his version of the
essential unity of doctrines or to prove his teachings' universal
appropriateness by testing them with extreme cases such as
murder. His thought is held together by experience of life, not
by abstract logic. The centre of this life-experience is the
intuition which links the human heart with the universe, the
satori: 'You can advance all kinds of argument but how can this
be expressed adequately in words?'

Baigan's highest objective was 'to know the heart' and for this
it was necessary to cast aside the narrow 'heart of the self'
(*shishin*) and find the original 'heart of things' (*kokoro*). This
essence, which can be given the name Principle, feeling or
virtue, 'is the single thing which harmonizes the self and the
universe'. His account of *kokoro*, which in some ways resembles
the 'mind' of the Wang Yangming school, is not very systematic,
but it is possible to discern two points of salient importance.
First is the importance of selflessness, *mushi*, the freeing of the
heart from personal desires. In terms of behaviour this implies a
range from relatively passive stoicism to active self-sacrifice.
Stoicism is based on an absolute submission to the ethics of
thrift; self-sacrifice finds its basis in the virtues of absolute
loyalty and filial piety.

The other important point of Baigan's thought is that the
universal *kokoro* is related to the *kokoro* of the various beings in
the universe but that the *kokoro* of each individual is of a
different form. Thus the differences in behaviour of animals,

insects and birds derive not from differences between their 'personal' *kokoro*, but from differences in the 'form' in which the universal *kokoro* has been granted to them. This principle of nature (*shizen no ri*) involves a natural order that is continuous with the social order. Thus individuals in society may be different in the 'form' of their life (in terms of their class and role in society) while sharing in the overall 'principle' of society. 'If we look at things in this light, the careers of all people in today's world are of a fixed form.' Thus to become aware of the essence of things is also to realize that this essence expresses itself in fixed forms and that one of these forms is social position. *Satori* allows one to 'know one's place' and 'be satisfied with one's lot'. The hierarchy will be respected and the merchant's energy devoted to a diligent, honest and successful pursuit of his business interests.

The values which *satori* reveals in *Shingaku* are all of this world. Where the *chōnin* such as Saikaku had developed secularism into a kind of hedonism, Baigan linked it with self-denial to create a 'Way of the *chōnin*'. Moreover, the working out of these values in behaviour took place within the framework of the family and the domain, structured as they were around hierarchical relationships. Baigan made no attempt to examine the possibility of altering the structure of the group to which he belonged (as Shōeki did) nor did he consider the possibility of leaving the group (as the *bunjin* did). For him the individual's involvement in the group was a given, and his thought developed from there. In his assumption Baigan was like the majority of the people who lived under the Tokugawa system. What distinguished him was his positive advocacy of 'knowing one's place' as a way of maintaining order within the group as well as loyalty and filial piety to ensure its smooth running. In opposition to these positive values he identified the 'selfish heart' as a quality which threatened the group's order and function. All these values he interiorized by his use of the concept of *kokoro*. The essence of secularism he saw expressed as thrift, its non-essence as hedonism; the essence of group consciousness was expressed as 'knowing one's place' and loyalty and filial piety, its non-essence egoism.

Shingaku found its motivation undoubtedly in the reaction expressed in Baigan's question, 'Why are merchants alone despised and disliked?' This motivation is clearly connected with Baigan's personal experience as a draper's assistant and the overall phenomenon of a merchant class which from the end of the seventeenth century was rising in influence, despite the Kyōhō Reform. His attempt to legitimize the position of the *chōnin* appealed to a universal element that transcended their particularity. Internally this element was what he termed *kokoro* (and this can be thought of as basic human nature) and externally the existent social order was thought of as continuous with natural order. He did not erect a *chōnin* ideology in opposition to that of the ruling classes but used the dominant ideology itself. By support of the system and its ideas he found a place for the *chōnin* within them. Tactically this was no doubt clear-sighted and realistic.

For the ruling *samurai* this movement was extremely convenient. Thrift was a virtue they constantly extolled and occasionally (as in the case of Yoshimune's sumptuary laws) tried to impose. For the *chōnin* to know their place and be content with their lot could only help the administrators in their task and maintain the *samurai* in their position of dominance, as would the virtues of loyalty and filial piety. This was all the more important as, with the passage of time, *samurai* came to depend more and more on wealthy merchants. Official scholars, especially if they were employed by a domain or the Bakufu, were limited in their contact with classes other than the *samurai* and could not in any case communicate with *chōnin* in the persuasive style of Baigan and his successors. These factors all helped in the spread of *Shingaku* through all classes of society that took place in the years after the founder's death.

No more than fifty people, mainly Kyōto *chōnin*, ever came to Baigan's meetings, even in his later years, and converts were limited to the area around Kyōto and Ōsaka. In the later eighteenth century, however, five hundred people came to meetings held by Tejima Toan (1718–86), *Shingaku*'s influence had spread to seven provinces and among its converts it counted many peasants. By the time of Nakazawa Dōni (1725–1803) and Shibata Kyūō (1783–1839) *Shingaku* was at its height and its converts in almost thirty provinces included many *samurai*, even retainers of the *Shōgun* and *daimyō* in the Edo region where it was most successful. Eventually the lords and chief retainers of sixty-five domains were converted to *Shingaku* and the Bakufu had *Shingaku* teachers addressed vagrants gathered in for compulsory labour; the religion had literally permeated society from the rulers to the most wretched.

This success was not consequent on any great change in doctrine. The thought of both Toan and Dōni kept faithfully to that of Baigan, adding nothing fundamentally new. *Shingaku* went beyond its function as a vehicle for the *chōnin's* assertion of identity and appealed to all the social classes of Tokugawa Japan. Baigan, an outstanding *chōnin* teacher, was at the same time a typical Japanese, concentrating on the problem of how best to live within the order of a given group in the sublunary world and using the concept of unity between universe and self to support his solution. His concept of the universe was not far from Kamono Mabuchi's 'spontaneous being' and Bashō's 'nature', and the popularity of both *Shingaku* and Bashō from the Meiji period should be viewed against a background of certain aspects of the indigenous Japanese world-view – those of secularism and group consciousness – which have manifested themselves frequently in Japanese history, only masked or modified by the influence of foreign philosophical systems. For this world-view abstract ideologies are no more than convenient mechanisms to be employed when and however necessary. In *Dialogue on Town and Country* Baigan says that the important things 'cannot be expressed adequately in words'. And for a truly 'Japanese' Japanese, his statement that 'in Shintō, Buddhism and Confucianism there is only one essential *satori'* is not primarily an assertion of the essential unity of the three religions; this is a secondary matter compared to the primary fact of *satori*.

CHŪSHINGURA AND THE POPULAR NOVEL

For the fifty or so years after the death of Chikamatsu Monzaemon the puppet theatre continued to flourish, especially in Ōsaka where the two most successful theatres, Takemotoza and Toyotakeza, vied for supremacy. Plays which were successful on the puppet stage were adapted for *Kabuki* and during this phase of the relationship between *ningyō jōruri* and *Kabuki* it was the puppet theatre that was dominant. The close relationship continued throughout the Tokugawa period but in the later stages *Kabuki* gained greater popularity and by the later part of the eighteenth century had achieved supremacy, a development symbolized by the conversion of the Toyotakeza into a *Kabuki* theatre in 1765.

In its heyday *ningyō jōruri* had three distinctive features. Firstly, its centre was not the political and administrative centre of Edo but the commercial city of Ōsaka, and its audiences were not *samurai* or peasants but middle- and upper-class *chōnin*. *Samurai* kept to their interest in *Nō*, an interest that the *chōnin* for the most part did not share. Indeed throughout the Tokugawa period there was no performing art which was supported by all classes, as *sarugaku* and *dengaku* had been in the Muromachi period. Secondly, plays were increasingly often of joint authorship. Such plays obviously did not reflect the thought and feelings of an individual but became, in effect, the expression of the ideas and values of the entire *chōnin* class. Joint authorship also meant that the play had to follow conventions accepted by the authors, and the competition between groups of authors and theatre troupes for popular success encouraged the development of sophisticated and strictly regulated techniques of puppet manipulation and *jōruri* chanting. (This situation is analogous to that of *Nō* during the fifteenth century when Zeami was active. By the eighteenth century *Nō* had become established as the entertainment of the ruling class and had become institutionalized; no new works were produced but rather the exquisite aesthetic details were polished and perfected for a limited audience.) Little is known of the lives of the *jōruri* writers of this period. This anonymity suggests that they were *chōnin*. Puppet plays were, like the practical and mundane teachings of *Shingaku*, created by *chōnin* for *chōnin*.

Thirdly, the puppet plays of the time were formally somewhat different from the works of Chikamatsu. They were longer – typically of five acts – and had complicated plots with a great number of characters. At the same time there developed the tendency to write scenes which would have a striking visual effect when staged but would often be more or less irrelevant to the development of the plot. Long and complicated plots meant drawing on history and mixing it with some elements of domestic drama, as Chikamatsu had in *The Battles of Coxinga* – it would have been rather difficult to write a love-suicide piece as complex and spectacular as the public demanded. The great majority of the successful plays were therefore historical pieces. Among these is *Sugawara denju tenarai kagami* (The Secret of Sugawara's Calligraphy) jointly written by Takeda Izumo (1691–1756), Miyoshi Shōraku (1696–?) and Namiki Senryū (also known as Namiki Sōsuke, 1695–1751) and first performed at the Takemotoza in 1746; it is based on the legends surround-ing the life and death of the great Heian calligrapher and poet Sugawara Michizane. Another play of this type is *Yoshitsune senbonzakura* (Yoshitsune: The Thousand Cherry Trees) by the same team and first performed at the Takemotoza in 1747; it is a completely fictional story set in the twelfth century during the time of the Heike-Genji wars, with Yoshitsune as its central character. In these plays we find such conventional scenes as one in which a faithful retainer kills his own son in order to substitute the child for his lord's, who has been condemned to death by their enemies (the temple school scene in Act 4 of *The Secret of Sugawara's Calligraphy*); in *Yoshitsune: The Thousand Cherry Trees* we have a scene featuring a defeated general, Tairano Koremori, disguised as a *sushi*-shop apprentice in order to evade his enemies, the visual impact of a travel scene set against the massed cherry blossoms of Yoshino, and a spectacle in which a fox-spirit character turns into a real fox after listening to a hand-drum made of its mother's skin.

These characteristics became more pronounced in the later years of the century when the puppet theatre was trying to compete with the rising popularity of *Kabuki* with an ever greater stress on individual, separate and often visually striking scenes. In *Imoseyama onna teikin* (An Example of Noble Woman-hood) by Chikamatsu Hanji (1725–83), a leading writer of the time, and Miyoshi Shōraku, first performed at the Takemotoza in 1771, the struggle between Fujiwarano Kamatari and Sogano Iruka, which actually took place in the seventh century, is depicted with completely anachronistic Tokugawa-period cos-tumes and manners and with action revolving around the doomed love of a young couple, although this is almost com-pletely irrelevant to the dispute. The couple, whose parents are enemies, live in mansions on opposite banks of a river. The stage set is such that the river, in centre stage, provides a striking visual symbol of the separation of two lovers by the enmity of their parents. This part of the play stands apart from the rest of the play as a self-contained pictorial spectacle.

In both *Kabuki* and *ningyō jōruri* there are a large number of such scenes that stand apart from the overall plot of the play. Indeed it is probably true to say that the overall plot matters less than the scenes that it makes possible. Individual scenes are not integral parts of a larger framework; rather the plot is a string of independent scenes only faintly linked thematically or conceptually. Thus if a scene is performed in isolation its effectiveness is decreased little if at all, and for this reason it is customary today in both *Bunraku* (the modern name for *ningyō jōruri*) and *Kabuki* to choose the most popular and effective scenes from plays and perform them by themselves. This is scarcely conceivable in the case of classical Greek theatre or later European drama, Shakespeare for instance. (There are, of course, some exceptions. In Germany, it is not unknown to perform only part of a long play such as Schiller's *Wallenstein*. However, these abbreviated performances, rare though they are, take place more often than performances of a *Kabuki* or *Bunraku* piece in its entirety.)

The popular drama of the Tokugawa period was distinctive in prizing the part above the whole. This reflects a characteristic of Japanese culture, a characteristic already clearly evident in the way that traditional tales from China were rewritten by the Japanese in the Heian period, as a comparison between the Chinese collection *Fayuan zhulin* and the Japanese equivalent, *Nihon ryōiki*, will show. Later, the Heian tales and historical narratives such as the *Eiga monogatari* (about Fujiwarano Michinaga) also put more stress on individual details than the structure of the story as a whole; the same tendency can be seen in the occasional writings (*zuihitsu*) of the Kamakura and Muromachi periods. In other artistic fields we can point to the composition of *Yamato-e* paintings and the design of the mansions of the *daimyō* built in the early part of the Tokugawa period as having the same characteristics; and in music the *shamisen* accompaniments to *jōruri* depend for their effect not on the overall form of the piece but on the subtlety of the individual notes and the intervals between them. Japanese culture, to the extent that it was supported without by a philosophical framework imported from the mainland, has shown a marked tendency to take as its starting point the individual detail rather than the overall concept, and the popular theatre of the eighteenth century was no exception to the general rule.

The greatest *ningyō jōruri* produced in the period of its highest popularity, a work far surpassing these we have already cited, was *Kanadehon chūshingura* (The Syllabary Book of the Loyal Retainers), written by Takeda Izumo, Miyoshi Shōraku and Namiki Senryū and first performed at the Takemotoza in 1748. It is a part-fictional version of the revenge killing of Kira Kōzukenosuke Yoshinaka by the band of *rōnin* known as the Akō-rōshi (the *rōnin* of Akō domain). This band of loyal retainers became figures of legend for the populace along with the historical figures Sugawara Michizane and Minamotono Yoshitsune and joined them as heroes of the popular theatre of the time. The definitive form of the legend was *Chūshingura*, a play that achieved success at its first performance and has played to full houses ever since. No other Japanese play has caught and held the popular imagination for such a long time.

The historical facts are these. In 1701 Asano Takuminokami Naganori, lord of Akō, a fief of 53,500 *koku*, had the duty of receiving the Imperial messenger at Edo castle. In charge of the ceremony was Kira Kōzukenosuke Yoshinaka, the *Shōgun's* director of ceremonial. For some reason Asano became angry with Kira and attempted to attack him with drawn sword. (The reason for his anger is not clear but there had been a similar incident involving Kira and Kamei Korechika, chief of the Tsuwano clan in 1698. Perhaps Kira took advantage of his position to taunt the provincial lords.) Although Kira was scarcely injured by the attack it was a capital offence to draw a sword within the confines of Edo castle and Asano atoned for his crime by committing *seppuku*. His domain and Edo mansion were confiscated, as was to be expected. All of his retainers became *rōnin*, and the chief retainer, Ōishi Kuranosuke Yoshio, and forty-six of the clan *samurai* awaited their opportunity for revenge. (In fact one of them defected leaving only forty-six to attack Kira.) Their time came when early on a snowy morning in the twelfth month of 1702 they attacked the Kira mansion, killed Kira and took his head as an offering to their lord's grave at the

Edo temple Sengakuji. The band had prepared their attack carefully and afterwards waited calmly to see how the authorities would treat them. The Bakufu first divided the group into four and held them in separate houses; later they ordered them to kill themselves, which they did by ritual disembowelment on the fourth day of the second month of 1703.

Not all Confucianists called upon to consider the matter supported·this line of action. One opinion, that held by Ogyū Sorai, Dazai Shundai and others, was that the *rōnin* were culpable in breaking the law of the nation in pursuit of their private vengeance. But there was another group, including Muro Kyūsō and Itō Tōgai, that maintained that the *rōnin* had shown commendable loyalty in avenging their master's death. The vast majority of the populace condoned and admired the action of Ōishi and his men and a *Kabuki* version of the incident, lightly disguised as the night attack scene in the story of the twelfth-century Soga brothers, was staged only twelve days after the *rōnin* band killed themselves. This play, put on at the Nakamuraza in Edo, was banned after three days but it was by no means the last of such dramas. The oldest extant play based on the incident is Chikamatsu Monzaemon's *jōruri*, *Goban Taiheiki* (first performed at the Takemotoza in 1706) and this was followed by a *Kabuki* version also staged in Ōsaka, *Onishikage musashi abumi* (1710), and a *jōruri* of the same title by Kino Kaion performed at the Toyotakeza in 1713. Later there was a *jōruri* by Namiki Sōsuke and others, *Ōyakazu shi jūshichihon* (Toyotakeza, 1747), and this was followed in the next year by the *jōruri* *Kanadehon chūshingura*, the *Kabuki* version appearing in 1749.

Chūshingura (as *Kanadehon chūshingura* is almost always known) is ostensibly set in fourteenth-century Kamakura and the heroes' names are changed. Thus Kira becomes Kōno Moronao, Asano becomes En'ya Hangan and Ōishi becomes Ōboshi Yuranosuke. Although it begins with the argument and attack in the palace and ends with the revenge killing, the plot often has little to do with historical reality. 'Asano,' portrayed as a short-tempered man, is given a motive for his attack on 'Kira' by a scene in which he is insulted by him. There is no mention of the one *rōnin* who defected and in the play forty-seven *rōnin* present the enemy's head at their lord's grave. (This number is necessary at least for the title, which includes a reference to the forty-seven letters of the Japanese syllabary of the time.) Incidents invented by the authors include Ōishi/Ōboshi elaborately masking his true intention by a display of dissipation, a tragic love affair between the completely fictional characters Kanpei and O-karu, the wooing and winning of Kon'ami by Ōboshi's son and the family problems that ensue, and the devoted behaviour of the Sakai merchant Gihee, who supplies the weapons used in the attack. These invented incidents and characters make up the greater part of the play and are themselves independent of the overall structure, with no necessary or close connection with the *rōnin* band's preparations for vengeance. In this the construction of *Chūshingura* does not differ from the typical play of the time.

The characters of the wholly fictional parts are ostensibly *samurai* but the values expressed are clearly those of the *chōnin*. Ōboshi's frolickings among the 'blooms of Gion' (i.e. the prostitutes of Kyōto) take up the long seventh act. For *chōnin* enjoyment in the pleasure quarters was the highest value, and this is also reflected in, for instance, Saikaku's novels. There is, for example, the absolute love felt by O-karu for Kanpei. Kanpei kills himself because he mistakenly believes that he has accidentally killed O-karu's father, and it is Kanpei's death, rather than her father's, that causes O-karu intense grief. Of her father she says, 'He died a violent death but he was an old man.' For Kanpei she laments, 'How sad he must have been, how grief-stricken, how he must have longed to see me.' This elevation of personal feeling above the more social Confucian virtues and duties is reminiscent of Chikamatsu's love-suicide pieces. The *chōnin* who actually appears as such in the play, Gihee, is, however, a model of loyalty. When surrounded by 'police' who threaten his young son with death if he does not tell them how he is planning to send arms to the *rōnin*, Gihee refuses to reveal anything, declaring himself 'a manly man'. Fortunately the 'police' are revealed to be the *rōnin* themselves and they are greatly impressed by his triumph in this test of fidelity. Ōboshi says, 'Though they say there are no real men among the common people, there are real men even among the merchants.' And: 'Your qualities are such that it would be no bad thing if you ruled the entire province.' These statements are designed to please a *chōnin* audience already influenced by the

Shingaku view that though they may be of a different social class from the *samurai* they are not essentially inferior. These *chōnin* values, although irrelevant to the historical events, ran through *Chūshingura* and ensured its success with its *chōnin* audience.

Chūshingura's popularity and that of the historical figures did not wane with the disintegration of the *chōnin* class after the Meiji Restoration. What is the secret of this continuing popularity? Asano's reason for attacking Kira stemmed from personal feelings, as did his regret at not succeeding in killing him. The actions of the *rōnin* in fulfilling his dying wish by killing Kira were illegal and against public order. Both of these factors – personal feelings and an attack on authority – would be attractive to the ordinary man. To that extent there is a resemblance to the love-suicide where authority is defied from motives of personal feelings. In the love-suicide *jōruri* the suicide is not justified in terms of duty (*giri*), which was the form of social order which made it necessary, but the feelings (*ninjō*) involved with it are legitimized by the *michiyuki* with its intensely emotional *shamisen* accompaniment. The *rōnin* band's actions on the other hand can be justified in terms of duty, their loyalty to their lord, and thus *ninjō* can be justified in terms of *giri* by applying the notion of duty with unusual thoroughness. This justification was more than adequate for an audience who had no wish to alter the system in which they lived.

The cause of the band's popularity, then, was not their loyalty; there are many other stories, fictional and historical, of loyalty. Rather it was a case of the ordinary people identifying with the element of personal feeling which could, under the guise of duty, go against public order while remaining within the limits of the system in which they found themselves. Another important element here is the group. This was not a vendetta carried out by one man but by forty-seven (forty-six) men acting in unison. Feelings of solidarity which in normal times lie latent and are masked by such things as love, dissipation and affection between parent and child, are manifested in a crisis when the demands of the group override all others. (Throughout the play these feelings of solidarity and the crisis that will inevitably provoke them are always present if not overtly expressed; the audience knows that the *samurai* and the other characters are moving towards the climax of group action.) The main attraction for the audience is in the strength of these feelings of attachment to a group, not in the (relatively un-worthy) objective. The incident begins in one man's short temper and ends with the death of Kira, sixteen of his retainers and the forty-seven themselves but is in itself rather unimportant. The popularity of *Chūshingura* can be expected to continue as long as the Japanese possess the characteristic of forming a unified front against outside challenge without questioning why they are doing so. The play was epoch-making not in being a play of loyalty but in being a marvellously concentrated expression of the feeling of belonging to a group, of solidarity, of, in short, the fundamental experience of Japanese society.

The amusements of the ordinary *chōnin* were not limited to *ningyō jōruri* and *Kabuki*. After the commercial success of Saikaku's novels there appeared a number of publishers who put on sale novels of a similar nature written by authors they themselves employed. The most successful of these was Hachi-monjiya of Kyōto whose most notable author was Ejima Kiseki (1667–1736), the son of an Ōsaka merchant. He is said to have been saved from dissipation and disgrace by the third master of Hachimonjiya, Jishō, and set to work as a novelist. As a way of becoming a novelist this differs considerably from that of Saikaku who chose to change from writing *haikai* to writing novels and took his material directly from the life of the *chōnin*. Kiseki, required to write to earn his living and satisfy his employer, imitated Saikaku to a considerable degree, his personal contribution being in adaptation and modification.

It is not surprising, therefore, that Kiseki's novels follow Saikaku's in being of two types, one being erotic and set in the pleasure quarters, *Keisei kintanki* (Courtesans Should Not Be Short-tempered, 1711), for example, and the other being anecdotal descriptions of the daily life of the *chōnin*. These latter, known as *katagi-mono* (character pieces), are short, realistic, slightly ironic descriptions in which the character and quirks of a *chōnin* type are outlined. They appeared as collections grouped according to subject. Thus the first was *Seken musuko katagi* (Characters of Young Men of Our Society, 1715) and this was followed by *Seken musume katagi* (Characters of Young Women of Our Society, 1717), *Ukiyo oyaji katagi* (Characters of Fathers of the Floating World, 1720), *Seken tedai katagi* (Characters of Shopmen of Our Society, 1730) and so on.

Kiseki's erotic novels, which take the hedonism expressed in

Saikaku's works as an assumption, chiefly consist of detailed descriptions of contemporary manners in the pleasure quarters. Similarly the novels of *chōnin* life take it (literally) as read that honesty, diligence and thrift bring success to a merchant and are in the main descriptions of the customs of the time. In neither of them is there any sign of the new way that the *chōnin* were beginning to think about themselves and their position. Nor do Saikaku's later perceptions – that hedonism eventually leads to a sense of futility and that wealth does not come from diligence but capital – find any expression in Kiseki's work. Kiseki did not develop what Saikaku had pioneered; he used it to create simplifications and stereotypes.

This does not mean however that Kiseki added nothing new to the Saikaku style of novel. One thing he did introduce was an element of parody. For instance the first two of the six volumes of *Courtesans Should Not Be Short-tempered* discuss the relative merits of male and female prostitutes (*yarō* and *keisei*) in the form of a dialogue which is a parody of a discussion of the relative merits of the Nichiren and Jōdo sects of Buddhism. One section, *Yakei no ryōshū azuchiron* (The *yaro-keisei* Azuchi Dialogue), is based on the Azuchi dialogues arranged for Oda Nobunaga in 1579 in which the Jōdo and Nichiren sects disputed. Similarly a pun on Ōhara (a place name) and *ōhara* ('a big belly') allows a parody of the Ōhara dialogues of 1186 (in which the founder of the Jōdo Sect first expounded his beliefs to the priests of Kyōto) in terms of pregnancy and the prostitute. There are also elements of humour in the 'laughing story' vein, found for example in *Characters of Young Men* in the description of the sons of merchant families variously fixated on martial arts, poetry composition and antiques. In these there is something akin to the 'punchline' (*ochi*) of *rakugo* stories. Compared with most of Saikaku's work the popular novel seems to have been coming closer to the ordinary humorous stories that could be heard on the street. The spirit of the laughing story, related to that of the humorous verses *kyōka* and *senryū*, was by no means anti-authoritarian. Rather it afforded the average *chōnin* momentary release from the rigid restraints of a system of which he by and large approved. He was diverted by the playful breaking of taboos, which could be physical (and broken by indecent and 'rude' language), cultural or occasionally social. Once the spasm of release was past, authority stood as solid as before. For a consistent attack on cultural authority we must look to Tominaga Nakamoto and for a direct attack on social authority to Andō Shōeki; they are not to be found in the thought and attitudes of Baigan, Takeda Izumo or Kiseki.

Kiseki's material was taken from the same group as his readership, the upper- and middle-class *chōnin*; he did not write about the *samurai* or peasants and showed no interest in the history or future of society, and thus he is more limited than Saikaku. But like Saikaku his writing is realistic and detailed (from it we learn a lot about the dress and speech of courtesans and the *chōnin*'s economic life and amusements) and there are no elements of invention or fantasy, no curiosities or marvels. While *Chūshingura* represented the ideals of the *chōnin* public, the popular novels of the same period described in detail their life as it really was.

There must also have been a public demand for and curiosity about fantastic and supernatural phenomena in the imaginative world. The novelists who dealt in the marvellous took their material from the colloquial (*bai hua*) fiction of China. Among the first people to study the colloquial Chinese novel was Okajima Kanzan (1674–1728), a Nagasaki interpreter who taught Sorai and his circle Chinese conversation and told them something of the novels, which up to this time had been virtually unknown in Japan. (They were written in a colloquial Chinese somewhat different from the classical style used for most other texts.) He also prepared some novels to be read in Japanese by adding reading marks and published translations. The Chinese name for this kind of novel is *xiao shuo*, which is read in Japanese as *shōsetsu* (the word used nowadays for *novel*), and Kanzan and the other Confucianists of the time who spoke and lectured on Chinese colloquial fiction became known as *shōsetsuka* ('novelists').

Writers, too, began to adapt the Chinese colloquial novels. One of the earliest to do so was the Ōsaka physician Tsuga Teishō (dates of birth and death unknown) who, under the pen-name Kinro Gyōja, produced the short novel *Kokin kidan hanabusa zōshi* (Weird Tales of Now and Long Ago, 1749) based on the Chinese collection *Jingshi tongyan*. Later the long Chinese novel *Shui hu juan* (The Water Margin) was partially adapted as *Honchō suikoden* (The Japanese Water Margin, Vol. 1, published 1773, unfinished) by Takebe Ayatari (1719–74), a littérateur-*samurai* of the Hirosaki domain who studied National Learning (*kokugaku*) under Kamono Mabuchi. Another National Learning scholar, Ueda Akinari (1734–1809), produced the most skilful blend of Chinese and Japanese in works such as *Ugetsu monogatari* (1776) and we shall discuss his work in more detail later.

Apart from the tales of the supernatural taken from Chinese novels there were two other new forms of fiction in the late eighteenth century. One was the fantastic and satirical novel typified by *Fūryū shidōken-den* and *Nenashigusa-den* (both 1763) by Hiraga Gennai (1728–79); the other was a kind of adult comic strip called *kibyōshi*, a picture book with a certain amount of text, mostly dialogue, with minimal narrative passages. Most of these were concerned with the pleasure quarters, the ideal 'man about town' (*tsūjin*) and how to enjoy yourself, and were written and published mainly in Edo. The first writer and illustrator of note in this style was Koikawa Harumachi (1744–89) and he was followed by the much more significant figure of Santō Kyōden (1761–1816), who was also a print artist of *ukiyo-e* under the name of Kitao Masanobu. Harumachi, who belonged to the Suruga Kojima domain and lived in the clan mansion in Edo, wrote what is usually regarded as the first work in the *kibyōshi* comic-strip style, *Kinkin-sensei eiga no yume* (Mr. Posh's Dream of Glory, 1775). Kyōden wrote many works in this style, *Edo mumare uwaki no kabayaki* (The Love Affairs of an Edo Lad, 1785), for instance, and in the slightly different style of *sharebon* (slightly longer and with more text), *Keiseikai shijūhatte* (The Forty-eight Ways of Buying a Courtesan, 1790) and *Seiro hiru no sekai, nishiki no ura* (Behind the Brocade: The World of the House of Pleasure in the Daytime, 1791). Shortly after the latter was published the entire novel form was banned and Kyōden was sentenced to fifty days in handcuffs.

Harumachi's *Mr Posh's Dream of Glory* is (like the Nō play *Kantan*) based on the Chinese fable 'The Dream of Handan'. The hero, a poor man from the provinces on his way to Edo, dozing as the owner of a teahouse prepares his meal, dreams that he is adopted by a wealthy man, only to spend all his money on whoring and be driven out of the family again. This short text, principally but not exclusively dialogue, speaks for the hopes and ambitions of the *chōnin* masses. The hero of *The Love Affairs of an Edo Lad* is the son of a well-off family who, although unattractive, wishes to be known as a great lover and, among other devices, pays money to women to put on charades that will give that impression. It should be noted that the reputation of being a great lover was as important, if not more so, than actual success. Such a reputation was a social necessity for a 'real man'. It was this kind of society that gave birth to works such as *The Forty-eight Ways of Buying a Courtesan*, which differs from the guides to the pleasure quarters that were its literary predecessors in portraying the relationships between various courtesans and their clients through the medium of dialogue. After a variety of scenes involving the guiles and wiles of the ladies of the night the last scene we overhear is between a couple who are truly in love:

GUEST: Why do you bewilder me like this? You're cruel! (*He draws her to him.*)

WOMAN (smiling): Why did you make me love you?
(*She slides her hand under the guest's pillow and nibbles his lips.*) I haven't had my period for two months, it's really worrying. (*She puts her hand on his back.*) Oh, you cheeky thing. Undo your sash. (*She undoes the man's sash and pulls it free of the bedclothes, undoes her own sash and they embrace skin to skin. Bong! goes the six o'clock bell.*)
The author *Kyōden* speaks: Lucky devil!

In the following passage of 'comment' Kyōden writes: 'This all might seem very silly from the outside but once you're in this position, it'll seem absolutely right.' It was indeed 'absolutely right' in that it was an ideal of *chōnin* society which ran right through the entire Tokugawa period.

Knowledge of European culture obtained through contact with the Dutch had widened the horizons of a section of the intelligentsia of the late eighteenth century. Meanwhile the majority of the *chōnin* continued to be under the influence of *Shingaku*. Only the popular novel actually narrowed its field of vision, from the pleasure quarter as a whole to the lovers' bedroom. The values of the *chōnin* were split between the virtues of thrift, honesty and diligence taught by Baigan and his successors and the pleasures of the profligate, great lover and man about town described by Kyōden and his fellow novelists. To achieve a balance between these two was the central (and subtly difficult) problem of *chōnin* life. It was not a matter of one set of values being open and the other covert – both were quite open and one could as easily read one of Kyōden's books (or frequent Yoshiwara) as attend a meeting held by Toan. The *samurai* who favoured a system of morality split into public uprightness and covert pleasure seem to have found this dragging of private pleasures into the open distasteful and subjected the author of *Behind the Brocade* to a severe and shaming punishment although the work, which takes some of its characters (Yūgiri and Izaemon for example) from *jōruri*, is in itself scarcely pornographic, less so even than the portion of *The Forty-eight Ways of Buying a Courtesan* quoted above.

HIRAGA GENNAI AND THE 'DUTCH SCHOLARS'

There were two sides to Hiraga Gennai (1728?–79); he was both a member of the literati and an engineer. As a literatus he followed a cultural tradition from the earlier part of the century but as an engineer he was part of a trend which developed in the latter half and which was characterized by attempts to learn scientific techniques from the Dutch at Nagasaki and their books, a much more direct way than through Chinese translations as had been usual before. Thus both an appreciation of tradition and a vision of the future were combined in this extraordinary man who seemed to embody the entirety of Edo culture from the mid-seventeenth to the mid-nineteenth century.

Gennai had many pen-names including Fūrai Sanjin and Kyūkei. The son of a minor *samurai* of the Takamatsu domain, he entered the service of the domain for ten years until 1761, when he resigned to spend the rest of his life (which ended in prison after he had stabbed a pupil to death) as a *rōnin*. When he first visited Edo in 1754 for study he was interested chiefly in botany. Between 1757 and 1762 he held five meetings with groups of people of similar interests to examine and discuss various natural materials, mainly used in medicine, and later wrote a descriptive catalogue of three hundred such materials from Japan, China and the West, *Butsuruihinshitsu* (1763). The materials included flora, fauna, marine life, insects, minerals and stones, and he appended a separate volume of sketches of the rarer of these and a volume of instruction for growing carrots and sweet potatoes which, according to his own introduction, would benefit society greatly.

He became a pupil of the National Learning scholar Kamono Mabuchi in 1763 and wrote two satirical novels *Nenashigusa* (Rootless Grass, in two volumes, 1763 and 1768) and *Fūryū Shidōken-den* (The Elegant Tale of Shidōken, 1763) and later bitter comments on the times such as *Naemara in'itsu-den* (The Tale of a Limp Prick in Seclusion, 1768) and *Hōhi-ron* (On Flatulence, two volumes, 1774, 1777). He also wrote many *jōruri*, beginning with *Shinrei yaguchi no watashi* (1770). None of these works shows any western influence although Gennai had obviously been interested in the West since the time of his descriptive catalogue. He was sent to study at Nagasaki twice, once by his domain in 1752 and once by the Bakufu in 1769, and after 1761 he was in frequent contact with the Dutch in Edo. Among his friends were Sugita Genpaku (1733–1817), a brilliant scholar of western medicine, and Shiba Kōkan (1738?–1818) a painter in the western style.

Gennai's achievements as an engineer include the making of asbestos in 1768 and the construction of a thermometer and a friction device to generate static electricity after the Dutch model he had seen in Nagasaki in 1773. He was also an engineer on a larger scale involved in the development of mining, searching for a suitable site for a copper mine at the invitation of the Akita domain (supposedly with the assistance of Shiba Kōkan) and trying unsuccessfully to set up an iron-ore mine in Chichibu just to the north-west of Edo, where he also undertook with greater success some work on opening the Ara River to navigation. Gennai spent his last years in Edo, dying from an illness in prison after killing a pupil in obscure circumstances.

Gennai, while he did occasionally undertake work for the Bakufu, was content to be a *rōnin* and live independently of *samurai* bureaucracy and *chōnin* commercialism. In this and the multiplicity of his artistic interests and his association with other artists such as Shiba Kōkan and Ōta Nanpo (1749–1823), the *kyōka* poet and playwright, he clearly was following the traditions of the literati. His work, however, was less like previous literati in a way that was characteristic of his time and the culture of Edo. He composed no Chinese verse but wrote *jōruri*; in place of classical Chinese prose he wrote humorous works in colloquial Japanese; he practised neither calligraphy nor ink painting but painted in a 'realistic' western style. (There remains an oil painting by him of a western lady.)

Gennai's *jōruri* are all historical pieces, mainly derived from the *Taiheiki* and *Heike monogatari*, and his *Shinrei yaguchi no watashi* has most of the characteristics typical of the later pieces: the theme is the relationship between lord and retainer, and one of the climaxes of the play comes when a retainer sacrifices his own son in place of his lord's. These works are in short an expression of conventional *samurai* values with no original element. What is new about them is the use of the tone and colloquialisms of Edo speech. The style of the collection *Fūrai rokubushū* (1780?; it includes *On Flatulence* and *Tale of a Limp Prick*) is an original mixture of slang, witty comments and parodies of the classics. In it Gennai criticizes contemporary mores and defends his position as a recluse. For example, in the second chapter of *On Flatulence* he praises the 'peace of mind' of the *rōnin* and gives vent to his hate of a world which, 'spoilt and dependent on universal peace, has its eyes focused on only one thing, money'. This is an attitude typical of the literati. The peace of mind of the *rōnin* came from 'a handful of rice and gravy, a gourdful of *sake* and no fixed property; instead, without the wasteful luxury of a master and sticky grains of rice to hinder his feet he can rush off where he pleases and mock the unpleasant things [of the world]. To be free all your life is, at the least, better than not.' To mock the unpleasant things of the world is, however, something more typical of an urban dweller who finds recreation in words rather than a literatus who finds escape in painting and writing. In a world dominated by Confucianism in which 'learning is thought of as just a matter of reading books and the principles of things are thought to be a matter of abstruse theory', for Gennai 'to use up all my property, give up my stipend, concentrate all my inventiveness and use up all my money...to make a static electricity generator and work for the public good' has only resulted 'in my being labelled a fraud....I might as well call my device a fartorator.' In the introduction to the second volume of *On*

Flatulence Gennai gives a scatological burlesque of the myth of the Shintō deity Yamato-takeru-no-mikoto and in *Tale of a Limp Prick* he compares the gorgeous gilded Buddhist 'erections' with his own state of impotence in a world where even the great sages of Confucian antiquity would have been unable or unwilling to ram their points home. Thus it is clear that he is not content with the life of an artistic recluse but uses and parodies the convention to express his dissatisfaction and rage at the state of the world.

Rootless Grass is set in the world of the pleasure quarters and *Kabuki* and in the hell which appears to the hero in his dreams. There are bitter attacks on the ways of Confucianists, doctors and priests and a mocking parody of the relationship between the *Shōgun* and the *daimyō*. The satirical novel *The Elegant Tale of Shidōken* is a far more substantial and coherently structured work. The hero, Shidōken, is an old man who tells humorous stories on a street in the Asakusa district of Edo. He tells the story of how long ago when he was young he met a magician who gave him a magic feather fan which allowed him to travel all over the world. He first went around Edo and then to a land of giants, a land of small people, a land of long-armed people, a land of long-legged people and a land where the people had a hole in the middle of their chests. He later visited the concubines' quarters of the Emperor of China and went on to Nyogo-no-shima, the mythical island populated by women. All men who come ashore on Nyogo-no-shima are rounded up to serve as prostitutes in a pleasure quarter that bears a strong if inverted resemblance to the pleasure quarters of Edo. Just as this was about to happen to our hero, the magician reappeared and pointed out to him that everything is relative and that he should now have understood the true nature of human feelings. He should therefore return to Japan to 'gather people to listen to fairy stories which pierce the shell which hides the reality of the life of this world and thus give great instruction to the people'. As Shidōken heard this he found himself 'sitting abstractedly on a bench' in Asakusa. The wizard's last admonition was that he should attack Confucianists who worship anything written by the Chinese and stress instead the importance of Japanese ways. 'Because Japan is by nature a country which follows righteousness and humanity, peace is preserved without [any need for] the creation of saints....Because Japan is a faithful and righteous country...there is no other country where the Emperor is so truly an Emperor.' Thus the relativity of local customs is used as grounds for an attack on Confucianists who worship inappropriate foreign writing but not to attack the tendency to absolutize Japanese mores.

This perhaps shows the influence of Gennai's exposure to National Learning. More probably it is a reflection of the nationalism of the masses as in Chikamatsu's The Battles of Coxinga. Certainly the nationalistic tone of his novels and the stress on fidelity in his jōruri seem to overlap. When writing for the masses Gennai could not advance any values that diverged substantially from the consensus. In The Elegant Tale of Shidōken he did, however, satirize certain aspects of Japan, the brothel system for instance, and his vision of Brobdingnagian and Lilliputian societies is certainly subversive of a fixed view of society. It could only be someone with a dawning and ever keener realization of the existence of cultures other than Japan and China who could write, 'the Japanese look upon the people of the isle of little people as insects while the giants regard the Japanese as freaks.' Gennai's jōruri have no connection with the world of engineering and scientific devices but the man who wrote the novels was not completely divorced from the man who was capable of discussing Sugita Genpaku and western techniques of dissection.

Japanese intellectuals gained access to Dutch books through the translation made by interpreters at Nagasaki such as Motoki Yoshinaga (1735–94) who produced a work on Japanese and Dutch maps of the world and translated a 1666 astronomical work by the Dutchman W. J. Blaeu, both of which touched upon Copernican astronomical theories. In 1784 Shizuki Tadao (1760–1806), another Nagasaki interpreter, translated a Dutch summary of Newton's theory of gravitation, itself a 1741 translation of the 1708 work by the Englishman John Keill. Motoki Ryōi (1628–97) translated a Dutch translation made in 1667 of a dissection manual by the German J. Remmelin and later Sugita Genpaku and Maeno Ryōtaku (1723–1803) prepared Kaitai shinsho (1774), a much more detailed and practical manual from a Dutch translation of the Anatomische Tabellen (1725) of the German J.A. Kulmus, supplemented and revised to some extent by reference to other western works.

At least one significant work on dissection had already been written by a Japanese – Yamawaki Tōyō's *Zōshi* in 1759 – and dissection itself had been attempted occasionally. But the team led by Genpaku was the first to use information from western books to dissect the human body (in 1771) and to realize the accuracy of the information and the misconceptions of traditional oriental medicine. This led them to the translation and publication of the first western manual of dissection.

In reminiscences he wrote late in his life, *Rangaku kotohajime* (The Beginning of Dutch Studies), Genpaku recalled the difficulties they faced: 'When Ryōtaku and I performed a dissection following the Japanese version of the Dutch manual, we found nothing that did not correspond to the illustration – it was all there.... So, when we finished that day's dissection I thought that I should definitely examine the shape of bones and so I collected bleached bones from the execution ground where they are left exposed and when I looked at many of them, they were different in some ways from how they had traditionally been described and, to my surprise, were exactly the same as the Dutch illustrations.'

This led Genpaku to announce his intention of translating in its entirety the foreign manual to Maeno Ryōtaku – who was studying Dutch – and a physician from his own domain, Nakagawa Junan (1739–86). This was indeed a historic moment; for the first time a Japanese collected bleached bones and thought not of the impermanence of human life, but of the structure of the human body.

For the Office of Calendars of the Bakufu, astronomy was no more than a matter of arranging the calendar; it was, and is, however, basically involved with man's view of nature in its entirety. Similarly, dissection of the human body, even if it for the doctor involved no more than something necessary to devise treatment of diseases, is inevitably involved with the fundamentals of man's view of himself. Both the structure of the universe and of the microcosm (the human body) differed from the age-old theories of Buddhism and Confucianism and, in particular, contradicted the natural order posited by Neo-Confucianism. What were the reactions of the late eighteenth-century Japanese intellectuals to this contradiction?

Shizuki Tadao seems to have concentrated on explicating Newton's theories of molecules and dynamics using the Neo-

Confucian concepts of Ether and *yinyang*. Sugita Genpaku limited himself to a practical concern with anatomy without questioning the significance of the new information in the wider context of natural philosophy. Hiraga Gennai, as an engineer, concentrated his efforts on reproducing the foreign devices which he had seen or had seen plans of and probably felt no need to revise his view of the universe. He was no theorist and like the majority of his contemporaries was aware that he could live without the doctrines of Confucianism and Buddhism. But there were a few thinkers who did wish to construct a comprehensive philosophical system that would link man and nature, and for this they employed Neo-Confucianist metaphysical concepts. For them western thought made necessary a reassessment of all previous theories and the construction of their own system. Typical examples of such thinkers are Miura Baien and Yamagata Bantō, both of whom were in contact with Motoki Yoshinaga at Nagasaki. Baien and Bantō both tried to resolve the contradictions between Confucianism and western thought, at least within the field of science. Not only did contact with western thought bring a challenge to Confucianism, it seems also to have been used to advance the cause of the Japanese world-view, and in this the outstanding figure was Motoori Norinaga.

MIURA BAIEN AND YAMAGATA BANTŌ

Miura Baien (1723–89) was a student of natural philosophy. The son of a doctor and a doctor himself, he was born and spent his entire life in the village of Tominaga on the Kunisaki peninsula of Kyūshū. His father seems to have been a man of culture, at least to the extent of writing *haikai*, a few of which survive. Baien was a devoted son who visited his father's grave every day in all weathers. Although Baien visited Nagasaki twice, as a young man in 1742 when he constructed a celestial globe and once as an old man in 1787, he seems never to have travelled beyond Kyūshū. His circle of acquaintances included the 'Dutch scholar' Asada Gōryū (1734–99) and he is known to have borrowed a dissection manual from a pupil of Yamawaki Tōyō and a copy of Arai Hakuseki's book on the Ainu, *Ezoshi*, from the Ōsaka

Confucianist Nakai Riken (1732–1817). Baien wrote extensively, revising and rewriting his more important works over many years. His magnus opus *Gengo* (Mysterious Words, 1753–74) took him more than twenty laborious years to write, during which time he thought of abandoning it on at least two occasions.

We may imagine Baien's daily life in the small village he scarcely ever left, except for rare and short journeys, as tranquil and extremely regulated; perhaps like his contemporary in Königsberg, Immanuel Kant, he went for a stroll of the same distance at the same time each day. The drama of his life did not take place in the exterior world but within his own spirit. Had this not been so he could scarcely have devoted twenty years of his life to producing one book. The simplicity of his way of life also meant that he must have been in close contact with the peasants of his native village and have known, unlike the vast majority of his contemporary thinkers, what the life of the ordinary man was like.

He described the conditions of the time in *Heigo fūji* (Confidential Report, 1786), prepared at the request of the lord of the domain. He was also in touch with Nagasaki and the modern versions of astronomy, medicine and geography brought by the Dutch; these were strong influences on his thought.

Baien's other works include *Zeigo* (Superfluous Words, 1756–89), which supplements the natural philosophy of *Mysterious Words*, and *Kango* (Daring Words, 1760–67, published 1773), which is a work on ethics independent of the other two. These three works, all written in Chinese, are known collectively as the 'Three Words'. He wrote a summary in Japanese of his early thought, *Genkiron* (Broad Principles, 1759), and a commentary on his later thought, *Taga Bokukei no sho ni kotau* (Reply to Taga Bokukei's Letter), as well as a medical treatise, *Shinseiyotan* (Further Writings on Natural Life, 1763–64), a work on economics, *Kagen* (The Origin of Value, 1773), and a memoir of his second trip to Nagasaki, *Kisanroku* (A Record of My Return, 1778). All of these works reflect some aspect of Baien's thought and with the exception of *Further Writings*, which is in Chinese, they are in Japanese.

Baien's intellectual background was traditional and Confucianist, the Confucianist classics for the most part interpreted through Neo-Confucianist theories. But his use of Neo-Confucianist theory was quite unlike that of his contemporaries who for the most part reduced the comprehensive metaphysical system to its constituent parts which could then be used in the examination of specific fields such as politics, ethics, rhetoric and prosody. Baien alone took as the object of his intellectual investigations the establishment of the existence of a rule or principle that could explain the universe, the *jōri* or 'logic' as he termed it. For him it was not enough to describe phenomena individually; they had to be explained with reference to a universal logic. He wrote in *Reply to Taga Bokukei's Letter* that although specialized knowledge was useful in its place, a view of the universe that explained the movements of the heavens by saying 'they are so because they are so' was all too superficial. At the same time the explanations provided by Neo-Confucianists for astronomical and geographical phenomena were clearly inferior in some cases to the western theories brought by the Dutch. The intellectual tradition of centuries was by no means without error. Even the words of Buddha and Confucius could not be accepted uncritically: 'The proponents of the comprehensive views of the universe whether they be called Buddha or sage are basically human beings; I make them my companions in debate and examination. My teacher is the universe.... Look for yourself, do not be confused by the mistaken theories of the ancients.' The main aim of Baien's thought was to make his own system of natural philosophy, distinct from the Neo-Confucian world-view, and to discover the 'logic' of the universe.

From western astronomy, geography and medicine Baien learned the effectiveness of the scientific method of examining phenomena directly, but he took his terminology to a large extent from the rich store of Neo-Confucianist concepts, especially the concepts of Ether, Principle and *yinyang*. Thus in *Mysterious Words* the universe is described in terms of the movements and states of *yinyang* and Ether. This Ether is, however, much more tangible than the ethereal and abstract substance in Zhu Xi's metaphysics, being in fact closer to matter in the sense that it was understood in the early days of physics. One illustration he used was that of a container of water: if the water leaks from one hole what enters another hole is Ether. In this case Ether is clearly what we would identify as air. Ether as well as being substantial is also universal. There is no such thing as a vacuum; if there were the sun, moon, clouds and rain would have nothing to support them. The argument is in its way quite scientific: 'Ether fills the solid mass of the earth and the emptiness of space; there is no chink in its fabric' (*Reply to Taga Bokukei's Letter*).

The main difference between this theory and those of the later Neo-Confucianists lies in the replacing of the notion of the abstract Principle, which for a Neo-Confucian is 'above shape' (i.e. metaphysical) with the notion of 'logic' inherent in the Ether itself. This 'logic' is expressed in the form of 'opposition and unity'. Ether can be in many states ('rough', 'empty', 'rising' etc.), each of which has its opposite ('smooth', 'full', 'falling' etc.); similarly, 'left' opposes 'right', 'line' opposes 'area', 'black' opposes 'white'. Each of these opposing pairs is *yinyang*, that is each complements and requires the other. The ultimate *yinyang* pair is the heaven and earth that make up the universe.

Thus when considering any phenomenon it is necessary to perceive simultaneously both the oppositions within it and also the unity which these oppositions create, and beyond this to the higher truth (heaven and earth) which comprehends them. In short, *Mysterious Words* seeks to explain the universe as an almost Hegelian dialectical development of matter: 'Individual things are *yin* or *yang* and are created thus by [inner] logic. Ether is split into individual things but is of itself a unity and, thus, a unity of division. Since Ether must be then *yinyang* and the entirety of heaven and earth is [made up from] things, heaven and earth, *yin* and *yang* are constant and inseparable.' This 'logic' is something that is inherent in the universe and can be perceived objectively. There is no need of sages to show the way, and 'if the sages came back to life would they be able to accept this?'

Although the argument of *Mysterious Words* stresses the importance of objective observation it does not in fact include many observations from nature. Rather the main proposition is intuited from a relatively small number of observed facts and the argument is developed along the lines of 'perceiving unity in opposites' to reach the conclusion. In this sense Baien's method, although rationally organized, was philosophical rather than positivistic. Baien was probably the only Japanese thinker since Kūkai (in *Jūjū shinron*) to have such a mastery of the ordering of abstract concepts. The beauty that he brought to Japanese letters was an architectonic beauty, an ordered building up of concepts of natural philosophy.

Baien's views on ethics, politics and economics have little direct connection with the philosophy of *Mysterious Words*. They seem to have derived more directly from his experience of life in a farming village. His ethical views are not dependent on considerations of social position but rather on a wider concept of human relationship, and he stresses the virtues of 'filial piety, brotherly love, loyalty, etiquette, righteousness, modesty and shame'. But his experience of the farmers and officials with whom he came into contact seems to have convinced him that self-interest could not be ignored as a basic human motivation, and he considered Mencius's view that self-interest is contradictory to humanity and righteousness to be mistaken. In *Daring Words* he says, 'It is human nature to act from likes and dislikes. And when it comes to likes and dislikes, self-interest is everything.... Self-interest which is the inevitable result of likes and dislikes, is the basis of humanity and righteousness.' The practical problem is whether one's actions are for the benefit of the community as a whole or for oneself alone. 'There is no greater Way than to ensure the security of the many, no greater virtue than to benefit the many.'

In his work on economics, *The Origin of Value*, Baien recognizes the necessity of money as a means of exchanging property but criticizes the tendency of money, which 'is needed alike by all four classes', to accumulate in the cities and in the hands of merchants. He regards the cause of the gulf between poor and rich to have been brought about by there being too much money in circulation. Behind this opinion is the belief that the most precious things for the people of the country are not gold and silver but food, drink and clothing. This belief in all probability comes from his experience in an agricultural community rather than an urban commercial community. Unlike Shōeki, however, Baien did not assert the primacy of agriculture or attack the social system, but merely requested his lord to economize rather than borrow from merchants and hoped for a policy which would allow the peasants to accumulate some non-monetary savings.

The political views which Baien sets forth in *Confidential Report* begin with 'Calm the people's minds, consult them and be aware of how they feel'. Probably he did in fact know how the local people felt better than did the local officials. He appends to this section is a very detailed list of things that need to be examined such as the population of the villages, the soil and the state of agricultural production. Speaking of taxation he has many sharp words on the subject of the poverty of the peasants and the amount of tax they pay in a year: 'When people are deprived of too much they sell their children and their wives and their lives are squeezed from them by hardship and suffering. I think there may be many who through the sufferings of poverty cannot eat real food but drag out their lives for a few days eating the plants and the bark of trees before dying; their deaths cannot be put down to the will of Heaven.' But Baien did not think that any solution to this could be found in the riots which had occurred so frequently in recent years; instead he advocated petitioning the lord of the fief and obtaining a change in policy.

Here then was a man who directed a vast intellectual effort to the construction of a comprehensive natural philosophy through the use of abstract concepts and whose views on ethics, politics and economics derived from the particular circumstances of an agricultural village; a thinker who opened not only Japanese but also Chinese culture to comparative evaluation and who spoke for the peasants among whom he lived against the *chōnin* of the cities. On one hand was Nagasaki and a view of the wide world – and Baien undoubtedly learned more than astronomy, geography and dissection from the interpreters there. In *A Record of My Return* he touches upon the religions of the West (Christianity and Islam), the languages (and the existence of a purely phonetic script) and the family system ('generally there is no divorce. If a wife is nevertheless divorced she is given half the man's property'.) and ethics ('Abortion is not allowed. . . . People who murder are not allowed to live. Suicide is considered a great sin.'). The multifarious cultures visible through the 'window' of Nagasaki made inevitable a comparative evaluation of Sino-Japanese cultural traditions, and Baien and his contemporaries were markedly different from previous generations of thinkers precisely because they perceived this. On the other hand, Baien lived in the rural village of Tominaga, completely isolated from the wealthy cities and the culture of the age. The peasants lived a life of poverty in a self-contained community with its own pressing problems. Miura Baien was pulled one way by Nagasaki and the other by Tominaga.

Yamagata Bantō (1748–1821) was the chief clerk of a wealthy Ōsaka merchant. He was born in Banshū (present-day Hyōgo Prefecture) the son of a peasant who was probably also a local merchant, and came to Ōsaka at an early age to become the successor to his uncle as chief clerk. He was successful in his job especially in dealing with the Sendai and other domains in the conversion of their rice incomes into money. He attended the Kaitoku-dō Confucian school where he was taught by the two Nakai brothers, Chikuzan and Riken, both of whom played a part in the writing of his major work *Yume no yo* (Daydreams; Chikuzan looked over the first draft; Riken contributed many opinions). He was taught astronomy by Asada Gōryū, an acquaintance of Miura Baien. He was widely read and examined some Japanese translations of Dutch medical works. *Daydreams*, which he wrote in later life from 1802 to 1820 (although it remained unpublished until 1916), is an exposition of a distinctive materialistic world-view.

In this combination of Edo commercial background, education at the Kaitoku-dō and a distinctive world-view Bantō shows himself to be a successor to Tominaga Nakamoto; he was in fact his only one. But one decisive difference between the two was that whereas Nakamoto was never significantly exposed to western thought, Bantō, who was a contemporary of Baien, was greatly influenced by it. Their work also differed in that while Nakamoto was critical of all three doctrines he was most critical of Buddhism (at least as far as can be judged from his extant writings) whereas Bantō was most generous towards Confucianism, reserving his sharpest attacks for the other two doctrines. This difference may be explained by the differences in their lives – although Nakamoto was born into a merchant family he left it and was not close to the centres of power in the same way as the chief clerk of a company that dealt with *daimyō* – and by the changes in the way that Confucianism was taught at the Kaitoku-dō. After the foundation of the *chōnin* Confucian schools the content of the education turned from a stress on ethical matters to a more positivistic approach. However this may be, *Daydreams,* although not published during the Tokugawa period, was copied and passed around widely (more than forty such copies are known) and its fate was completely different from that of Nakamoto's *Discourse on Errors,* which seems to have been suppressed.

What Bantō found in western thought was the positivistic approach that it embodied and in this he was similar to Baien. Baien stated in *The Origin of Value* that 'westerners base their thought on observation', referring to their astronomy, geography and medicine, and Bantō says of western geography that 'they do not discuss or make maps of places they have not been' and of astronomy that 'they make observations and take measurements as they go to and fro between various countries'. In medicine, 'The Chinese carelessly say things riddled with error without checking them and India and Japan accept them.... Practitioners of Sino-Japanese medicine cling to their old books and know nothing of the accurate observations and practical efficacy achieved by western medicine.' For Baien the relativization of the traditional intellectual authority opened the way to his own natural philosophy, but he concentrated his efforts exclusively on the construction of a consistent theory to explain the natural world and did not deal directly with history or society except in traditional terms. Bantō took what he needed in terms of information from Dutch Studies for his damaging attacks on Buddhism and the myths and popular beliefs of Shintō that he made from a positivistic standpoint. That he made no strong attack on Confucianism in *Daydreams* was probably because it seemed to him that the major propositions of the philosophy did not contradict his own positivistic views, not because he acknowledged the unchallengeable authority of China. When he criticized Chinese doctors for abstruse speculation there is little doubt that he had the whole of the Chinese traditional culture in mind.

Another thing that Bantō gained from western thought was a keen appreciation of the provinciality and insularity of Japan's culture. It was, after all, westerners who had discovered that the world was round and Japan was only one of many countries – facts that were not widely appreciated in Japan. 'The sun is said to rise from the "land of the *fusang* trees [i.e. Japan]" and our "land of the rising sun" derives its name from this ... but how

can there be a place on a round earth from which the sun rises?'
The idea is obviously nonsensical.

When pointing out the closed nature of the Japanese consciousness he is also concerned to warn of the consequences of this: 'We do not have even a general idea of the countries of the world. Would it not be regrettable to go through the world thinking only the ways of Japan and the way things are now to be right and when anything happens abroad in this weird and wonderful world not to understand it but to regard it with fear and wonderment?'

It may have been a desire to shatter the insular nationalism of the Japanese that made Bantō write *Daydreams*. It is a theme that runs through the book and is extended to involve the relativization of all cultures. All religions – Christianity, Islam, Confucianism, Pure Land Buddhism and other sects – he regarded as peculiar to certain areas. 'All of them are prevalent in and peculiar to certain countries. They are similar to the Tenmangū and Inari cults in Japan today.' Similarly, although each country has its own system of law there is no universal or natural law, no 'heavenly reward or heavenly punishment'. 'Fundamentally there is no unvarying law for the world,' he says. It is in this realization of the complete relativity of culture, including that of Japan, that Bantō shows himself a worthy successor of Nakamoto, and there is no doubt that he owed this to his contact with western scientific thought.

Daydreams includes detailed accounts of the western thought that Bantō had encountered through Japanese translations. These though perhaps not original are wide-ranging and accurate and include virtually everything that had been learned by Japanese intellectuals of the late eighteenth century. He explains the heliocentric universe and the western calendar, the movement of the tides and the moon's orbit around the earth (although his version of the connection between the two has it that when the moon approaches the earth it pushes the sea down) and mentions Newton's theories of dynamics. 'The basis of western theories of the movement of the earth and their measurements and observations of the planets and the stars is the theory of attraction and mass.' This is not expressed mathematically, but Bantō consistently attempts to explain astronomical phenomena (he includes lightning) in a scientific way and to refute anthropomorphic explanations. His remark in Volume 1 that 'Lightning kills people but how could it know whether the person is good or bad? Even King Wen, Wu, the Duke of Zhou and Confucius would not survive if they were struck' is one example of this attitude.

The geographical information given in the book is detailed on the topography and customs of the Japanese archipelago and nearby islands and shows a knowledge of the world, particularly Europe. Africa and South America are dismissed as places 'where few people go', but details such as the Cape of Good Hope are mentioned. There are also pointed and detailed references to the colonies of the European powers, of *Horutogaru*, *Hisuhaniya*, *Furansu*, *Engerando* and *Horurando*, and he comments in Volume 2 that 'In this way the countries of Europe are seizing other countries to make them their colonies, installing governors and ruling them.' He describes the 'idea behind this' as 'frightening'. This danger had already been pointed out in Shizuki Tadao's *Bankoku kanki* (A Glimpse of the Countries of the World, completed 1782) and *Daydreams* does little more than echo the warning. But for most intellectuals of the time the threat posed by western imperialism was only dimly perceived. Bantō knew of the 'evil cunning of the red-haired people' through the trade at Nagasaki and his direct perception of colonialism was limited to the 'various plans' that *Musukohia* (i.e. Muscovy) had for Hokkaidō. In medicine he shows a detailed knowledge of human reproduction and mentions such things as identical and non-identical twins, extra-uterine pregnancy and Caesarian section. He also describes in detail measles and smallpox and the various types of vaccination.

One distinctive feature of Bantō's thought was his atheism, which he expounds in the second and eleventh volumes of *Daydreams*. He begins by referring to a Chinese anecdote in which Ruan Zhan won an argument with a visitor who claimed that supernatural beings existed. The guest then changed into a supernatural being and vanished. Ruan Zhan fell ill and died a year later. Bantō's objections to this were that if the guest was truly a ghost then it is odd that he lost the argument over his own existence, that Ruan Zhan's death was too long after the apparition to be attributed directly to it and that it was strange for ghosts to appear in clothes; if ghosts did exist they would be naked. 'As for ghosts who appear in official uniform or ordinary clothes – those clothes should still be in the drawers [where they left them]. How could they get them out and put them on?' Were the clothes themselves ghostly? 'After death many people are cremated. Thus their clothes and their bodies are reduced to ash. How could they then take shape?' Accounts by people who had 'really seen a ghost' are all 'superstitions'.

Bantō advances three main arguments against the existence of all ghosts, goblins, gods and Buddhas. Firstly, 'proof' derived from classical texts is irrelevant. 'The arguments that the Cheng brothers and Zhu Xi advance for the existence of ghosts and spirits all depend on other books and are not soundly based. They quote various books and offer this as evidence but how could this be adequate as proof?' Secondly, even if one insults the gods and Buddhas one does not incur divine punishment. 'Amaterasu has been regarded from the oldest times as taking the form of the sun or a woman; ... however, if one defiles or insults these symbols there comes no divine punishment nor any message from the god that in fact these are not her true image.... If gods really existed would she let this pass? This is proof that gods and spirits do not exist.' Thirdly, the indissoluble connection between the body and the soul means that it is impossible for the soul to exist after the body's death, let alone have miraculous powers. 'The body has five organs, six entrails and many other minor parts. They do not function after death.' How much less then can things of wood and stone, pictures and images have any miraculous powers?

These arguments are consistent with a cosmology based on the functions of *yinyang*. The error of believing in ghosts arises from a misunderstanding of the theory that a human soul is a concentration of Ether which disperses at death. Bantō argues in Volume 10 that 'It is possible to say that existence is to be alive and that non-existence is to be dead.... It is clearer if we speak not of the concentration and dispersion of Ether but of existence and non-existence. When we say that coming and going, contracting and expanding, life and death, day and night are the functions and virtues of the "two Ethers" we mean that they are *yinyang*.' None of these arguments looks to classical texts for support; Bantō had already found these unreliable in astronomy, geography and medicine compared with western writings. They show Bantō applying the positivistic methods he had learned from western thought, but the arguments themselves are not taken from the West. In fact he applies them to subjects which the people of Europe, at least the overwhelming majority of them, would certainly have not. Bantō was a contemporary of the French Encyclopedists but their theories of materialism were as yet completely unknown in Japan.

If there are no gods or spirits then the motives of the priests who proclaim their powers are obvious. They do so 'to deceive the vulgar, to support their own wives and children from them, to make money and make a living'. These bandits, according to Volume 11, use demons and goblins to frighten and mystify the people simply in order to 'grab property and ensnare women.... Since the beginning of Japan's history there has been the superstitious belief in demons. Later came goblins and magic foxes. All of these were popular in a certain age to frighten people and the foolish were taken in by them. How can these "marvels" really exist in the world?' It was not only the foolish but even the wise who discoursed on gods and spirits and were taken in by marvels. It was the opinion of Bantō that 'if we consider this it seems that in all ages an independently minded gentleman is a rare thing.'

If there is no divine authority then the basis for human behaviour must be sought in the secular world. Bantō, in Volume 8, found the framework for his set of moral values in traditional Confucian ethics: 'The classics are teachings on how to control the self and rule the people,... this is the Great Way for humanity and what should one seek other than this?' Although he was himself a merchant he thought that 'peasants are the basis of the country' and that state policies should 'encourage agriculture and discourage commerce and craft'. 'Every lord should use frugality alone.' These views are conservative and close to being a regression from the opinions of Ishida Baigan. The only part of *Daydreams* that clearly reflects the author's commercial background is a passage in Volume 6 which argues that the government should stop intervening and allow the market mechanism to settle the price of rice.

In the afterword of this magnum opus Bantō included the following poem:

> No hell no heaven no self
> The only things that are
> Are man and the universe.

We also find:

> In this world where there are no gods Buddhas or monsters
> Still less is there anything strange and marvellous.

These form a perfect summary of the whole work. Neither, however, was there anything strange and marvellous in the social order. 'Lords, retainers, fathers, sons. What can you want other than this?' He had found success within the social order; no 'black ships' had come to threaten the order from outside; there was as yet no hint that the Tokugawa regime would ever end.

MOTOORI NORINAGA AND NATIONAL LEARNING

The epoch-making achievement of Motoori Norinaga (1730–1801) was to raise to the level of intellectually sophisticated thought an indigenous world-view free from Confucianism and Buddhism, within a culture deeply influenced by both of these. Using Hegelian terms we can say that in Norinaga's thought the indigenous world-view became for the first time 'for itself' rather than 'of itself'. He expressed his thought in his original form of scholarship (known as *kokugaku* or National Learning), in polemic writings and in the sayings recorded by his pupils. His studies of ancient Japan were wholly unlike previous attempts to impose an artificial and unnatural system onto ancient myths, indigenous beliefs and rituals using the conceptual tools of Buddhism or Confucianism; rather they took the form of a rigorous historico-linguistic examination of ancient texts (the *Kojiki* in particular) and profound insights into the heart of the culture peculiar to the Japanese masses.

Before Norinaga, in the early part of the eighteenth century, Arai Hakuseki had attempted to describe Japanese history objectively, using textual criticism, and Kamono Mabuchi had attempted to explicate the *Manyōshū*, relying on studies of ancient Japanese. It was a desire to bring the studies of the latter to bear on the *Kojiki* that decided the particular direction of Norinaga's scholarship. Ogyū Sorai had already employed positivistic historico-linguistic methods in interpreting classical Confucian texts, and Tominaga Nakamoto, perhaps influenced by Sorai, had provided a critical account of the various Buddhist and Confucianist doctrines within a framework of the historical development of thought. It is certain that Norinaga had a high opinion of their methods. Thus both the areas of scholarly study explored in the early eighteenth century (ancient languages and ancient history) and the new methods (a positivistic approach) were continued in the latter part of the century by Norinaga and, in a sense, brought to fruition.

Hakuseki had provided an account of ancient history but not of ancient thought, and Mabuchi's studies, which were mainly linguistic, only touched upon one limited aspect of thought. Sorai and Nakamoto were historians of ideas but directed their attention to the histories of Confucianism and Buddhism, scarcely discussing indigenous thought. Norinaga was the first figure to attempt to clarify ancient Japanese thought in a scholarly way and that he did so was not simply due to the intellectual legacy he had inherited. His scholarly work consisted of a linguistic interpretation of the *Kojiki*, which he believed (in a religious sense) to be literally true. His studies no doubt strengthened his faith, and more particularly, his faith must have given support to his studies. However his faith was not a theoretically inevitable conclusion from his studies. At least there is nothing in his positivistic studies of the *Kojiki* to lead him to the conclusion that 'When they are recorded in writing, things that existed long ago are clearly seen.' (Indeed, Hakuseki had already pointed out from a comparison with Chinese texts that the *Kojiki* did not reflect what actually happened.)

How then was Norinaga led to this belief? In *Genji monogatari, tama no ogushi* (The Tale of Genji: The Precious Comb) he writes that if one 'searches thoroughly through the depths of the true hearts of people' there are many 'things which are feminine and trivial' and that many of the things which are 'masculine and intellectually clever' are merely 'an outward show on the surface'. By 'masculine and intellectually clever' is meant Confucianist values, which are on the surface of the consciousness, whereas at a deeper level – 'in the depths of the heart' – things are quite different. This deeper level, unaffected by Buddhism and Confucianism, can be regarded as similar to the hearts and minds of people of ancient times, before the advent of the two faiths. Norinaga gazed into the depths of his own heart and of those of the people around him and subsequently discovered the same characteristics in the *Kojiki*. It was this that caused him to believe in the literal truth of its history. His insights into the human heart were not a consequence of his studies of ancient history. The characteristics of the indigenous mentality – what he called the 'Japanese heart' or *Yamatogokoro* – were evident in ancient texts and also in the 'depths of the heart' of himself and each person with whom he came into contact. This belief, and accordingly the originality of his thought, sprang from the deeper levels of consciousness which he, as a provincial doctor, shared with the mass of his contemporaries. In this he was quite unlike previous scholars.

Norinaga was born the second son of a merchant family in Matsuzaka in the province of Ise (present-day Mie Prefecture). Although earlier generations had been *samurai*, the family had declined and was apparently poor during Norinaga's early years. It is apparent from the reminiscences *Ie no mukashi monogatari* (The Tale of My Family's Ancient Past, 1798), which he wrote in his last years, that he was always conscious of these ancestors. He refers to merchants as 'an ignoble people', and to his own becoming a doctor as 'getting away from the ranks of the business people'; being 'known to the people of the world' by his scholarship and writings was the 'great honour' of his life. He began medicine and his other studies at an early age. At first he was adopted into a merchant family, but he terminated this arrangement after two years and went home, soon afterwards moving to Kyōto to study medicine. He was in Kyōto for five years, between the ages of twenty-two and twenty-seven (1752–57) and it was during this period – exactly when is not known – that he wrote his first major work, *Ashiwake obune* (Small Boat Parting the Reeds), in which he developed his original theories of poetry. After this and until 1792 when he took service with the domain of Kii (present-day Wakayama Prefecture) with a five-man stipend, Norinaga practised as a doctor in the small town of Matsuzaka. His medical techniques were based on Chinese medicine, unaffected by Dutch medical theories, and he specialized in paediatrics.

It would have been a professional necessity for him, in his contact with a wide range of patients and their families outside *samurai* society, to become familiar with their customs, feelings and thoughts and to achieve an insight into 'the depths of their hearts'. Moreover although Norinaga regarded the merchants as an 'ignoble people' he was fond of the *chōnin* society of Matsuzaka. He liked bustling crowded places rather than peaceful mountains and forests ('only crowded, lively places are pleasant for me', he writes) and he loved the customs and manners of his home town, which resembled those of the capital ('it is good that both men and women have no rusticity'). When he discussed the hearts and minds of the people of Matsuzaka he must have done so with a certainty based on long experience: 'Peoples' hearts are not good, but proud and with little sincerity.' Norinaga intellectually objectified this experience, concentrating not on the Buddhistic 'further shore' but on the sublunary world-view of the Japanese and investigating not the Confucianist contradiction between notions of good and evil but the harmony of the indigenous cultural tradition.

The temple to which the Motoori family belonged was of the Pure Land faith and Norinaga's father and mother were devout believers, as he himself seems to have been in his early years. It was because of this deep connection with Buddhism, not despite it, that there is an emphasis in his work on the need to sweep Buddhism aside – this may have been a form of resistance to his parents. On the other hand, the language in which the majority of his contemporary thinkers expressed themselves relied heavily on Confucian terminology, particularly that of Neo-Confucianism, and this had strong connections with *samurai* society. (The overwhelming majority of the Bakufu and domain schools in the early eighteenth century did not admit *chōnin*, and even in the latter part of the century the majority of the pupils were *samurai*.) Norinaga, being a *chōnin*, studied Confucianism at a private school. Therefore undoubtedly he would have been unable to identify himself as a scholar with Confucianism, the ideology of *samurai* society. This perhaps is one reason that his thought as a whole appears completely antithetical to Confucianism and that his consistently violent attacks on Confucianism have about them the tone of inflammatory polemic.

When Norinaga criticized Buddhism and Confucianism this was not merely an *ad hominem* attack on their followers but rather a way of purging those elements of Buddhist and Confucian thought still within him, in order to establish his own identity, and this meant that his attacks were inevitably persistent and aggressive.

However, although Norinaga could not identify with *samurai* society neither could he identify with the society of the merchants, those 'ignoble people'. This second son of an ex-*samurai* family, neither *samurai* nor *chōnin*, had no choice but to define himself as a Japanese. Probably Norinaga's nationalism (or 'Japanism') sprang from this. Norinaga is not the only person whose inability to become integrated with an existing group (*samurai* or *chōnin*) has led him to identify ideologically with a higher and abstract group (the Japanese nation) and at the same time to form his own smaller group and to emphasize the experience and feelings of fellowship. His extreme nationalism and the nonsense that he wrote with unwavering persistence from this standpoint were not the result of his scholarly studies but derived from a psychological need. He began lecturing in Matsuzaka, gathered people with similar interests around him, took pupils and formed a group, not only because there was a demand for this on the part of the pupils but also because it was inevitable that he should do so.

Norinaga was by no means the first *chōnin* scholar. Before him there had been such figures as Tominaga Nakamoto, who died young, Itō Jinsai and Ishida Baigan. Itō Jinsai had maintained his position in the field of Confucianism, the province of *samurai* society, through acquiring and deploying overwhelming learning; Baigan had become a popular *chōnin* teacher by translating the Confucianism of *samurai* society into the language of the merchants.. Norinaga, it can be said, found a third solution, to sweep away the ideology of the *samurai* and establish his own National Learning.

Norinaga began to practise as a paediatrician in Matsuzaka in 1757, divorced his first wife in 1760, remarried in 1762 and became the father of two sons and three daughters (both of his sons, Haruniwa and Harumura, followed in their father's footsteps and became scholars); he seldom travelled and lived in his home town dividing his time between medicine and scholarship. His *chef d'oeuvre* is *Kojiki-den* (The Story of the *Kojiki*, forty-four volumes, written between 1764 and 1798). Its first volume contains the general argument, discusses the making of the *Kojiki*, its various editions and their language, and gives a summary of the 'Way of Truth' that he had derived from his reading of the history. The final section of this volume is *Naobi no mitama* (The Spirit of Purity, completed around 1771). The second volume consists of a commentary on the preface of the *Kojiki*, and the other volumes provide commentaries on the main text. The fruits of Norinaga's thirty years of linguistic research are concentrated in these last forty-two volumes. This work is not only epoch-making in being the first detailed study of the *Kojiki* but also original in its use of the positivistic method of making a comparative examination of all the usages of each word. It is an enduring achievement, still the point of departure for any commentary on the *Kojiki*.

One of its important subjects, for instance, is the *kami* ('god', 'superior being'), and Norinaga examines in Volume 3 what this word meant in the system of indigenous beliefs before the arrival of the strong continental influence: 'In the first place *kami* meant the various gods of heaven and earth found in the ancient writings; these spirits when enshrined in shrines that celebrate them and also not only people but such things as birds, beasts, trees and plants, oceans and mountains – anything that is out of the ordinary and outstanding, anything that inspires wonder, is called a *kami*.'

This interpretation is in agreement with what Arai Hakuseki had pointed out a hundred years before in *Koshitsū* (Knowing Ancient History): 'A *kami* is a person. Generally in the customs of this country *kami* is used to denote a person held in reverence. The word is the same now as of old.' However, the interpretation in *The Story of the Kojiki* is wider than Hakuseki's. Norinaga divides *kami* into three types: the gods of heaven and earth mentioned in such works as the *Kojiki*, human beings, and natural things other than humanity. No modern discussion of the meaning of the word *kami* essentially goes beyond these. What later scholarship has added is background in terms of etymology, comparative religion and ethnology.

Norinaga's works other than *The Story of the Kojiki* cover six fields. First, there are linguistic works such as *Kotoba no tama no o* (The Precious Thread of Language, 1779) which is a detailed discussion of the particles and conjunctions of Japanese in comparison with their equivalents in Chinese. He puts forward the view that the Japanese form of particle is a characteristic of the language. Even in linguistics, however, once his nationalistic ideology intervenes he falls into self-contradiction. For instance, he says that he will not write on the phonology of languages other than Chinese as he does not know them, and, later, that spoken Japanese is laudably precise and the finest in the world.

Second, there are his philosophical theories, summed up in the section 'The Spirit of Purity' in *The Story of the Kojiki* and also in *Tamakushige* (The Precious Comb, 1787) in the magnum opus of his later years, *Tamakatsuma* (The Precious Basket, begun 1793, published 1795–1811), and to some degree in *Suzunoya tōmonroku* (Suzunoya Dialogues, 1801). In *Uiyamabumi* (Uiyama Writings, 1798) he concentrates on expounding his scholarly methodology and his world-view.

Third, there are his works on aesthetics, including *Ashiwaki obune*, which is mainly about *waka*, *Isonokami no sasamegoto* (Isonokami Whispers, 1763), and his commentary *The Tale of Genji: The Precious Comb* (1793–96). This last contains Norinaga's well-known theory of *mono no aware*, 'the aesthetic empathy of things and feelings'. Fourth, there are his polemic works of nationalistic ideology, the most representative being *Karaosame no uretamigoto* (Resentful Words on Restraining the Chinese Barbarians, 1778) and *Kuzuhana* (Kuzu Flower, 1780). In the main he directed his criticism at Confucianism and Confucianists but he also had a lively exchange with Ueda Akinari, the student of National Learning. Fifth, Norinaga wrote on contemporary social and political problems in *Hihon tama no kushige* (The Precious Comb-case: The Secret Volume, 1787, published 1851), a work of detailed arguments which he presented to the lord of Kii and Ise provinces, Tokugawa Harusada, at a time when the area was troubled by famine, peasant risings and the fiscal difficulties of the domain government. Sixth, Norinaga produced personal writings as well, including his reminiscences *The Tale of My family's Ancient Past* and *Yuigonsho* (Last Testament), written about a year before his death. The former of these is important as biographical material, the latter curious in that it requests a Buddhist funeral and a Shintō grave.

Central to Norinaga's philosophy is 'the human heart as it really is' (as he puts it in his commentary on *The Tale of Genji*), the natural state of humanity. People are born able to do anything. In 'The Spirit of Purity' he says that 'Just as they are born they know spontaneously and can do well everything that it is in them to do'. Both good and evil are contained in this capacity just as the gods perform both good and evil: 'There are both good and evil gods and their actions accord to this.' The relationship between humanity and the gods is continuous; the gods (especially Musubi-no-kami) not only control natural phenomena ('the changes of the seasons, such things as the falling of the rain and the blowing of the wind') but also social phenomena ('all the myriad things, good and evil, of the country and the people ... each and every one of these is the work of a god'). There is a certain order to this world created by humanity and the gods, an order to which he gives a name taken from Confucianism, 'the Way'. It is, or should be, possible to find this natural state in Japan as it was before extensive contact with China; 'the human heart as it really is' can thus be equated with the 'Japanese heart'.

In order to precisely identify this 'Japanese heart' it is necessary to sweep away the 'Chinese heart' and attempt, through philological investigation, to restore conditions as they previously were. The *Kojiki* is the work that best transmits the ancient age of Japan, and according to Norinaga it is 'the greatest among all existing historical works'. This means that understanding the *Kojiki* is the ultimate aim of scholarship. As we have said, Norinaga's methods were a continuation of Sorai's lexicography of ancient texts. As Norinaga himself put it 'heart, fact and word are all things that are equivalent to each other.' In order to know the 'heart' of the ancient times, (the 'Japanese heart') and the 'facts', it is necessary to study the 'words'. Therefore Norinaga approached the language in its entirety – in poetry, invocations and prayers, and imperial edicts – attempting to read the Japanized Chinese in the form which he considered closest to ancient Japanese. Accordingly he divides the *Kojiki* into parts 'written in *kana*', parts 'written like imperial edicts', parts 'written in Chinese but like ancient Japanese' and those 'written in Chinese and unlike ancient Japanese'. He also examines, in addition to vocabulary, the continuation and connections of the style, pronunciation of consonants, accents and intonations and the Japanese readings of the Chinese particles. This was the most positivistic philological study of the entire Tokugawa era.

A positivistic approach was not the only technique Norinaga brought to philology. It was essential to use imagination and intuition to discover what were the 'true feelings' of the people of old. And it was his own intellect and emotions, already purged of the 'Chinese heart' and close to the 'Japanese heart' that guided his imagination and made his intuition accurate. In order to reach this state it was necessary to become familiar with the Japanese classics and to read, and write, *waka*: 'Unless you compose *waka* it is impossible to know the beautiful heart of ancient Japan or the essence of elegance.' This is because *waka* are direct expressions of the feelings and thus are expressions of *mono no aware*. The same thing can be said of the 'tales' written during the Heian period, and these too 'show *mono no aware*'. An evaluation of tales and poetry purely in terms of how well they express 'true feeling', 'the human heart' and *mono no aware* is of course independent of political or moral values: 'The basic nature of poetry is not to assist in governing nor to govern oneself, but simply and only to express the things felt by the heart.' Also: 'In a tale it is good when the goodness or badness of the workings of a person's heart ... shows *mono no aware*, is sympathetic and accords to the feelings of people in the world.' Further the question of 'whether it accords or not with people's feelings' is 'very often not the same as Confucian and Buddhist notions of what is good and evil'.

This respect for 'the real feelings of people' expressed itself in political conservatism and advocacy of tolerant policies. *The Precious Comb-case: The Secret Volume* has it that 'all things in the world, whatever they may be, good or bad, depend on the trend of the times.' Since 'it is beyond human power' to change this trend one should 'without ignoring the state of the age follow the forms as handed down from former occasions', and 'in most cases there is no harm in following the old ways'. The implementation of new laws on the basis of theoretical logic, being the mode of the Confucianists, must be rejected. Rather 'it is a good thing in accordance with the ancient and generous thought of Japan' to 'leave a law as law', even when it does not suit the age, and to devise some appropriate way of applying it. On the other hand the 'trends of the time', being above Confucianist notions of good and evil, are impossible to change by armed force or deal with by laws and punishments. 'It is good that punishments should be lenient and light' and even in the case of a peasant rising 'it is vital to avoid circumstances which lead these to occur.' The reason for peasant risings is of course the poverty of the peasants. To deal with this Norinaga proposed that taxes should be lessened and that the peasants should refrain from any luxury above their station, a policy of no special originality. However he did point out the 'rapidity with which the poor are getting poorer and the rich richer' and the passage in which he says that it would be a 'benevolent policy' to use the money of the wealthy to succour the poor shows the particular way in which his sensitivity reacted to the 'pattern of the age'. He did not, however, ask the government to use force to obtain the money of the rich but merely to be as generous as was possible to the peasants within the framework of existing laws.

It is fundamentally difficult to demonstrate moral norms while still showing respect for things 'as they are', and Norinaga's thought is indeed lacking on this point. He recommended in *Uiyama Writing* no more than to 'follow the rules of the government of the time', 'to behave as your parents behaved in former days' and to act 'no different from the custom of the world'. This has much to do with the fact that the 'essence of the Way back to ancient times' on which Norinaga sought to depend was incapable of achieving normative consciousness equal in intellectual sophistication to that of Buddhism or Confucianism. In this, too, Norinaga's understanding of the 'Japanese heart' was correct.

There is only one place in which the human heart 'as it really exists' and the 'trend of the times' can manifest themselves and operate – the sublunary world. The gods intervene in this world but their will is incalculable. Thus Norinaga's world is the reality of the everyday world, the world as we experience it beyond the 'wisdom of one man' to grasp and beyond 'human power' to change. For one living in this world no other world exists. 'The people of this world high and low, good and bad, each and every one, go inevitably to the Lower World when they die, a very sad thing indeed.' We do not know what this 'Lower World' is and therefore in the end 'it is impossible to know what happens after death.' Thus in his *Last Testament* Norinaga makes no mention of his own death or the world after death while including considerable detail about the funeral and the gravestone. Norinaga's concern was with this world and its happenings even if he himself should have died. This thorough secularism and almost technological practicality is in marked contrast to the Buddhist concepts of the dual universe ('this shore' and the 'further shore') and the rationalism of the Neo-Confucianists.

Norinaga perceived the basic form of the pre-Buddhist, pre-Confucianist indigenous world-view in the *Kojiki* and, with this, gave a new meaning to the Japanese cultural legacy – literary values on the aesthetic levels, conservative tolerance in the field of government. Or to put it another way he offered proof of the continuity of the indigenous world-view which had remained alive 'in the depths of the true heart' despite Buddhism and Confucianism, until the time of Norinaga. Such an original interpretation of historical culture was given direction by this Matsuzaka doctor's profound insight into the hearts of the merchant or peasant housewives who came to visit him, and was confirmed in the depths of his own heart. What Norinaga perceived there was the sensibility of the Japanese masses, the antiquity which still lived on.

If one examines the depths of the true human heart there is much that is feminine and unstable; the masculine and clever things are added, when we have become conscious of ourselves, in order to keep up appearances. When we are doing such things as talk to other people we act more and more so as to show a surface which is arranged to impress rather than bringing out what is really there.

This, from *The Tale of Genji: The Precious Comb*, is probably the keenest socio-psychological insight of the entire Tokugawa period and the first writing to point clearly to the connections between the Japanese 'surface' and 'depths', the expressed and true feelings, conscious values and unconscious psychological tendencies and foreign ideologies and the traditional world-view. It is here that his thought is at its most profound and accurate and most capable of transcending the age in which he lived.

But his successors in National Learning inherited, apart from the technical aspects of philological methodology, two of Norinaga's weakpoints. One was a confusion between myth and history (and this led to the rendering of the Emperor into a mysterious and unapproachable figure). The other was the confusion between the particularity of different cultures and the universality of ideas (and this led to a nationalism notable for its inconsistency of thought). The second of these appeared clearly in the written debate he had with his contemporary, the National Learning scholar Ueda Akinari.

UEDA AKINARI

During the latter part of the eighteenth century the number of followers of Motoori Norinaga rose to about five hundred, most of these being *chōnin*, peasants and Shintō priests, with only one in seven being a *samurai*. In the first part of the nineteenth century Hirata Atsutane (1776–1843), a self-professed continuator of Norinaga's thought, had five hundred pupils, one third of whom were *samurai*. In that it developed within the merchant classes and then gradually spread throughout the *samurai* class National Learning resembled *Shingaku* which Ishida Baigan first spread among the merchants and which only attracted *samurai* support at the time of his successor, Tejima Toan. The same trend is shown in the adoption by the *samurai* Sakai Hōitsu (1761–1828) of the painting style developed a century earlier by Ogata Kōrin. One of the most interesting social changes of the eighteenth century was the reversal of the flow of culture from 'above' (the *samurai*) to 'below' (the *chōnin*). The flow came to be from below to above.

However, National Learning was substantially a transfer of the humanistic learning already defined by *samurai* Confucianism to the study of the Japanese classics. Confucianists annotated and commented upon the Chinese classics, wrote verse and prose in classical Chinese and subscribed, to a greater or lesser extent, to Confucian ideology. The National Learning scholars annotated and commented on the Japanese classics (*Kojiki*, *Manyōshū*, *Kokinshū* and *Ise monogatari* and *The Tale of Genji* in particular), wrote verse in Japanese and adopted various Shintoist positions, according to their own interpretation of Shintō. Some involved the sweeping away of Buddhism and Confucianism, the deification of the Emperor and 'Japanism'; others, while relativizing Confucianism and Buddhism, emphasized a kind of practicality divorced from any ideology. There were also variations in the stress that various thinkers put on each of the activities that they all shared – the study of classical language and literature, the writing of verse and other artistic pursuits and the assertion of Shintoist ideology. For instance, the early nineteenth-century figure Kagawa Kageki (1768–1843) was primarily a classical scholar and poet while Hirata Atsutane was a classicist and a Shintō ideologue.

Of the scholars of National Learning of the latter part of the eighteenth century, two – Motoori Norinaga and Ueda Akinari (1734–1809) – are notable for being markedly different on almost every point. Norinaga was born a *chōnin* but his family had in earlier generations been *samurai*. Akinari never knew his father and talked little about his mother (who, according to some sources, was employed in the Sonezaki licensed quarter); he was adopted and brought up by the Ōsaka merchant family of Ueda. Norinaga was a successful doctor, gathered a number of pupils as a teacher of National Learning and formed a school (known as the Suzunoya school). Akinari only worked for thirteen years as a doctor, lived in relative poverty and was an isolated figure in the world of National Learning, never surrounded by disciples.

Norinaga did not think of the myths recorded in the histories *Kojiki* and *Nihon shoki* as just one set among the many myths of many countries. He regarded them as the single truth. In his work *Kakaika* he says, 'Although in each country there are tales of the earliest antiquity, foreign traditions are not correct ... moreover the traditional stories of our imperial land are different in kind from those of foreign countries, being the accurate account of the truth. They are things which the people of all countries, not only this one, should believe.' Amaterasu is the sun, which shines on every country. Therefore Japan, the country of Amaterasu is 'the imperial country', the land which is

'the ultimate centre of faith for all the countries of the four seas'.
Indeed, that Japan is 'superior and worthy of reverence' is plain
to see; there are for instance 'the unbroken succession of the
imperial line' and the 'beauty of the crops', it has 'never been
ravaged by foreign countries' and 'the population being dense,
it is wealthy, prosperous and flourishing'. So for a scholar it is
'essential to hold firmly to the Japanese spirit'.

On his portrait Norinaga wrote the following well-known
poem:

> If someone asks
> What is the heart of Yamato:
> Shining in the morning sun,
> Blossom of the mountain cherry.

Akinari recognized that other countries had their own myths
and he thought it impossible to transfer Japanese myths to
them: 'Each one of the writings has a separate account of the
creation of the universe for each country ... and even if one
transfers them to other countries they would not be accepted,
being self-regarding accounts.' This is all the more so when
Japan, as seen on the Dutch maps of the world, is no more than
'a small island, like a tiny leaf which has fallen onto a vast lake'.
It would be difficult to persuade other countries that this was
the country from which came the sun and moon, with whose
light they were all blessed. Akinari notes in his *Tandai shōshinroku* that it was only 'old' tales that give the sun and moon human
forms; in fact 'seen through the telescope they call a *zongarasu*
the sun, which flames, and the moon, which boils, are nothing
of the sort'. He dismisses Norinaga's theories as 'the talk of a
sheltered rustic' and 'the cant of an indigent priest'. 'The
"Japanese spirit" is something without meaning. In any country
the "spirit" of that country is its stench.' He adds a verse:

> Again all that mumbo-jumbo
> About the heart of Yamato
> And cherry-blossom.

Norinaga's verse was popular in the militarist Japan of the
nineteen-thirties and forties and remains well-known today,
while few people are familiar with Akinari's poem. The reason

for this is that there is little chance of such trenchant criticism of nationalism as 'In any country the "spirit" of that country is its stench' being highly valued in this homogeneous society. Norinaga's originality lay in his bringing to the popular consciousness a sense of values which previously had been shared unconsciously. The originality of Akinari's keen observations lay in their denial of the overt 'common wisdom' of the society. The difference in attitude probably derived from the fact that while one sought to identify himself with society the other sought to and indeed could not help but, live a life of alienation.

Akinari's major work of his late years, *Tandai shōshinroku* (written 1808, unpublished in his lifetime) is a collection of fragmentary pieces on people and history mixed with his own views and opinions and personal recollections. Akinari's views on people, including of course Norinaga, are often harsh. He terms Bashō a 'fake' and Sorai's scholarship 'the quick calculations of a terminal age'. Of Katō Chikage (1735–1808), then called the greatest poet of the age, he writes, 'his verse is poor, he is illiterate'. On painting he comments, 'the members of the Kanō school are all incompetent', and about Chinese verse he says, 'the poets' students keep on gushing but there is nothing of worth'. In his historical research he did not take the myths as literal fact but attempted to estimate what people of later ages may have added. 'The tales of the age of the gods in Japan are things which have been invented and added to and should not be handed on.' He also thought that the sixteen arhats (enlightened ones) of Buddhist lore and Confucius's ten greatest disciples were all made up by 'manipulators'. Looking back on his life he writes that when he was a doctor in Ōsaka he consistently avoided becoming a flatterer, and that when he gave up medicine he began a life of dispassionate poverty, earning his living even after the age of seventy from 'things which the publishers ask me to do' (editing *Ochitsubo monogatari* and *Yamato monogatari*). He adds at the end, 'Since there is nothing I can do, I'll just drink my tea and wait for death.' There are few examples of such keen and cutting self-irony. To be ironical about oneself does not necessarily mean that one lacks self-confidence. This next passage castigates commercially minded scholars and poets: 'Confucianists and poets are all businessmen. In the end they won't be able to enter a life of tranquility as I have. Pitiful people.'

Running through *Tandai shōshinroku* are an anti-authoritarian attitude, a pitilessly trenchant critical spirit and the will to live his own life whatever the price. Because of these the work shines out from the rest of Tokugawa literature.

Norinaga went on relentlessly composing incompetent verse; Akinari produced two collections of excellent short stories, *Ugetsu monogatari* (Tales of the Rain and Moon, completed 1768, published 1776), and *Harusame monogatari* (Tales of Spring Rain, posthumous). Each of these contains nine short stories. The first collection is mainly adaptations from two Chinese collections, *Jiandeng xinhua* (New Tales Under Lamplight, written in literary Chinese), and *Jingshu tongyin* (Tales to Warn the World, written in colloquial Chinese). The later collection takes its material from a wide range of Japanese sources. *Tales of the Rain and Moon* is written in a Sinicized style with an admixture of the Japanese style of the Heian tales, while the later collection is in a more colloquial Japanese.

All the stories in *Tales of the Rain and Moon* are of the abnormal and supernatural. The heroes meet ghosts of historical personages, as in *Shiramine* (White Peak) and *Buppōsō*, or the ghost of one of the characters appears to another, as in *Kikka no chigiri* (The Chrysanthemum Pledge), *Asaji ga yado* (The Inn at Asaji), *Kibitsu no kama* (The Cauldron of Kibitsu) and *Aozukin* (The Blue Hood). All of these events involve communication between the dead and the world of the living. The other three stories are also not only about the people of this world; in *Muō no rigyo* (The Carp That Made Dreams Come True) characters turn into fish, in *Jasei no in* (As Lascivious as a Snake) snakes turn into people and in *Hinpukuron* (Rich and Poor) the spirit of gold appears.

In 'The Chrysanthemum Pledge' a man unable to go to his friend's house because he has been imprisoned kills himself so that his ghost can escape and fulfil the pledge. His friend now waiting with fading hopes as the day of the pledge draws to its close goes outside to see if he is coming but there is no one approaching: 'the moon had been darkened by the crest of a hill and thinking it too late he made to go in and close the door when he suddenly saw something. There was a figure in a dark shadow and as he looked in amazement it approached as if floating on the wind'. It was his friend. 'I am delighted that you have been able to come as you promised,' he says and shows him in. The man 'merely nodded and did not say anything'. There is an unusual power and life in these few lines of description.

'The Cauldron of Kibitsu' is the story of a man who leaves his wife to run off with a prostitute. The wife dies and her spirit possesses the prostitute who herself dies. Later the man meets a beautiful woman, in fact the ghost of his wife, who says she will get her revenge on him. The man visits a soothsayer and follows his instructions to seal his door with talismans until forty-nine days since his wife's death have passed. The ghost of the dead woman circles the house every night uttering hideous screams of anger. Towards dawn on the forty-ninth night the man speaks through the wall to his neighbour who has been watching over him, and deciding that it must now be safe goes out. His neighbour hears a scream from the neighbouring house, and 'snatching up an axe he went out onto the main road. The night which he had said had ended was still dark, although the moon was high partially dispelling the shadows, and the wind was cold.' The door of the house is open but there is no sign of the man. Thinking he may have fled inside he enters, but it is not the sort of place where anyone could hide.

> Wondering what had happened he felt suspicious and then afraid. When he lighted a torch and looked around here and there, the light revealed fresh blood by the door, trickling down to the ground. However no body or bones could be seen. When he looked by the light of the moon he saw something under the eave. He lifted up the torch and it illuminated only a man's topknot. There was nothing else at all.

This one passage is perhaps all it takes to show the descriptive powers of the author of *Tales of the Rain and Moon*.

Why was Akinari so skilful in his descriptions of ghosts, supernatural animals and weird manifestations? The most probable reason is that he himself believed in them: 'There are obvious cases of people being possessed by foxes and raccoon dogs and it is the heaven-given nature of foxes or whatever to be superior to humans,' he says in *Tandai shōshinroku*. The Confucianist of the Osaka *chōnin* school Kaitoku-dō, Nakai Riken, responded to Akinari's telling of ghost stories with the words 'there's no such thing as possession by foxes or ghosts'. This, according to Akinari, merely showed that he, being secluded within the school and concerned only with Confucian theory, knew little of the world outside: 'He is immersed in the obscurities of the Way and finds this impossible to understand.' Akinari believed that ghosts and possession by foxes were facts, things that were experienced in the world at large. When a ghost appears in *Tales of the Rain and Moon* it is for him not fantastic and impossible but something that exists in the real world, a characteristic which produces a kind of chilling weirdness.

Akinari believed the gods of Shintō to be real in the same way as foxes and racoon-dogs. It was possible for men to become Buddhas or (Confucian) sages through religious diligence and austerity. Therefore such things as human goodness and evil, right and wrong were appropriate in the world of religion and philosophy. However, '[Shintō] gods are gods, not something that humans can become through training.' Therefore consideration of goodness and evil is not appropriate. 'They help those who are kind to them and afflict those who hurt them.' Akinari is here opposing the normative qualities of Buddhism and Confucianism with the non-normative nature of the indigenous system of beliefs. Borrowing Norinaga's term for the non-normative character of the indigenous beliefs, this is 'the Japanese heart as it really is'. Norinaga's rejection of the 'Chinese spirit' which makes rigorous distinctions between good and evil is not essentially different from Akinari's attitude here. Even in the stories in *Tales of the Rain and Moon*, where the plots are taken from Chinese sources, the power of description which is their original element is connected with the basic indigenous world-view that Akinari had perceived.

Tales of Spring Rain contains nine short stories and a short treatise on poetry, *Uta no homare* (In Praise of Poetry), which is concerned with the *Manyōshū*. *Mehitotsu no kami* (The One-eyed God), in which a *kami*, a mountain priest and a Buddhist priest perform wonders, is the only one of the stories that deals with supernatural phenomena. The others are concerned with the world of men and women. Three of them – *Chikatabira* (The Bloody Robe), *Amatsu otome* (The Amatsu Maid) and *Kaizoku* (Pirate) – feature people from history; the other five are based on popular tales and true stories: *Nise no en* (The Marriage Bond), *Shinikubi no egao* (The Smile on the Face of the Corpse), *Suteishimaru*, *Miyagi ga tsuka* (The Grave of Miyagi) and *Hankai*. The characters of the people who appear in these stories show a range and development not seen in any fiction of the Tokugawa period since Saikaku. For instance, there is the hero of *The Bloody Robe*, Emperor Heizei, constantly unable to decide among the opinions offered by those around him, and the opportunist Henshō of *The Amatsu Maid* who draws close to the centre of power without disclosing his political views. When the holder of power to whom he has become so close dies and conditions in the court are against him, he vanishes to become a priest, reappearing when things are more favourable, to get himself elevated to abbot. There is also the eponymous hero of 'Hankai', a thief who roams Japan alone, a powerful man of no ambition, careless of money and seeking no followers. These are not the usual types of characters to appear in Japanese fiction. In the case of Hankai, if we replace physical with intellectual power and lack of concern for finding followers with lack of concern for finding pupils, we have a character not unlike Akinari himself. And again the opportunism of Henshō of 'The Amatsu Maid' is the same as that which Akinari hated and despised in many contemporary poets and scholars. The characters of these stories are given life and clearly delineated by the sympathy or dislike that the author feels for them.

Akinari's views on Buddhism and Confucianism are also evident from *Tales of Spring Rain*. The words spoken by one of the characters in 'The Bloody Robe' without doubt reflect the views of the author: 'When the teachings of Confucianism first came to Japan it was expected that our faults would be corrected by this intellectually clever doctrine. But the only result has been a tendency to make pettifogging arguments. Although the Confucianists flourish age by age the world does not become better.' His view of the cleverness and pettifogging arguments of Confucianism is the same as that of Norinaga but Akinari does not think Confucianism is bad enough to be swept away entirely. He is harsher on the subject of Buddhism even than Norinaga. In 'The Marriage Bond' a priest is dug from his grave when he is heard ringing a bell as part of his Buddhist devotions. His faith was strong enough for him to continue this form of devotion even after he had been buried, but he is now without memory, revelation or hope. In short: 'the Teachings of Buddha are nothing more than nonsense'. In the same village there is an old woman of eighty on her death-bed whose son says to her: 'I entreat you to pray to the Buddha that he might allow you to end your life in peace.' She bursts out to the doctor in attendance, 'Listen to that; what an idiot! I don't even want to pray to be born again well!' and goes on to say that if she does go to the Way of Beasts and becomes a cow or a horse this will not displease her as human life is by no means all enjoyment and it will make no great difference. Meanwhile the man rescued from the grave 'continues with his bitter life, running around no less than any horse or ox'. This story mocks and caricatures the heaven and hell of popular Buddhism.

The concern of the author of *Tales of Spring Rain* was focused on the sublunary world, without any Buddhistic 'further shore' and on the variety of human character and behaviour, not simply according to the moral norms of Confucianism but of human society as it was. That it did focus on these things shows that Akinari too was conscious of the 'Japanese heart' which had lived on since before the influence of Buddhism and Confucianism and which Norinaga had made articulate and given a theoretical framework to. The scope of his concern, which extended beyond everyday experience to history, was due perhaps to his learning in both Japanese and Chinese.

Thus Akinari's two collections of short stories form a complementary pair. *Tales of the Rain and Moon* describes how the spirits of the dead can move between 'this world and the world beyond' and how they involve themselves with the living. *Tales of Spring Rain* describes the behaviour of people in this world and relationships between the living.

In both cases the works are underpinned by the critical spirit which this solitary scholar had taken as far as was possible within the framework of a sublunary, down-to-earth 'Japanese' world-view.

Tales of Spring Rain was not published until the twentieth century and so had no influence on contemporary writers. *Tales of the Rain and Moon* became an influential example of successful adaptation of Chinese fiction some years later, when Santō Kyōden and Takizawa Bakin were writing their own adaptations, the *yomihon*.

KABUKI AND PICTURES OF THE 'FLOATING WORLD'

Kabuki had developed from the beginning of the eighteenth century maintaining a close relationship with the puppet theatre. In the latter part of the century, when the centre of *chōnin* culture moved to Edo, it became more strongly a drama of verbal dialogue and spectacular productions, featuring popular actors who attracted large audiences. This outstanding *chōnin* theatrical form (which was both drama and spectacle) is different in many ways from *Nō* and *Kyōgen* and differs fundamentally from western drama as it has been since the sixteenth century. Its characteristics can be seen clearly in relatively early works, among them three plays we have already mentioned as being successfully staged for the puppet theatre: *Chūshingura* (first performed as *Kabuki* in 1748), *The Secret of Sugawara's Calligraphy* (1746) and *Yoshitsune: The Thousand Cherry Trees* (1747).

An entire *Kabuki* play is typically made up of a series of anecdotal episodes, with no particularly significant plot to link them. Each scene is not part of an overall convergence to a final climax but has its own individual build-up and resolution, as we have already mentioned in the case of *Chūshingura*. The story of revenge was basically a pretext for a series of spectacular scenes. *Yoshitsune: The Thousand Cherry Trees* is a collection of scenes from popular tales about Yoshitsune and the war leaders of the house of Taira with almost no thematic or narrative linkage. Naturally enough the audience would watch each scene of this long work as an independent spectacle, and this has given rise to the distinctive custom of performing individual scenes completely detached from the rest of the play. The plays were written by more than one playwright (usually two or three, sometimes as many as four or five) attached to the theatre. Each of these would take charge of a particular section. This meant of course that the resulting play was markedly different from, for instance, the *jōruri* of Chikamatsu, especially the domestic pieces with their tight dramatic structure.

The dialogue of *Kabuki*, unlike *jōruri* which provides commentary and narrative, is limited to the actors. The action of the scenes depends on this. This does not mean, however, that the beautiful and affecting language of *jōruri* has been put into the mouths of the characters on the stage. Rather the establishment of *Kabuki* as a theatre of dialogue coincided with an almost complete loss of 'the power of language'. The lines of *Kabuki* merely explain the situation or express the characters' feelings in a simple and mundane way; the dialogue itself is incapable of moving the audience. There is nothing in it of the universal, the paradoxical or the abstract, and its intellectual content is extremely thin. To confirm this one only has to look at famous *Kabuki* lines which have become popular catch-phrases. These are all connected to the feelings of a specific character in specific circumstances and say nothing about human feelings in general or about the human condition. Thus most of them include a mention of some particular character ('Has Yunosuke not come yet?' etc.). This is in sharp contrast to, for example, the lines of Shakespeare with which most English-speaking people are familiar. No *Kabuki* actor ever utters lines of such universal significance as the 'All the world's a stage' speech. Why not? Probably the *chōnin* of the Tokugawa period in their daily conversation talked mostly about specific people and seldom about humanity in general. Their interest was in specific subjects, not universal considerations. Accustomed to communicating within a small group they had long taken wordless communication and intuitive understanding as the ideal. The idea that verbal communication is limited and that everything important is communicated without words had permeated Japanese culture, and two of the features which characterize Japanese society in general, and the society of the Tokugawa period in particular, are a close link between the thing communicated and the specific circumstance, and a relatively minor importance attached to language as a means of communication. These were, inevitably, reflected in the dialogue of the *Kabuki* stage.

This limitation of dialogue to an expression of specific emotions under specific circumstances robs the plot of intellectual interest and severely restricts characterization. The character of Ōboshi Yuranosuke, the leader of the faithful forty-seven *rōnin*, is not of a complexity that requires him to re-examine the purpose of revenge. Sugawarano Michizane and Yoshitsune have no personalities as such but are merely cases of misfortune. The faithful retainers who frequently appear in *Kabuki* are often torn between their duty to their lord and their personal feelings – but not one of them is moved by this personal emotional experience to criticize or re-examine the existing social order. The strain between the exterior rational order and the interior emotional needs never leads to the interiorization of the rational order, nor to the rationalization and thus the externalization of emotion. No confrontation arises between interpretations of the law derived from differing personal and emotional experience. This is probably the reason that there are so few court scenes in *Kabuki*. The heroes and villains do not confront each other, like Shylock and Portia, in a public court; they encounter each other in private, personal scenes where it is money, brute force or plotting that counts. They never appeal to the audience of people in general; their justification is something that concerns them alone and has no theoretical backing that can convince a third party. *Kabuki* generals do not attempt, like Mark Antony and Brutus, to justify themselves by address-ing the crowd in a public square; they get on with the fighting. There are no questions and no answers. This has inevitable consequences for the quality of the dialogue.

Yet the confrontation itself, although verbally impoverished, can, depending on the ability of the actors, become a concen-trated expression of extreme psychological strain. One typical instance is *Kanjinchō* (The Subscription Roll), an adaptation of the *Nō* play *Ataka* first suggested by Ichikawa Danjūrō VII (1791–1859), who also produced it and took the main role of Benkei. (The script was by Namiki Gohei III.) Benkei, who has forced Yoshitsune to disguise himself as a porter and has himself adopted the disguise of a mountain priest in order that they might escape into Ōshū, confronts Togashi, who is in charge of the Ataka barrier through which they must pass and has been ordered to capture Yoshitsune. One of Togashi's subordinates becomes suspicious of Yoshitsune's disguise. Hav-ing no internal passport Benkei pretends to read a subscription roll in order to prove that they are itinerant priests (and thus free to travel) and attempts to show that his 'servant' is not Yoshi-tsune by abusing and striking him. Togashi sees through Ben-kei's ruse but pretends to be deceived and allows the party to pass. For his part Benkei, although he realizes that he is no longer deceiving Togashi, has to continue with his act. Togashi's subordinates at least must accept the disguise. The mutual understanding between Benkei and Togashi is established without the use of words but solely from the situation. If this mutual comprehension is not achieved one of them will die, Benkei at the hands of the enemies that he and his lord are fleeing, or Togashi as a result of his disregard of orders. Their tacit understanding goes beyond language. This, however, is one of relatively few examples.

The forte of *Kabuki* is not its dialogue but the performances of its actors. It is, after all, a spectacle. The highly formalized performance can, when skilfully done, produce a feeling that is half dramatic and half aesthetic. The aesthetic and sensual effect is strengthened visually by gorgeous and sophisticated costumes and changes of scene made by advanced stage equipment. Indeed, the Japanese theatres of the late eighteenth century had stage equipment, including revolving stages, which was probably in advance of that of any other country in the world.

This kind of theatre flourished in the *chōnin* society from the middle of the eighteenth to the early years of the nineteenth century. Almost all those who went to see it were *chōnin*, for the *samurai* of the domain mansions in Edo and their families were publicly forbidden to watch it. Many of the important playwrights from Sakurada Jisuke (1734–1806) to Tsuruya Nanboku (1755–1829) were also *chōnin*. The subjects of their plays, like Chikamatsu's *jōruri*, were taken from either popular historical stories or contemporary events. The historical tales were already well-known from the popular war-classics *Heike monogatari*, *Gikeiki*, *Soga monogatari*, and *Taiheiki*, and characters from these works, like Yoshitsune and the Soga brothers, appear frequently. Contemporary events treated could involve either *chōnin* or *samurai*. Typically the *samurai* pieces concerned 'family disputes' or power struggles within an influential family, and it was usual, for obvious reasons, to set the story in an earlier age, at least superficially. The story of the forty-seven faithful Akō retainers is of course 'disguised' in this way. Typical of the plays featuring *chōnin* are those about love-suicide, many of which are set in the licensed quarters. Examples of these are the stories of Yūgiri and Izaemon and of O-hatsu and Tokubee.

What were the values of the merchant classes reflected in these plays? In Chikamatsu's love-suicide pieces when 'human feelings' were in direct confrontation with 'duty' they were affirmed through death. During the following century the values of 'duty', sponsored by the *samurai* classes, had permeated the merchant classes, had been systematized as a social principle and seem to have become more flexible, at least in some ways. Certainly its level of tolerance was at its greatest within the clearly circumscribed world of the Yoshiwara pleasure quarter. After the middle of the eighteenth century in *Kabuki* the affirmation of 'human feelings' did not necessarily require lovers to die. The eponymous hero of *Sukeroku*, a 'chivalrous commoner' from Asakusa, is a master of picturesque and salty repartee, undaunted at the wealth and power of Ikyū, his enemy and rival for the hand of the courtesan Agemaki. The play is set in Yoshiwara and the story has it that Sukeroku is really Soga Gorō, but this is a merely superficial detail in what is an expression of the ideals of the Edo *chōnin*. His loved one Agemaki as usual in *Kabuki* is more positive than he in their love affair, even more so than usual in that she is a courtesan. This feature in itself was not new in the *Kabuki* of Edo. However the woman who defends and hides her lover from his pursuers with the defiant words 'If the end of that pole should so much as touch me the whole of Yoshiwara will be plunged into darkness,' and 'Well, you just deal with me. Deal with Agemaki,' is far from the women who set off for suicide with their lovers. Within Yoshiwara the Edo *chōnin* affirmed their pride in being *chōnin*, lovers affirmed the rights of love and *chōnin* affirmed values that they were realizing were their own; death was no longer necessary.

Kabuki at its peak produced heroes that were in effect egotistical villains who considered the ends justified any means. The definition of villainy depended on existing ethical values. In other words, the villain did not criticize or embody a criticism of the traditional social order but accepted it; his role was to produce a strong sensual stimulation within the given social and moral framework. Thus in *Kabuki* there was a profusion of bloody, cruel and perverted tortures and killings, separate from the overall plot of the play, the weakness of which we have already noted. When stimulation is repeated its effectiveness lessens. Thus there is always a need for new devices. Blood must flow more copiously and more bloodily. Actors must play many parts and learn quick-change techniques by which they switch costumes and stage manner to emerge as completely different characters. Stage equipment must be used to the limit of its possibilities, spectral appearances become increasingly grotesque.

The man who best represented the authors of such spectacles was Tsuruya Nanboku. Of the more than one hundred plays that Nanboku wrote the one most often performed today is *Tōkaidō yotsuya kaidan* (The Ghost of Yotsuya, first performed in 1825). The villain, a *rōnin* by the name of Tamiya Iemon, kills the father of his wife, O-iwa, in an Asakusa rice field. At the same time the eel fisherman Naosuke Gonbei attempts to kill Yomoshichi, the husband of the old man's other daughter O-sode, but, deceived by a disguise, kills the wrong man. O-iwa and O-sode however believe that both men have been killed. Meanwhile the daughter of a neighbour has fallen in love with Iemon and in an effort to bring the two together her father gives O-iwa poison, which disfigures her face. Iemon leaves O-iwa and their newly born child and attempts to fabricate evidence of her adultery so that he can divorce her. In rage and despair O-iwa stabs herself in the throat and dies. Iemon then kills the man whom he had accused of being O-iwa's lover and tying his corpse and that of O-iwa to opposite sides of a board throws them into the river. Iemon has now killed two people, or three, if we include O-iwa whose death he caused. The story continues with a series of weird scenes in which he is haunted by the ghost of O-iwa. For example, the face of his new love turns to that of O-iwa, and he strikes at it with his sword only to find he has beheaded his wife-to-be. Similar things happen to the father who poisoned O-iwa. A further complication to the story is a triangular relationship between Naosuke, O-sode and Yomoshichi. O-sode marries Naosuke in return for his promise that he will take revenge on her former husband's murderer. When Yomoshichi appears, apparently from the grave, it is discovered that O-sode and Naosuke are in fact brother and sister and that their relationship is incestuous. There is also an episode connected with *Chūshingura* but this is of minor importance.

The story is unconcerned with the overall conditions of society and remains completely a purely personal matter of those involved. Iemon alone is a clearly drawn character, the others, including O-iwa, being nothing more than *Kabuki* stock characters. There is a plethora of murder but motives are no more complex than simple mundane ambition or the complications of a triangular relationship. There is hardly any perceptible moral lesson for those who might seek one. People utter Buddhist prayers but there is no sign of Buddhistic elements in the relationship with death. For instance there is no attempt to pacify O-iwa's ghost with incantations and prayers. By this time Buddhism could no longer perform this kind of magical function.

At the same time there is a wealth of invention in the details of the grotesque and cruel scenes. Fingers are cut off on stage, fingernails are torn off, the poisoned O-iwa's face changes from beautiful to ugly and her hair falls out, a corpse nailed to a board speaks, the water in a pitcher turns to blood out of which appears a hand, a huge rat runs here and there, O-iwa's ghost appears from inside a lantern (a later innovation). Scenes which provide unnatural and sadistic excitement include Iemon's treatment of O-iwa, the actions of the masseur who insinuates himself into O-iwa's confidence when she has become ugly and the incest scenes. *The Ghost of Yotsuya* takes the bloodlust present in the completely personal sphere of the secular *chōnin* society to the limits of possibility. Iemon is not a villain because he is bad but because it is necessary to have murders and therefore a murderer. O-iwa does not become a ghost because of her jealousy; the jealousy is needed to make the haunting possible. A culture which stressed the part rather than the whole, which made the forms of action sophisticated without questioning their purpose and which sought strength of excitement rather than depth of feeling culminated in *The Ghost of Yotsuya*. Such *Kabuki* plays, however, were not the only thing that this society produced.

Just as there was a close connection between *Kabuki* and the pleasure quarter of Yoshiwara, so the art of woodblock-printed *ukiyo-e* ('pictures of the floating world') developed with connections to both the world of the theatre and the world of the ladies of pleasure. A revolution in woodblock-printing technique took place during the second half of the eighteenth century. This was the polychrome print or 'brocade picture', and most of the pictures produced employing this were of 'beauties' or actors.

The beauties depicted were not always courtesans; some were *chōnin* belles. The most distinguished print artists of the time included Suzuki Harunobu (1725–70), Torii Kiyonaga (1752–1815) and Kitagawa Utamaro (1753–1806). They along with virtually all other *ukiyo-e* artists also produced 'secret pictures' of rather more specialized interest. In this sense too there was a close connection between the prints and the world of the pleasure quarters. The pictures of actors which showed them in their famous scenes usually feature the whole figure or upper half of one man, with extremely few showing a group of more than two. Print artists in this style included Katsukawa Shunshō (1726–92), Tōshūsai Sharaku (dates of birth and death unknown, active 1794–95) and Utagawa Toyokuni (1769–1825). The landscape prints of Katsushika Hokusai (1760–1849) and Andō Hiroshige (1797–1858) appeared later than the portraits of beauties and actors, from the end of the century. The aesthetics of the *chōnin* of the latter part of the eighteenth century were concentrated in the city rather than the provinces and directed not at the forms of nature but those of man.

The subject was not the only thing which characterized the polychrome print. The lines of the folds and the outlines of the kimono have a flow which is almost the ultimate of refinement (as for instance in the work of Harunobu and Kiyonaga). There is great originality in the use of colour, especially in the handling of homogeneous shades such as black and grey (in the work of Shunshō and Sharaku). The original composition in which secondary surfaces are separated and composed through the use of either a somewhat geometrical line (particularly in the crests of the kimono of Shunshō's actors) or of a highly expressive line (as in the hands of Sharaku's actors) is something which has hardly been surpassed in the history of Japanese art. This visual beauty owed something if not everything to the *Kabuki* stage.

Thus the *chōnin* society of the latter part of the eighteenth century did not only seek sensual excitement but aesthetic refinement of sensual experience. It can also be said that, musically, this can be appreciated in the music of the *shamisen* – developed in the pleasure quarters and the theatre.

The appeal of the play was not in the overall form or story but in the details of individual scenes. The attraction of the *shamisen* is not in the abstract structure of the entire musical piece but in the way an interval is made between individual instants and by the way each note is played. In both play and music success or failure is decided at each instant in the flow of time. The flow of time is not organized into beginning, continuation, climax and conclusion but is a series of individual instants in the present. Woodblock prints defined the sensual experience of the instant in visual language as *haikai* did in verbal language. This was the reason that both woodblock prints and *haikai* were both popular among the educated merchants of Edo.

What came after this? Kawatake Mokuami (1816–93) reviewed previous *Kabuki*, by then a form with no further possibilities for development, and brought the various elements together. The authors of *ninjōbon* ('stories of human feelings') wrote of the customs of the pleasure quarters and the delicate workings of the emotions. Hiroshige returned the woodblock print, as Kobayashi Issa (1763–1827) did the *haikai*, to the everyday world of the *chōnin*. But there is another noteworthy form of self-expression developed by the *chōnin* under the dictatorship of the *samurai*: this was the form of comic verse known as *senryū*. The age of *Kabuki* and *ukiyo-e* was also the age of the *Haifū yanagidaru* collection.

THE LITERATURE OF LAUGHTER

In the late eighteenth century the higher-class *chōnin* not only increased their financial power in the *samurai*-ruled system as production came more and more to involve commerce and a national market developed; they also became a greater creative force in cultural terms with the development of *chōnin* schools and the rise of *Kabuki* and the culture associated with the pleasure quarters. This was accompanied by an easing of the tension between the values of duty that the *samurai* sought to impose on them and the values of 'human feelings' that they themselves emphasized; eventually the two achieved a more relaxed accommodation. The tragedy of the love-suicide pieces was joined by the humour of comic verse (*kyōku* and *kyōka*) and stories (*kobanashi*). Here for example is a *kyōku* about the pleasure quarters:

A man and a warrior!
... Then why does he turn *chōnin*
And come here?

(*Haifū yanagidaru*)

The tone is clearly one of superiority towards the *samurai* who should be above such pleasures as those offered by the houses of Yoshiwara but in fact is not. This superior attitude would not of course be directed towards the values adumbrated in the phrase 'a man and a warrior' and still less would there be any opposition to the society which held these values, the society outside the private world of Yoshiwara. The *chōnin* did not resist the system or its *samurai* rulers but they had realized that within that system they did have some power – this realization was expressed in their humour.

As the eighteenth century continued more *samurai* abandoned the social position they had inherited and joined the ranks of the *chōnin*. A larger number remained *samurai* but devoted their spare time to interests which were part of the *chōnin* culture. The finances of the domains were often straitened and the life of their lower-grade *samurai* bitterly impoverished.

The *chōnin* culture offered an emotional outlet and must have seemed not unattractive when compared with the ritualistic severity and rigid Confucian ethics of *samurai* life. By the late eighteenth century the *samurai* too had developed two parallel cultures, one 'official' (or overt) and the other 'unofficial' (or covert). The latter ranged from the cultural diversions of the Sorai group through the sophisticated elegance of Yanagisawa Kien to the plays and comic verse of Shokusanjin, and can be seen as the *samurai* culture drawing closer in some ways to the *chōnin* culture. To strike a balance between the strict official ethical culture and the private culture of the emotions required above all intellectual distancing. This was expressed as humour. The humour of the *samurai*, unlike that of the *chōnin*, was in part satire directed against the social order and the authorities, but little of this was as sharp and hostile as Ueda Akinari's, no doubt because the fact that the writer was himself a *samurai* restrained him from any wholesale attack on a system that he and his kind dominated. These writers were, however, critical of certain aspects of *samurai* society and the policies of the

Bakufu and the domains, and this gave them a certain scope for satire.

> *Yo no naka ni ka hodo urusaki mono wa nashi*
> *bunbu to iute yoru mo nerarezu*
> There's nothing as annoying as a mosquito;
> You can't sleep at night for its buzzing.

This verse is a fairly meaningless little comment until one takes into account the pun between the sound that the mosquito is said to make (*bunbu*) and the word that sums up the twin accomplishments, literary (*bun*) and martial arts (*bu*) that *samurai* were supposed to master. The author of this squib seems to have been a *samurai* but on the very periphery of his class.

For the *samurai* and *chōnin* of the late eighteenth century there were many causes for laughter. Not so for the peasants. The peasants did not find humour an adequate way of expressing their reactions to life; instead they killed newborn children they could not afford to feed, abandoned farms they could not afford to run and rose in riot against the authorities that would not or could not alleviate their sufferings.

Both *samurai* and *chōnin* believed that the social system in which they lived was absolutely permanent and prized tradition in style above innovation. There were three main forms of humorous literature in the latter half of the eighteenth century and not one of them was new. The origins of the *kyōku* (a kind of humorous *haikai* without *haikai* conventions) can be traced back to the *Inu tsukubashū*, and those of the *kyōka* (a humorous form of the *tanka*) to the humorous *odoke uta* poems of the Heian period. As for the *kobanashi* stories, extant works show that they have a history dating back at least to *Yesterday Happenings Are Today's Tales* and remained popular until the end of the Tokugawa period. The *chōnin*, and those *samurai* who wrote humorous verse, used these well-established forms enlarging the range of subjects and changing to some extent the nature of the humour to produce a cultural form which was appropriate to and typical of their age.

Karai Senryū (1718–90), an Edo *chōnin*, published the first part of the *kyōku* collection *Haifū yanagidaru* in 1765; the minor *samurai* and *kyōka* poet Kimura Bōun (1719–83) made a collection of *kobanashi* which was published under the title *Kanoko mochi* in 1772 and Yomono Akara (1749–1823) compiled one of the first *kyōka* collections, *Bansai kyōkashū* (A Collection of a Myriad *Kyōka*), in 1783. Yomono Akara, the central literary figure of this period, was the pen-name (another one was Shokusanjin) of a minor Bakufu official, Ōta Nanpo.

Senryū made 23 more collections in the years before his death and the fact that 167 other collections were made says something about the popularity of the form. The poet gave his name to this kind of verse and *kyōku* have been known since his time as *senryū*. The authorship of the verses in the early volumes of *Haifū yanagidaru* is unknown. Most of the subject matter is taken from the daily life of Edo but there are also verses concerning historical figures well-known to the reader through *Nō*, *Kabuki* and popular classics such as the *Taiheiki* and *Ise monogatari*.

The everyday *chōnin* subjects cover a wide range, including family relationships (between husband and wife, parent and child, wife and mother-in-law), hairdressers, carpenters, mendicant priests, wet nurses, maids, Buddhist prayer-meetings, plays and food and drink. For instance this verse of a visit to a poverty-stricken invalid is sharply perceptive of human nature:

> When the 'special medicine' is opened –
> Inside . . . a gold coin.
>
> (*Haifū yanagidaru*, Vol. 1)

This is a well-known verse on a less than successful marriage:

> In the shop there is one man
> Who does not know –
> The husband.
>
> (ibid., Vol. 7)

However, most of the *senryū* are about sexual relationships. There are many about Yoshiwara and several about love-suicide. Others concern the *Shōgun's* lady attendants and their aphrodisiacs, dildos and contraceptives. The life of the peasants and the scenery of the provinces are almost completely ignored. There are a few verses mocking rustics on visits to Edo but hardly any about life in rural villages. Similarly there are few verses about travel. The world of the Edo *chōnin* as it is reflected in the *senryū* is self-sufficient, unmindful of the world to come and hardly conscious of the world outside Edo.

Samurai however came in for their share of mockery as in the first *senryū* quoted above. *Samurai* were officials, and

> An official is on his mettle
> When riding in a *choki*.

A *choki* is a small boat used to go to and from Yoshiwara. Like 'a man and a warrior' this verse gives full expression to the *chōnin*'s keen and down-to-earth appraisal of the *samurai* officials. Priests and doctors are also satirized:

> Having praised the
> Dead man's final poem
> The doctor departs.
>
> (ibid., Vol. 2)

Buddhism is gently mocked:

> No Chinese have been put into
> This picture of hell.
>
> (ibid., Vol. 1)

> After praying to the bronze Buddha –
> Tap it
>
> (ibid., Vol. 2)

The first of these makes an amusing point; the second is keenly perceptive about the way people behave.

The historical characters in *Haifū yanagidaru* are drawn into this everyday world. The battles of Tairano Tomomori become the brawls of apprentices. The heroism of the lady-warrior Tomoe Gozen is like the bustle of a housewife.

The humour of these pieces derives from the deliberate anachronism often accompanied by an iconoclastic nuance. For instance, there is the old tale about Fukakusano Shōshō who has fallen in love with the poetess Onono Komachi, who has promised to fulfil his desire after he visits her for one hundred nights; he dies on the ninety-ninth night. This had been treated in the *Nō* plays *Kayoi Komachi* and *Sotoba Komachi*. In *Haifū yanagidaru* the story is transformed – Komachi becomes a Yoshiwara courtesan with a list of regular clients and the lover, far from ardent, neglects her so that

> On the ninety-ninth night
> She erased him
> From the lovers' register.

The same story is parodied in the *kobanashi* collection *Kanoko mochi*. A man who sends love letters to an aristocratic lady is eventually told that she will grant him her favours if he comes to her house every night for a hundred nights and, as proof, leaves a mark on the carriage stand outside the front gate. Every night, through wind and rain the man appears to make his mark and so impressed is the lady with his devotion that on the ninety-ninth night she sends her maid down to invite him to her chamber. The man is strangely reluctant and somewhat taken aback and when the maid presses him confesses: 'Well, the thing is that I'm just employed by the day to put these marks here.'

As these examples show, *senryū* and *kobanashi* have many similarities in subjects and humour. Both use puns and word-play, jokes about everyday matters, and small psychological misunderstandings, gentle mockery, deliberate anachronism, and the occasional flouting of authority especially of the authority of sexual conventions. Only rarely is the humour satiric in nature. The *kobanashi* were told on the streets or at small public performances and also sold as small pamphlets. They are obviously the predecessors of the *rakugo* comic monologues which remain popular today but they are much shorter (the Onono Komachi parody is if anything on the long side). Most of them end with a 'punch-line' that gives a twist to the story.

Kyōka were somewhat different from these forms. Perhaps the most famous period for these comic versions of *tanka* was the Tenmei era (1781–88) when they enjoyed great popularity among *samurai* intellectuals, and some of the more literary *chōnin*. Unlike *senryū*, *kyōka* were attributed to specific poets when they were printed in collections, although of course the poets did not use their real names but invented antique pen-names. The names of the best-known poets of the period are to be found in the collection *Azumaburi kyōka bunko* (The Azumaburi *Kyōka* Library) edited by Yadoyano Meshimori (1753–1830), with portraits by Kitao Masanobu (the popular novelist mentioned earlier, Santō Kyo8den) and calligraphy by Yomono Akara. This contains a portrait of each of fifty poets and a *kyōka* by each of them. Half of them are *samurai*, half chōnin. The *samurai* are for the most part minor Bakufu officials; apart from Ōta Nanpo (pen-name Yomono Akara), there are Yamazaki Kagetsura (Akera Kankō, 1740–1800) and Kimuro Bōun (Hakurikan Bōun). There is also one poet from a distinguished *samurai* family – Sakai Hōitsu (Shiriyakino Sarundo, 1761–1828), the younger brother of the lord of Himeji castle and also an outstanding painter of the Kōrin school.

The extent of the popularity of *kyōka* among educated *samurai* can be judged from an anecdote recounted in one of the essays in *Kasshi yawa* (first volume completed 1821, whole work completed 1827) by Matsura Seizan (1760–1841). Ōta Nanpo, the central figure of the *kyōka* circle, was forced to give up writing because of the reforms imposed on society in the Kansei era which followed Tenmei. These reforms were largely the work of Matsudaira Sadanobu, who became president of the Council of Elders in 1787. Even Sadanobu, however, would write *kyōka* when the occasion presented itself. While he was in Edo he heard that his castle had been the scene of a fire and continually received messengers 'like plucking teeth from a comb', as *Kasshi yawa* has it, to be kept informed of the extent of the damage. Soon a chief retainer came from his domain in a state of some apprehension to be greeted by Sadanobu with the angry comment that he already knew the details of the fire and did the chief retainer have anything to add. The retainer could think of nothing and remained mute and miserable. Sadanobu reached for his inkstone, wrote briefly and, throwing the paper in the direction of the wretched man, retired to his private rooms. The man found, instead of a strong hint that suicide might be the only course for a dutiful retainer, the following *kyōka*:

> Now that it's done
> And you've done it to a turn
> No need to overdo it yourself.

The retainer left with a great sense of relief and an intact abdomen.

Kyōka were written by the scholars Hanawa Hokiichi (1746–1821, pen-name Hayatomono Mekari) and Hiraga Gennai (Fūrai Sanjin), by painters of the Kanō school, by actors such as Ichikawa Danjūrō V and by courtesans.

Chōnin poets came from many walks of life – ward officials (*nanushi*), landlords, innkeepers, owners of brothels, bathhouses, oilshops, exchange houses, bookshops, wine shops and sellers of fish and of adzuki-bean soup. The writing of *kyōka* required a certain amount of literary education, however, and this meant that they were unlikely to become very popular among the *chōnin*. At the same time it is clear that the denial of certain features of culture to the lower classes which had hitherto been a feature of the Tokugawa system was now crumbling. In Edo at this time *samurai* and *chōnin* went to the same poetry meetings, criticized each other's work and were published together. This did not happen in the seventeenth century or before. The favourite form of the *kyōka* was parody of famous *tanka*, particularly those of the thirteenth-century collection *Ogura hyakunin isshu*. This for example is a famous poem by Fujiwarano Toshinari:

> Night and autumn chill
> Seep into my body.
> The village of Fukakusa
> Where the quail cry.

Here is the *kyōka*, the work of Yomono Akara:

> One is taken, then two
> Till none remain to eat.
> The village of Fukakusa
> Where the quail fry.

We have mentioned that it was possible for *kyōka* to contain political criticism and social satire but these were in fact rare exceptions. Japanese lyrical verse traditionally avoided political and social comment and *kyōka* largely kept within this tradition. The world of *kyōka*, like that of *waka*, was mundane and this-worldly and it was informed by down-to-earth and hedonistic values. To this extent *kyōka* did not differ from *senryū*. The central concerns of the *kyōka* poets were love, wine and money. As Yomono Akara puts it:

> In this world sex and drink are our foes
> And foes we would gladly encounter.

And:

> In this world white rice and
> Moonlit nights are commonplace
> But money ...

Senryū are rich in concrete descriptions of customs and things whereas *kyōka*, as these two examples show, tend to be more general and abstract in tone. The descriptions of love in *kyōka* for instance are more oblique than those in *senryū* which are often direct and concrete.

There is however a more important difference between *kyōka* and *senryū; kyōka* are typically ironic about the poet and his life, *senryū* seldom so. *Kyōka* are concerned with the basic and constant aspects of human life, not just single scenes, fortuitous incidents and phenomena. One could say that *senryū* deal with the experiences of a certain day and a certain place while *kyōka* often deal with the experiences of a lifetime. This indicates how far the *kyōka* poets were able to stand outside their own personal experience of life within an apparently eternal and inescapable social system. It was impossible to cut oneself off from this system and the etiquette that dictated how one should conduct even the most trifling parts of one's life. Trapped in a fine net of petty concerns the poet's opportunity for adventure was limited indeed and the realization of this prompted an attitude of mockery towards the self caught in such a life, as can be seen in the following caustic definitions:

> Asleep or awake nothing much happens –
> This is 'reward for a past life'.

> (Yomono Akara)

> Happiness is cherry blossoms in spring
> The moon in autumn
> And a man and wife eating together three times
> Without arguing.
>
> (Hanamichi Tsurane)

These have no bitterness in their self-mockery. Rather the despair, disillusion and pettiness of life are dispelled and transformed by humour and objectified by the traditional form. This device to remove the bitterness from self-mockery was at the heart of the style adopted by the warrior-official of the time. The word *sharenomesu* (humorous) sums up the tone of this work, and it can be said that the *kyōka* poets were products of a humorous society.

There were at that time no religious values or beliefs that could prevent the *kyōka* poets regarding their own death with the same eye. The culture of the time was secular and had been so long enough for the secularism to have attained a great degree of sophistication.

> Eat, get hungry again,
> Sleep, then wake.
> That's life.
> Perhaps it'll be interesting
> To die for a change.
>
> (Hakurikan Bōun)

This is the death-bed poem of an intelligent *kyōka* poet. A joke is stronger than death. Humour in the face of death is a feature of many cultures of various ages (Villon's poems, for instance); in Japanese literature it is in the *kyōka* poets of the late eighteenth century that it reaches its highest point, in what was the finest Japanese humorous writing.

Senryū and *kyōka* continued to be popular until the middle of the nineteenth century. In prose there was a division. Comic monologues developed into the longer more sophisticated and more formalized *rakugo* and there appeared great comic novels such as *The Bath-house of the Floating World* and *Shanks' Pony along the Tōkaidō*, to be discussed later. The merits of these works were found not in their innovations in terms of humour but rather in their observations of contemporary mores. Essentially the limits of Japanese humour had been reached in the late eighteenth century. Never again was humour to be such an essential element of the culture. In the nineteenth century, particularly in the middle years, the Tokugawa system was shaken by a combination of domestic problems and external threats. The efforts to defend or attack the system were not regarded as humorous.

Bibliographical Notes

This bibliography has been prepared by the translator to serve as a guide to accurate and relatively easily available texts and translations of the major works referred to in the History. It is not comprehensive, nor are the editions cited here necessarily the ones used by the author. For Japanese texts of verse, fiction, drama and belles-lettres before 1868, the Nihon Koten Bungaku Taikei (NKBT) series published by Iwanami Shoten, Tōkyō, offers well-annotated and accurate materials. The Nihon Shisō Taikei (NST) series from the same publisher performs a similar service for major philosophical texts. Nihon Koten Bungaku Zenshū from Shōgakkan, Tōkyō, is another well-annotated series covering an area similar to that of NKBT.

Further details about translated works can be found in bibliographies such as *Studies in Japanese Literature and Language*, a bibliography of English materials compiled by Yasuhiro Yoshizaki (Tōkyō: Nichigai Associates, 1979) and *Modern Japanese Literature in Translation*, a bibliography compiled by the International House of Japan Library (Tōkyō: Kodansha International, 1979). Japanese sources are given in the *K.B.S. Bibliography of Standard Reference Books for Japanese Studies with Descriptive Notes* (Tōkyō: Kokusai Bunka Shinkokai, 1967).

This bibliography lists very few volumes of translated poetry. There are no western translators closely connected with any of the great Japanese poets. Rather, *haiku* are published in collections of translation, of which there are now at least one hundred and fifty, too many to cite here.

Andō Shōeki
Andō Shōeki, Satō Nobuhiro. NST. Tōkyō: Iwanami Shoten, 1977.

Arai Hakuseki

Arai Hakuseki. NST. Tōkyō: Iwanami Shoten, 1975.
Tales Around a Brushwood Fire: The Autobiography of Arai Hakuseki.
  Translated with an introduction and notes by Joyce Ackroyd.
  Tōkyō: University of Tokyo Press, 1979.

Bashō
See Matsuo Bashō.

Buson
See Yosa Buson.

Chikamatsu

Chikamatsu Monzaemon zenshū. Edited by Takano Tatsuyuki and
  Koroki Kanzō. Tōkyō: Shun'yōdō, 1922.
Major Plays of Chikamatsu. Translated by Donald Keene. New
  York and London: Columbia University Press, 1961.

Christian and anti-Christian writings

Kirishitansho, haiyasho. NST. Tōkyō: Iwanami Shōten, 1970.
Boxer, C.R. *The Christian Century in Japan.* Cambridge: Cambridge University Press, 1951.

Chūshingura

Kanedehon chūshingura. Edited by Fujino Yoshio. Tōkyō: Ōfūsha,
  1975.
Chūshingura: The Treasury of Loyal Retainers. Translated by
  Donald Keene. New York: Columbia University Press, 1971.

Dazai Shundai (and the school of Sorai)
Sorai gaku-ha. NST. Tōkyō: Iwanami Shoten, 1972.

Fujiwara Seika
Fujiwara Seika, Hayashi Razan. NST. Tōkyō: Iwanami Shoten,
  1975.

Haifū-yanagidaru
Selection in *Senryū kyōkashū.* NKBT. Tōkyō: Iwanami Shoten,
  1958.

Haikai

Abe Jirō, Komiya Toyotaka, et al. *Saikaku haikai kenkyū*. Tōkyō: Kaizōsha, 1935.

Hakuin

Hakuin Oshō zenshū. Edited by Mori Taikyō. Tōkyō: Ryūginsha, 1934–35.

Hakuin hōgoshū. Tōkyō: Ichōbonkankō-kai, 1953.

The Zen Master Hakuin: Selected Writings. Translated by Philip B. Yampofsky. New York: Columbia University Press, 1971.

The Embossed Tea Kettle: Orate Gama and Other Works of Hakuin Zenji. Translated by R. D. M. Shaw. London: Allen and Unwin, 1963.

Hiraga Gennai

Fūrai sanjinshū. NKBT. Tōkyō: Iwanami Shoten, 1961.

Hiraga Gennai zenshū. Tōkyō: Meichō Kankō-kai, 1970.

Hirata Atsutane

In *Hirata Atsutane, Ban Nobutomo, Ōkuni Takamasa*. NSTK. Tōkyō: Iwanami Shoten, 1973.

Ihara Saikaku

Teihon Saikaku zenshū. Edited by Ebara Taiyō, Teruoka Yasutaka, Noma Kōshin. Tōkyō: Chuōkōronsha, 1950–51.

The Japanese Family Storehouse or the Millionaire's Gospel Modernized. (Nippon eitaigura). Translated by G. W. Sargent. London and New York: Cambridge University Press, 1959.

The Life of an Amorous Woman and Other Writings by Ihara Saikaku. Translated by Ivan Morris. London: Chapman and Hall, 1963.

Some Final Words of Advice. Translated by Peter Nosco. Rutland, Vt., and Tōkyō: Tuttle, 1980.

Tales of Japanese Justice. Translated by Thomas M. Kondo and Alfred H. Marks. Honolulu: University Press of Hawaii, 1980.

This Scheming World. Translated by Masanori Takatsuka and David C. Stubbs. Rutland, Vt., and Tōkyō: Tuttle, 1965.

Ishida Baigan, Toan and *Shingaku*
Shingaku dōwa-shū. Edited by Shibata Kyūō. Yūhōdō Bunko series no. 60. Tōkyō: Yūhōdō Shoten, 1917.
Sekimon shingaku. NST. Tōkyō: Iwanami Shoten, 1971.

Itō Jinsai
Itō Jinsai, Itō Tōgai. Edited by Yoshikawa Kōjirō and Shimizu Shigeru. NST. Tōkyō: Iwanami Shoten, 1971.
Itō Jinsai: A Philosopher, Educator and Sinologist of the Tokugawa Period. Spae, Joseph John. Monumenta Serica Monograph series. Peiping: Catholic University of Peking, 1948.

Jippensha Ikku
Tōkaidōchū hizakurige. NKBT. Tōkyō: Iwanami Shoten, 1958.
Satchell, Thomas R. *Shanks' Mare*. Rutland, Vt., and Tōkyō: Tuttle, 1960.

Kabuki
Kabuki kyakuhonshū. Edited by Urayama Masao and Matsuzaki. Tōkyō: Iwanami Shoten, 1960.
Kawatake Shigetoshi. *Kabuki meisakushū*. Tōkyō: Kōdansha, 1936.
Brandon, James R., trans. *Kabuki: Five Classic Plays*. Cambridge, Mass., and London: Harvard University Press, 1975.

Kaibara Ekiken
The Way of Contentment. Translated by Ken Hoshino. The Wisdom of the East series. London: John Murray, 1913.
Women and Wisdom of Japan (parts of Onna daigaku). Translated by B. H. Chamberlain. London, 1909.
Kaibara Ekiken Muro Kyūsō. NST. Tōkyō: Iwanami Shoten, 1970.

Kawatake Mokuami
Mokuami zenshū. Edited by Kawatake Shigetoshi. Tōkyō: Shun'yōdō, 1924–26.
Translated by Frank T. Motofuji *The Love of Izayoi and Seishin* (Izayoiseishin) Rutland, Vt., and Tōkyō: Tuttle, 1966.

Kibyōshi and Santō Kyōden
Kibyōshi sharebonshū. NKBT. Tōkyō: Iwanami Shoten, 1958.

Kino wa kyō no monogatari
In *Edo shōwashū*. NKBT. Tōkyō: Iwanami Shoten, 1966.

Kobayashi Issa
Issa Sōsho. Edited by Shinano Kyōiku-kai. 11 vols. Tōkyo: Kokon Shoin, 1926–28.
Buson-shū, Issa-shū. NKBT. Tōkyō: Iwanami Shoten, 1959.
Lewis, Richard. *Of This World: A Poet's Life in Poetry*. New York: Dial Press, 1968.
Mackenzie, Lewis. *Issa: The Autumn Wind*. New York: Paragon, 1957.
Mackenzie, Lewis. *Orphan Sparrow*. London: John Murray, 1958.

Kumamoto Bansan
Kumamoto Bansan. NST. Tōkyō: Iwanami Shoten, 1971.
Inumakura, Nisemonogatari, Chikuzai. In *Kanazōshi*. NKBT. Tōkyō: Iwanami Shoten, 1965.

Matsuo Bashō
Kōhon Bashō zenshū. Edited by Komiya Toyotaka et al. Tōkyō: Kadokawa Shoten, 1962.
Back Roads to Far Towns: Basho's Oku no hosomichi. Translated by Cid Corman and Kamaike Susumu. New York: Grossman, 1968.
Ueda Makoto. *Matsuo Bashō*. Boston: Twayne Publishers, 1970.
Yuasa Nobuyuki. *Basho: The Narrow Road to the Deep North and Other Travel Sketches*. London: Penguin Books, 1967.
Andrews, J. D. *Full Moon Is Rising – Lost Haiku of Matsuo Basho and Travel Haiku of Basho: A New Rendering*. Boston: Branden Press, 1977.

Miura Baien
Miura Baien-shū. Edited by Saigusu Hiroto. Iwanami Bunko series no. 2229. Tōkyō: Iwanami Shoten, 1953.

Miyamoto Musashi
Gorin no sho. In *Kinsei geidōron*. NST. Tōkyō: Iwanami Shoten, 1972.
A Book of Five Rings. Translated by Victor Harris. London: Allison and Busby, 1974.

Motoori Norinaga
Motoori Norinaga zenshū. Edited by Motoori Seizō. 13 vols. Tōkyō: Yoshikawa Kobundō, 1926–28.
Motoori Norinaga. NST. Tōkyō: Iwanami Shoten, 1978.
Matsumoto Shigeru. *Motoori Norinaga.* Cambridge, Mass.: Harvard University Press, 1970.

Ogyū Sorai
Ogyū Sorai. NST. Tōkyō: Iwanami Shoten, 1973.
Distinguishing the Way (Bendō). Translated by Olaf G. Lindin. Monumentica Nipponica monograph series. Tōkyō: Sophia University, 1970.
Lindin, Olaf G. *The Life of Ogyū Sorai: A Tokugawa Confucian Philosopher.* Lund: Studentlitterateur, 1973.
McEwan, J. R. *The Political Writings of Ogyū Sorai.* Cambridge: Cambridge University Press, 1962.

Peasants
Minshū undo no shisō. NST. Tōkyō: Iwanami Shoten, 1970.

Poets. *Kanshi*
Edo kanshishū. NKBT. Tōkyō: Iwanami Shoten, 1966.

Saikaku
See Ihara Saikaku.

Sekkyōbushi
Sekkyōbushi shōhonshū. Edited by Yokoyama Jū and Fujiwara Hiroshi. Tōkyō: Ōokayama Shoten, 1936.

Senryū
Blyth, R. H. *Senryū: Japanese Satirical Verses.* Tōkyō: Hokuseido Press, 1949. Reprint. Westport, Conn: Greenwood, 1971.
Senryū kyōka-shū. Edited by Sugimoto Nagashige and Hamada Giichirō. NKBT. Tōkyō: Iwanami Shoten, 1958.

Shikitei Sanba
Ukiyoburo. NKBT. Tōkyō: Iwanami Shoten, 1957.
Ukiyodoko. Edited by Nakanishi Zenzō. Nihon Koten Zenshū series. Tōkyō: Asahi Shinbunsha, 1955.

Sugita Genpaku
In *Taionki, Oritakushiba no ki, Rantō kotohajime*. NKBT. Tōkyō: Iwanami Shoten, 1964.
Matsunoto Ryōzo and Kiyooka Giichi. *Dawn of Western Science in Japan* (Rangaku kotohajime). Tōkyō: Hokuseido Press, 1969.

Takizawa Bakin
Chinsetsu Yumiharizuki. NKBT. Tōkyō: Iwanami Shoten, 1958 –62.
Nansō Satomi hakkenden. Iwanami Bunko series. Tōkyō: Iwanami Shoten, 1937–41.
Zolbrod, Leon. *Takizawa Bakin*. Boston: Twayne, 1964.

Takuan
In *Bujutsu sōsho* (vol. 138). Tōkyō: Hayakawa Junsaburō, 1915.

Tominaga Nakamoto
Tominaga Nakamoto, Yamagata Bantō. NST. Tōkyō: Iwanami Shoten, 1973.
Kato, Shuichi. *Tominaga Nakamoto: A Tokugawa Iconoclast*. Vancouver: University of British Columbia Press, 1967.

Tsuruya Nanboku
Dai Nanboku zenshū. Edited by Tsubouchi Shōyō and Atsumi Seitarō. Tōkyō: Shun'yōdō, 1925–27.

Ueda Akinari
Ueda Akinari-shū. NKBT. Tōkyō: Iwanami Shoten, 1959.
Tales of the Spring Rain. Translated by Barry Jackman. Tōkyō: University of Tokyo Press, 1975.
Ugetsu Monogatari: Tales of Moonlight and Rain. Translated by Leon Zolbrod. Vancouver: University of British Columbia Press, 1975. London: Allen and Unwin, 1975. Rutland, Vt., and Tōkyō: Tuttle, 1977.

Watanabe Kazan
Watanabe Kazan, Takano Chōei, Sakuma Shōzan, Yokoi Shōnan, Hashimoto San'ai. NST. Tōkyō: Iwanami Shoten, 1971.

Yamazaki Ansai, Kamono Mabuchi et al.
In *Kinsei shintō-ron, Zenki kokugaku.* Tōkyō: Iwanami Shoten, 1972.

Yanagisawa Kien
Hitorine. In *Kinsei zuisō-shū.* NKBT. Tōkyō: Iwanami Shoten, 1965.

Yosa Buson
Haisei Buson zenshū. Tōkyō: Shueikaku, 1921.

Index